Electoral Strategies
under Authoritarianism

RUSSIAN, EURASIAN, AND EASTERN EUROPEAN POLITICS

Series Editor: Michael O. Slobodchikoff, Troy University

Mission Statement

Following the collapse of the Soviet Union, little attention was paid to Russia, Eastern Europe, and the former Soviet Union. The United States and many Western governments reassigned their analysts to address different threats. Scholars began to focus much less on Russia, Eastern Europe and the former Soviet Union, instead turning their attention to East Asia among other regions. With the descent of Ukraine into civil war, scholars and governments have lamented the fact that there are not enough scholars studying Russia, Eurasia, and Eastern Europe. This series focuses on the Russian, Eurasian, and Eastern European region. We invite contributions addressing problems related to the politics and relations in this region. This series is open to contributions from scholars representing comparative politics, international relations, history, literature, linguistics, religious studies, and other disciplines whose work involves this important region. Successful proposals will be accessible to a multidisciplinary audience, and advance our understanding of Russia, Eurasia, and Eastern Europe.

Advisory Board

Books in the Series

Understanding International Relations: Russia and the World, edited by Natalia Tsvetkova

Geopolitical Prospects of the Russian Project of Eurasian Integration, by Natalya A. Vasilyeva and Maria L. Lagutina

Eurasia 2.0: Russian Geopolitics in the Age of New Media, edited by Mark Bassin and Mikhail Suslov

Executive Politics in Semi-Presidential Regimes: Power Distribution and Conflicts between Presidents and Prime Ministers, by Martin Carrier

Post-Soviet Legacies and Conflicting Values in Europe: Generation Why, by Lena M. Surzhko-Harned and Ekaterina Turkina

Through Times of Trouble: Conflict in Southeastern Ukraine Explained from Within, by Anna Matveeva

Eurasia on the Edge: Managing Complexity, by Piotr Dutkiewicz, Richard Sakwa, and Fyodor Lukyanov

Cultural Imperialism: Russian and Western Soft Power in Eastern Europe, by G. Doug Davis and Michael O. Slobodchikoff

Electoral Strategies under Authoritarianism: Evidence from the Former Soviet Union, by Megan Hauser

Electoral Strategies under Authoritarianism

Evidence from the Former Soviet Union

Megan Hauser

LEXINGTON BOOKS
Lanham • Boulder • New York • London

Published by Lexington Books
An imprint of The Rowman & Littlefield Publishing Group, Inc.
4501 Forbes Boulevard, Suite 200, Lanham, Maryland 20706
www.rowman.com

6 Tinworth Street, London SE11 5AL

British Library Cataloguing in Publication Information Available

Library of Congress Cataloging-in-Publication Data

Names: Hauser, Megan, author.
Title: Electoral strategies under authoritarianism : evidence from the former Soviet
  Union / Megan Hauser.
Description: Lanham : Lexington Books, [2019] | Series: Russian, Eurasian, and Eastern
  European politics | Includes bibliographical references and index.
Identifiers: LCCN 2018047459 (print) | LCCN 2018053905 (ebook) | ISBN
  9781498556729 (Electronic) | ISBN 9781498556712 (cloth) |
  ISBN 9781498556736 (pbk)
Subjects: LCSH: Elections—Former Soviet republics. | Authoritarianism—Former
  Soviet republics. | Former Soviet republics—Politics and government.
Classification: LCC JN6592 (ebook) | LCC JN6592 .H38 2018 (print) | DDC
  324.70947—dc23
LC record available at https://lccn.loc.gov/2018047459

Contents

Foreword

DEMOCRACY IN NON-DEMOCRATIC REGIMES

Following the collapse of the Soviet Union, little attention was paid to Russia, Eastern Europe, and the former Soviet Union. The United States and many Western governments reassigned their analysts to address different threats. Scholars began to focus much less on Russia, Eastern Europe, and the former Soviet Union, instead turning their attention to East Asia among other regions. With the descent of Ukraine into civil war, scholars and governments have lamented the fact that there are not enough scholars studying Russia, Eurasia, and Eastern Europe. Scholars must again turn their focus on this extremely important geographic area. There remains much misunderstanding about the politics of the region. With tensions between governments at heightened levels unprecedented since the Cold War, scholarship addressing the politics of the region is extremely vital. The Russian, Eurasian, and Eastern European Politics Book Series aims at remedying the deficiency in the study and understanding of the politics of Eurasia.

Democracy is a powerful norm. It grants legitimacy to any regime. Even authoritarian regimes strive to signal that they are democracies. They do this to ensure regime survival domestically while also signaling to international audiences that they are at least regimes that can cooperate and be open to relations with other states. Many of these regimes do hold contested, multiparty elections, which is an important aspect of a democratic regime. However, often authoritarian regimes turn to manipulating elections, even in cases where the outcome of the election is near certain. The strategy of manipulating elections has become a favored tactic by several post-Soviet states. Yet it is puzzling as to why leaders in authoritarian or non-liberal democracies would need to resort to manipulating elections.

In this very important book, Dr. Megan Hauser develops a theory of strategic decision making by both incumbent and opposition actors toward elections. She argues that rather than writing off elections in non-liberal democratic states as being a facade, the institution of elections is vital to regime stability. Her theory is extremely important in creating a systematic approach to understanding elections in the post-Soviet space rather than a more limited single-country analysis of specific elections. This is a must-read book for not only Eurasian specialists, but also for those who discount electoral politics in authoritarian regimes.

Michael O. Slobodchikoff
Series Editor
Lexington Russian, Eurasian, and Eastern European Politics Book Series

Chapter One

Electoral Strategies and Authoritarianism

Introduction and Background

Since 1991, contested, multiparty elections have served as the primary vehicle for filling government offices in Eastern Europe and Eurasia. Contested elections have introduced the classic dynamic of competition between incumbent candidates and parties, and opposition actors seeking office in most post-Soviet states. However, the behavior and electoral strategies of both incumbent and opposition political actors in these states have at times been puzzling.

Many of these elections have been conducted with significant interference from the ruling or incumbent regime. Election monitors continue to observe fraud and manipulation in elections regardless of the degree of competition in place. This means that monitors see manipulation in elections where the outcome is genuinely uncertain as well as in those where most expect the incumbent to win. In 2012, for example, Vladimir Putin was widely expected to easily win reelection to the presidency of the Russian Federation when he decided to seek a third, nonconsecutive term. And yet, international election monitors from the Organization for Security and Cooperation in Europe (OSCE) observed the rampant abuse of state resources during the pre-election campaign.[1] So, why would the regime actors, like Putin and his supporters, bother with manipulation at all? Why would incumbents engage in such activities given that their victory is so predictable?

A similar dynamic exists for opposition actors as well. Many of the opposition victories that have been witnessed in Eastern Europe and Eurasia occurred when multiple opposition actors and/or parties banded together to challenge election results and/or to challenge the incumbent regime during the election itself. Indeed, the highly publicized and studied Color Revolutions elections (Georgia's 2003 parliamentary election, Ukraine's 2004 presidential election, and Kyrgyzstan's 2005 parliamentary election) all contained a unified opposition after the disputed election results; furthermore, Ukraine's Orange Revolution also presented a case of a pre-election coalition of opposition actors throughout the campaign. If opposition unity or the formation of pre-election blocs have proven to be such useful strategies, then theoretically we might expect to see them in many or most elections. Yet this has not been the case. Pre-election opposition blocs, for example, have only been witnessed in 27% of elections within former Soviet states.[2] So what explains this relatively low rate?

In this book I explore the various dynamics at work in the selection of electoral strategies by both incumbent and opposition actors in these states. While a vast majority of states worldwide, including those that emerged after the collapse of the Soviet Union, hold some type of election to determine their political leadership, the presence of elections themselves does not guarantee democracy. Such recognition has led to a growing field of scholarship devoted to understanding the political dynamics of electoral authoritarian regimes, a distinct regime type from both consolidated democracies and fully authoritarian states. While fully autocratic states may hold elections that are often constrained to one political party or may limit the number of candidates on the ballot (Gandhi and Lust-Okar 2009; Hyde and Martinov 2011), the elections within electoral authoritarian states allow competition, but witness authoritarian practices by elites, including electoral fraud, interference and an unfair electoral playing field (Schedler 2013; Levitsky and Way 2010). Many of these studies note behavior similar to the examples cited above. Incumbent politicians and parties often engage in electoral manipulation even in elections they already know they will win, and sometimes even to a higher degree than when the election's outcome is in question (Schedler 2013; Simpser 2013). Opposition figures have also demonstrated variation in running well-coordinated campaigns that have proven crucial to their ability to achieve victory (Bunce and Wolchik 2011). Yet the majority of studies have explored these issues with a focus on one side or the other, ignoring the likely interconnections between opposition and incumbent forces as well as the interaction between incumbent strategies at electoral interference alongside legal attempts at voter persuasion.[3] As Boix (2009) reminds us, political parties and actors inherently consider the goals, strategies and behavior of their competitors in establishing their own programs as well as their campaign tactics. I consider this relationship to be especially important due to the lopsided scale of political conflict in electoral authoritarian regimes. This book explores these dynamics and develops a theory of electoral strategies for both incumbent and opposition actors within electoral authoritarian states.

When considering politics in electoral authoritarian states, the uneven power held by incumbent leaders, and often their party, significantly dominates the electoral and political landscape. Due to this power imbalance and the government's ability to hinder opposition development, both opposition and incumbent political actors face puzzling dilemmas. The opposition, like parties and candidates operating under more democratic circumstances, are theoretically interested in winning or building voter support. To do so, they should seek to persuade voters, often by differentiating themselves from their competition on policy positions and issue preferences, and by criticizing the incumbent regime. However, the political environment in electoral authoritarian regimes is marked by the uneven and often unfair electoral field of competition dominated by incumbents. If parties and candidates want to try to win votes away from such dominant political actors during electoral campaigns, they may risk regime blowback that could threaten their continued ability to exist or function normally. Therefore, opposition actors within electoral authoritarian regimes are confronted with the reality that the very behavior that can help them win votes may threaten their political future.

Incumbents in electoral authoritarian regimes, on the other hand, may have the legal ability to eliminate elections altogether, due to their significant institutional power. Instead, many choose to allow elections to continue, thus subjecting themselves to regular public scrutiny. Given this, incumbents face the dilemma of how much to focus on voter persuasion versus electoral manipulation during the election in seeking to ensure that they are victorious (Birch 2011a). This balance can be precarious, as highly visible electoral manipulation and fraud can threaten their popular support in the state and may trigger public unrest and demonstrations. The aforementioned Color Revolutions developed under precisely these circumstances, where popular outcry developed after the perception of rampant electoral fraud and the manipulation of the election's outcome. Therefore, incumbent and pro-regime actors are likely to seek a balance between their desire to win and their desire to prevent massive public outcry.

Despite these important and conflicting dilemmas, the present literature lacks a comprehensive theory explaining under which circumstances opposition and incumbent actors are likely to select a particular strategy or set of strategies. Given that the opposition seems to vary its selection of strategies, what influences such decisions? Why would opposition actors not form a pre-election bloc most of the time? Moreover, why would opposition actors in some instances pursue just the opposite: an election boycott that surrenders their chance to participate altogether? Turning to incumbent actors, manipulation and fraud can be both beneficial and costly electoral strategies. Given this, are they more likely to select some types of manipulation over others? And why do they bother with manipulation in predictable elections at all? I contend that, given these conflicting motivations, the electoral behaviors of both the opposition and incumbents within electoral authoritarian regimes are likely related to one another, and should be examined together.

To do this, I build upon the arguments of Tsebelis (1990) and Schedler (2013) that treat political phenomena as a series of nested games. This rational-choice approach argues that political actors operate strategically, considering not just the immediate goals and outcomes of a particular action, but the future optimal scenarios that may better serve their interests. This type of approach is especially useful for understanding behavior that may be seen as counterintuitive, such as the usage of electoral manipulation in elections no matter how predictable the outcome, as well as the decision to boycott an election and face guaranteed defeat. Building upon Schedler's (2013) framework of nested games in electoral authoritarian regimes, I argue that some strategies, such as certain types of manipulation, have greater short-term benefits but long-term costs, while others, including opposition boycotts, have explicit short-term costs but greater potential long-term benefits. From this perspective, we can better explain the selection of these strategies based on factors that affect an election's outcome itself, including the competitiveness of the election, the incumbent dominance in the state, and the type of election.

BACKGROUND AND IMPETUS FOR STUDY

Elections have long been scrutinized on multiple fronts. At their most basic level, they serve as a tool that determines the officeholders of various state positions. Elections inherently allow citizens to hold these officeholders accountable for their actions and decisions. This accountability typically produces competition and incorporates debate into the process of governing. And yet, elections historically have also been held in fully closed authoritarian states (Hermet, Rose, and Rouquie 1978). Under these circumstances, elections have been argued to provide a façade for democracy (Linz 2000). Yet such elections have also been argued to serve other functions. These include a communicative or informational purpose, as well as promoting competition and even generating legitimacy (Hermet, Rose, and Rouquie 1978; Simpser 2013; Schedler 2013; Cox 2009; Little, Tucker, and LaGatta 2015; Miller 2015). Elections can provide information to voters on the strength of the regime (Magaloni 2006; Simpser 2013; Schedler 2013) as well as a regime's weakness and lack of popularity (Little et al. 2015), causing voters to protest the results of elections perceived to be close and fraudulent. The practice of elections can also be used to reduce the capacity of the opposition. They may be enticed to join the regime, or be coopted by pro-government actors (Magaloni 2006; Reuter, Buckley, Shubenkova, and Garifullina 2016). Finally, election results can also spur policy shifts in electoral authoritarian regimes by demonstrating to the incumbent regime that voters are dissatisfied (Miller 2015).

The numerous functions of elections are important given that elections are now held in over eighty percent of states worldwide,[4] yet the same high rates of democratization have not been observed. Despite hope that elections could serve as the impetus to democratization (Lindberg 2009; Teorell and Hadenius 2009; Brownlee 2009b), this has not always been observed. Flores and Nooruddin (2016: 32) remark that "the democratizing power of elections depends on their integrity; not all elections are created equal." Instead, elections in so-called developing democracies are inherently problematic in enabling democracy, given the lack of legitimate and stable institutions (Flores and Nooruddin 2016) or that elections can ultimately be tools used to keep an authoritarian regime in power (Gandhi and Lust-Okar 2009). This has contributed to the burgeoning research on electoral authoritarian regimes. These states hold regular elections but also maintain more restrictions on civil and political liberties and routinely witness authoritarian incumbent behavior to a degree that precludes them from being considered "democratizing."[5] In these states, electoral unfairness is not the exception, but rather the norm, with elections that "exist and are meaningful, but (are) systematically violated in favor of the incumbent" (Levitsky and Way 2010:19). These elections can vary in terms of competition, sometimes yielding genuinely unpredictable contests while others lack any surprise concerning the outcome. It is within these states that much of the recent research on the informational or communicative role of elections has focused, as they can serve a functional role in these states in particular (Schedler 2002; Simpser 2013; Little et al 2015).

With all this considered, Morse (2012:179) reminds us that we still know relatively little about "the underpinnings that sustain electoral authoritarianism," with much still to be uncovered. As elections, they still require popular participation and voter support, even given the uneven playing field, with both incumbents and opposition figures still likely to select strategies that serve their interests. Given this reality, I am interested in how the electoral strategies of both incumbents and opposition actors may vary depending on the conditions present within the election. Previous studies have explored aspects of this, though more often producing questions rather than answers. Birch (2011a:56) suggests that all incumbents and governments have the opportunity to pursue "a package of fair and foul electoral strategies" in seeking victory. This decision, she argues, is likely based on considering the threshold of both needed to win and still maintain legitimacy. Scheder (2013) provides the most thorough investigative analysis into the selection of some incumbent and opposition strategies, revealing many conflicting and counterintuitive relationships. Many of these studies have illustrated that electoral manipulation often does not necessarily alter the outcome that would have been reached without any interference at all, which is puzzling. Simpser (2013) asserts that this is due to the informational role that manipulation serves within the context of the election. Therefore, much of the existing literature emphasizes the need to understand these phenomena, but provides mixed and sometimes conflicting conclusions.

The next section seeks to flesh out the broad relationships and observations made about electoral authoritarian regimes. It focuses on both incumbent and opposition behaviors, and how they fit into the dynamics of unfair elections, deficits in democratic institutions, and the potential for authoritarian strength. It does this through a regional account of both electoral manipulation and opposition electoral behaviors among post-Soviet states, which remain the focus of this book. It illustrates the variety of tactics available to incumbents and regime forces, and it demonstrates the similar patterns observed in both the regional power, Russia, and many of the smaller states that receive less scholarly attention.

ELECTORAL AUTHORITARIANISM IN PRACTICE

Manipulation Strategies in post-Soviet States

The post-Soviet region has seen no shortage of manipulation strategies initiated to support incumbent candidates and parties. Since the collapse of the Soviet Union in 1991, many patterns of manipulation emerged across the region. The vast majority of the scholarship on electoral manipulation has examined and analyzed such behavior on a case-by-case basis. This is understandable, as these phenomena are often incredibly complex and may require extensive data to understand. What this has meant is that no study of the post-Soviet region has produced a generalizable theory and explanation for the frequency and types of manipulation employed by incumbents in these states. Therefore, I first provide an overview of the trends observed and the explanations provided across these varied, typically case-specific studies.

Russia has received the largest share of attention on election manipulation. Many studies in particular have emphasized the many different strategies of manipulation observed in Russia over the last twenty-five years. One ubiquitous feature of Russian politics has been the growth and sustenance of patron-client networks, machine politics, and neo-patromonialism. The main thrust of such arguments rests on the provision of rents and resources to supporters through a single power structure to maintain unchallenged authority (Hale 2015; Gel'man 2016). Russian elections, both at the national and regional levels, have witnessed machine politics and clientelism (Hale 2007; Golosov 2011; Harvey 2016); government-associated workplaces have been especially susceptible to clientelistic efforts at voter mobilization (Frye, Reuter and Szakonyi 2014). Russia's immense geographic size has not deterred the success of patronal politics; instead, regions in which well-resourced elite maintain complex political machines are more likely to produce pro-government vote swings. Conversely, when Kremlin-appointed regional outsiders take power, regions often reveal a decline in support for pro-government candidates; this may be due to the outsiders' lacking access to previously established networks and machines (Reuter 2013).

Candidate registration laws have also seen manipulation in Russia, as they are often designed to be so broad that they can legally prevent any prospective candidate deemed problematic (Wilson 2005; Baekken 2015). Election laws have repeatedly been modified in Russia in ways that many argue have been designed to suppress or stymie opposition political power. Regional parties were effectively barred through laws that mandated membership in at least half of Russia's regions (Wilson 2006). Additionally, the electoral system for the State Duma was switched to an entirely proportional representation system with an increased minimum threshold of 7% for representation, and the direct election of governors was eliminated, which has also worked to limit opportunities for dissent and opposition challenges (Levitsky and Way 2010). Furthermore, regional electoral commissions across Russia, along with United Russia, the platform party that supports president Vladimir Putin, have exhibited different techniques in maintaining control over the electoral landscape. Their behaviors have varied from relatively permissive registration to the widespread denial of opposition registration to instances of intense fraud and falsification (Kynev 2015). Collectively, these types of registration manipulation have been observed to a greater degree in elections that are seen to be more competitive (Harvey 2016; Baekken 2015).

Election day fraud has also been widely observed and studied in Russia. Electoral fraud has a particular regional dimension in Russia. Fraud has been detected in Russia through especially high rates of voter turnout, especially when such rates spike in some regions, districts or republics but not others. Such behavior is particularly blatant when certain regions see their support for pro-government candidates grow immensely from one contest to the next, as was observed between Russia's 2000 and 2004 presidential elections. Ballot box stuffing as well as switching votes from one candidate or party to another also have occurred in Russia's elections, and are expected in polling places where election monitors are absent. Many of the ethnic autonomous regions and republics have been the sites of massive margins of the victory for Putin and pro-government forces (Myagkov, Ordeshook, and Shakin 2009; Goodnow, Moser, and Smith 2014). Moreover, the practices of inflated voter turnout and election day fraud in Russia have spread due to regional proximity, showing how regions neighboring those with excessive turnout will too witness such increases in subsequent elections (Moser and White 2017). Efforts at election monitoring by opposition parties and supporters have argued that the vote tabulation process is often either not transparent or fraudulent; in the 2003 parliamentary election, both the Yabloko and Union of Right Forces (SPS) parties would have received enough votes for representation were it not for fraudulent vote counting (Wilson 2006).[6] The 2011 parliamentary election also witnessed allegations of fraud and mismanagement at the polls, but clearly the blatant nature of such conduct was a step too far for many Russians, leading to the largest protests in twenty years (Petrov, Lipman, and Hale 2014). One unifying theme, however, is that while fraudulent vote counts, inflated turnout figures and ballot box malfeasances are regular occurrences, almost no observers consider such acts to be reversing the outcomes from a contest without manipulation. Pro-government forces thus far had been expected to prevail when they have; the fraud has only worked to produce more striking margins of victory.

While the volume is less, studies on elections in other post-Soviet states have also emphasized incumbent manipulation. Clientelism and patrimonial politics were common practice in Georgia both prior to and after 2003 (Timm 2012); such practices were also endemic to Ukraine's political system in the 1990s (Birch 1997; Pleines 2008). Informal oligarchic networks have continued to influence electoral politics in Ukraine, but their support has been divided among different regional elites, rather than all operating in support of the national government (Pleines 2012). Similarly, the heads of schools, universities, and other government entities were enlisted to engage in get-out-the-vote efforts in favor of the incumbent, Victor Yanukovych by putting pressure on employees and subordinates (Way 2005a). Patronage and the establishment of centralized power hierarchies have been clearly linked to the survival of authoritarian incumbent regimes in Belarus, Azerbaijan, Kazakhstan, and Tajikistan (Way 2005b; Hale 2015). The distribution of rents and support has been facilitated both through state-run enterprises as well as through informal connections to economic oligarchs; the presence of significant natural resource rents has proven to be pivotal in many cases as well (Hale 2015).

Explicit fraud has been especially visible in the post-Soviet region. The perception of such fraud served as the impetus for the Color Revolutions, which began as large and organized protests of the official election results. The actual practice of fraud varied. In Georgia, many people were denied ballots on election day, examples of group voting were observed and the official results seemed completely outlandish when compared to pre-election polls (Fairbanks 2004). Internal documents from Ukraine's 2004 presidential election now reveal extensive pre-meditated plans for electoral fraud, including ballot box stuffing, carousel voting, and the denial of a secret ballot, all in service of ensuring regime victory (Way 2005a). In Kyrgyzstan, opposition actors and supporters alleged that the fraudulent results were due to explicit government pressure and voting irregularities in addition to a fraudulent vote count (Abazov 2007). Protests against electoral fraud have occurred not just in states where the incumbent regime was toppled, but also in response to the perception of widespread fraud in Azerbaijan, Armenia, and Belarus (Bunce and Wolchik 2011), as well as in Moldova (Senyuva 2010).

Obstruction and suppression of opposition campaign activities have been prevalent as well. One shared characteristic among almost all post-Soviet states has been increased scrutiny and pressure on opposition parties, actors and activists (Bunce and Wolchik 2011), although the specific tactics of such efforts vary. Pressure on the opposition was a key strategy for the Kuchma regime in Ukraine, particularly the usage of tax police enforcement to economically hinder opposition efforts (Darden 2001; Darden 2008). The intimidation of the opposition actually increased in Georgia under Mikhail Saakashvili since its Rose Revolution in 2003, through efforts at campaign finance and regulations in the Electoral Code that disproportionately hurt opposition groups (Jawad 2012). Media restrictions have effectively eliminated the opposition from television in Azerbaijan (Fairbanks 2004), and laws have been passed to evict opposition forces from campaign offices (La Porte 2015). Laws designed to prevent certain opposition candidates from running at all have also proliferated across the region (Bunce and Wolchik 2011)

The practice of drafting and manipulating registration standards and election laws more generally has been observed across the region. In fact, the spread of election laws susceptible to political influence has been attributed to Russia's own practices, a so-called "authoritarian diffusion" of such laws (Bader 2014). More generally, there has been an alternative movement to Western democracy promotion through actions like the diffusion of authoritarian regulations and practices termed "autocracy promotion." Strategies to subvert democracy and maintain incumbent regime dominance have been emphasized and spread across the former Soviet Union (Cameron and Orenstein 2012). Russia has also been active in so-called 'Black Knight' support for authoritarian candidates within the region by offering guidance and models to follow for electoral manipulation and the weakening of democracy more generally (Tolstrup 2015; Levitsky and Way 2010). This behavior definitely introduces new strategies into elections, but it does not explain when one type of strategy may be introduced over another. Since this type of "autocracy promotion" has grown, especially over the last ten years, the frequency of some strategies may have increased as a result. The empirical models in chapters 3 and 4 will control for time to account for this.

Opposition Strategies

While the incumbent strategies of manipulation include multiple categories, sub-types, and behaviors, the strategies for the opposition are much more simplified. In the early years following the collapse of the Soviet Union, the political opposition in many states found ways to assert influence even if not fully in power; one pathway was through representation in the legislature (Remington 2001). The underdeveloped and skewed political environments of the former Soviet states often relegated opposition parties and actors to afterthoughts. However, it was the Color Revolutions that brought significant attention to one particular opposition strategy: the formation of opposition pre-electoral coalitions (McFaul 2005; Tucker 2007). These studies emphasized not just the specific role of the opposition in Georgia, Ukraine, and Kyrgyzstan, respectively, but also for the tactic's potential to more generally bring the opposition back into the political calculus. To clarify, while the opposition did unite into a pre-election coalition in Ukraine's 2004 presidential election, the same did not occur in Georgia or Kyrgyzstan. In Georgia, the opposition parties campaigned separately and did not present a unified front to voters (Fairbanks 2004). In Kyrgyzstan, candidates were not allowed to register officially with a party or coalition, and instead all ran as independents (Abazov 2007). Yet in these two cases, opposition or anti-regime candidates and parties did unite after the election in protest of the fraudulent election results.

As an electoral strategy, a pre-election coalition is easily identifiable and measurable across electoral contests. When seeking to unseat an incumbent, especially within the context of an electoral authoritarian regime, opposition parties and actors that combine forces and campaign together represent clear instances of this strategy. The formation of a pre-electoral coalition explicitly links at least two parties, factions and/or politicians into a temporary coalition, typically with the implicit or explicit goal of then governing together if victorious. The utility of this strategy as a device for toppling electoral authoritarian regimes emerged in Serbia's 2000 election, the so-called Bulldozer Revolution. As chapter 5 will show, the frequency of opposition pre-election coalitions has clearly increased in the post-Soviet region, and the diffusion of this strategy is evident. The zeitgeist aspect of this strategy has been explored by Bunce and Wolchik (2011) in their case studies of Ukraine, Georgia, Azerbaijan, Armenia, and Belarus. While the existence of a strategy of unification was already known, its success in some settings has helped opposition forces across the region learn from previous efforts, beginning with Serbia's example in 2000 (Beissinger 2007). Initially, opposition unification was somewhat of a rarity in the region (Huskey and Iskakova 2010), but its frequency has grown. In fact, the post-Soviet region is now considered home to the largest number of opposition pre-election coalitions overall, when compared with electoral authoritarian regimes in other regions (Gandhi and Reuter 2013).

Some attention to opposition pre-electoral coalitions have highlighted the importance of their internal composition in the post-Soviet region. Coalitions that included previous regime insiders that defected to the opposition have often been more successful. This was especially the case in Ukraine's 2004 presidential election, where Viktor Yushchenko, Yuliya Tymoshenko, Petro Poroshenko, and Oleksander Zinchenko had all previously worked in the incumbent regime. Mikhail Saakashvili of Georgia, and the leading force behind the 2003 Rose Revolution, had also publicly resigned from the previous incumbent's regime (Bunce and Wolchik 2011). Additionally, connections to Western democracy assistance and NGOs that sought to strengthen pro-democracy opposition actors has also been highlighted as a reason for the success of some opposition coalitions (Levitsky and Way 2010; Bunce and Wolchik 2011). This has also pointed to the need for a more nuanced approach beyond simply uniting against the incumbent regime. Bunce and Wolchik (2011) in particular argued that new and savvy campaign strategies as well as international democracy and civil society support were far more crucial in contributing to an opposition victory than unity alone.

The actual formation of an opposition pre-election coalition has been fraught with issues as well. While Kyrgyzstan was home to the Tulip Revolution, where opposition candidates united in protest of the election results, and where power has alternated multiple times in the last decade, a unified opposition has remained a complex issue. The election that produced the Tulip Revolution itself did not feature an opposition pre-electoral bloc; this was largely due to electoral rules that forced all candidates to run as independents. Since 2005, opposition actors have stated that political ambition as well as the temptation of government spoils and the pressure of regime oppression have all worked to hinder opposition unification (Huskey and Iskakova 2010). In Russia, many have noted that the more liberal opposition parties such as Yabloko and the now-defunct Union of Right Forces had been unable or unwilling to unite in elections. This lack of action has at times been blamed for their electoral exclusion from the Duma, particularly after the 2003 parliamentary election when each party won about 4%, just shy of the 5% threshold. Ambition and personal differences have been blamed for their continued rivalry and their failure to unify (Sakwa 2005). More recently, anti-corruption blogger and opposition activist Alexei Navalny saw his attempts to register as a candidate for Russia's 2018 presidential election rejected. He subsequently refused to join forces with the registered, purported opposition candidate Ksenia Sobchak.[7] Navalny considered Sobchak to be a spoiler and

Kremlin-approved candidate, while she argued that she arose from the same post-2011 Bolotnaya protest movement and supported similar issues.[8] This example highlights how the intense skepticism and exclusion among different opposition-identified candidates and parties have reduced the likelihood for any grand coalition in Russia.

Even when a unified opposition succeeds in winning the election and taking power, this is no guarantee of success. The Orange coalition in Ukraine, following the 2004 presidential election, collapsed after a few short years of governing collectively. This collapse has been attributed to the weak party system, the lack of cohesion over the policy agenda, personality clashes between Victor Yushchenko and Yuliya Tymoshenko, and the institutional structures of the political system (Thompson 2008).

A second opposition strategy of note is an electoral boycott. Because electoral authoritarian regimes are often built upon the foundations of unfair elections and government manipulation, opposition actors may understandably consider abandoning the charade entirely. Under the conditions of obstruction, repression, and repeated losses on election day, opposition actors may find the idea of boycotting appealing. Thus, an opposition boycott represents the extreme opposite of a pre-election opposition coalition. Major boycotts are events in which most or all of the existing opposition actors agree not to participate in the contest (Beaulieu 2014). Thus, instead of agreeing to work together in unseating an authoritarian incumbent, in this case they agree to sit out the election entirely. Boycotts have been observed within the post-Soviet region, although at a lesser frequency than pre-election coalitions. This alone is surprising, as it reveals that opposition actors generally prefer to participate in the unfair contests of electoral authoritarian regimes, rather than selecting the protest strategy of a boycott. Clearly, boycotts may be strategies of last resort, and this emphasizes the puzzle of what drives opposition actors to make such a drastic decision.

Boycotts have generally been studied through a cross-national and cross-regional approach. Many of these studies have focused on Africa, where almost two-thirds of the globe's election boycotts have taken place. Therefore, region-specific consideration of boycotts among post-Soviet states has been quite low. International election monitors have been linked to the presence or absence of boycotts, in both a cause and effect relationship (Beaulieu and Hyde 2009; Kelley 2011). In this vein, the participation of monitors has been attributed to the decision by most of the opposition in Azerbaijan not to boycott the 1998 presidential race (Cornell 2001). Those that did boycott this election attributed the politicized Central Election Commission as the reason for their abstention (Hyde and Beaulieu 2009). The elections included in this book were all observed by international election monitors, meaning that every observed boycott also coincided with the presence of such monitors.[9] Unlike the major boycotts typically witnessed in Africa, many of the boycotts in the post-Soviet region have been partial. At various times in Belarus, some opposition actors have decided to boycott, while others have participated, even forming a unified coalition themselves (White and Korosteleva-Polglase 2006). Such mixed messages may dilute the impact of this protest strategy.

In a different vein, Russia's 2004 presidential election featured either second (or third) tier candidates or boycotts from the systemic and non-systemic opposition, which did end up producing an especially lopsided victory for Vladimir Putin (Clark 2005). Russia's most recent 2018 presidential election also featured a prominent boycott from the aforementioned Navalny. This boycott looked different from others, as it came only after Navalny was not allowed to register as a candidate. From December 2016 until December of the following year, he behaved very much like a candidate, opening campaign offices across the country, holding rallies, and releasing policy position papers.[10] Once Navalny changed his message to a boycott, he repurposed his campaign operations to hold demonstrations and gatherings in support of a boycott. These events attracted significant negative attention from the regime, demonstrating the ability for a boycott to still engage with the incumbent regime during an election.[11] Boycotts at the regional level have also taken place within Russia, but these cases have been even more limited. One reason is that the systemic opposition generally has had more opportunities to genuinely take office in some particular regions (Turovsky 2015). Finally, boycotting actors can struggle to get their message out to the electorate. During Kazakhstan's 2011 presidential election, for example, opposition groups and actors that called for a boycott faced pressure from the regime and were largely prevented from promoting their endeavor in the media, similar to the experience of the boycott in Russia mentioned above.[12] Given the dearth of region-specific accounts of opposition boycotts, their occurrence and effects will be considered in greater depth in chapter 6.

EXISTING THEORIES OF ELECTORAL STRATEGIES

While no previous book has created a general theory of electoral strategies in electoral authoritarian states, many other studies have offered explanations for aspects of these strategies. However, some suggestions and theories have been developed regarding particular strategies. Therefore, I will consider explanations regarding the usage of the following strategies in any type of political regime: incumbent electoral manipulation, opposition pre-election blocs, and opposition boycotts.

Previous Explanations of Incumbent electoral manipulation

I begin with the previous scholarship on electoral manipulation. These studies have noted some patterns of when manipulation occurs, as well as distinguishing among the manipulation strategies witnessed. I classify these studies and findings into three categories: those that have focused on international, domestic, and election-level explanations for electoral manipulation.

At the international level, election monitoring is an increasingly common practice in all states, democratic, democratizing, or electoral authoritarian (Hyde 2011). Intergovernmental, domestic, and international nongovernmental monitoring agencies typically descend upon most elections globally, with the consent of the domestic regime. These monitors could theoretically have an impact on electoral manipulation, perhaps reducing its frequency. This has not been observed to be the case. Both Hyde (2011) and Kelley (2012) have found that manipulation does not go away in the presence of election monitors, even though the monitors are invited and granted official access to the elections. Simpser (2013) further observed that monitored elections are associated with higher levels of electoral manipulation than non-monitored contests. This does not mean that election monitoring has had no effect on incumbent and regime manipulation. The routinized practice of election monitoring seems to have shifted the manipulation from the actual day of voting back to the campaign period (LaPorte 2015). As a result, pre-election manipulation is now the most common type observed in elections (Donno and Roussias 2012). This suggests that regimes have learned from the presence of election monitors and have altered their practices as a result.

Another potential international factor on electoral manipulation is the receipt of international democracy assistance. Regimes that receive such aid may be compelled to reduce the practice of manipulation, as it by definition hinders the potential for democracy in the state. Of course, this explanation is somewhat problematic, a reality acknowledged by Birch (2011a). She notes that states receiving democracy aid may be less democratic by definition, and therefore we may expect elections in those states to be more problematic anyway. Yet Scott (2012) argues that democracy aid from the US Agency for International Development (USAID) has a positive relationship with subsequent democracy and human rights records. Birch's (2011a) analyses found that while democracy assistance had no effect on the overall practice of electoral manipulation, she did observe some differences among types of manipulation. Democracy assistance has a positive relationship with the manipulation of electoral rules, while it has a negative correlation with the manipulation of state resources, and no relationship with interference in the electoral administration. This suggests that democracy assistance may have mixed effects on the conduct of elections, and cannot be a primary explanation for manipulation.

Domestic-level explanations have also been provided to explain electoral manipulation. Factors such as the protection of civil liberties, civil society development, and corruption all could potentially influence the decision by incumbents and regimes to manipulate elections. Presumably, in states where civil liberties are respected and protected, those same governments may be less likely to interfere with the electoral process. A similar logic holds for civil society development: a more active and responsive civil society may be more likely to hold the regime accountable for its actions, which could lead actors to avoid or reduce electoral manipulation. Conversely, corruption could have a positive association with manipulation. The prevalence of corrupt activities could signify that the government lacks the capacity, or the will, to enforce the rule of law and limit corrupt activities. In her analyses, Birch (2011a) observed that corruption, media freedom, and the potential for protests have all had significant relationships with some types of electoral manipulation, but these relationships were not consistent across types. Still, the level of corruption has a positive association with the institutional, media, state resource, voter registration, and vote counting manipulation. On the other hand, civil society development has a negative relationship with voter, media, state resource, voter registration, and vote counting manipulation.

Political institutions present another set of national-level factors that may influence the practice of electoral manipulation. In particular, electoral systems that present the opportunity for a personal vote have been argued to increase electoral manipulation, as the votes cast can directly affect an individual candidate as opposed to a party (Hicken 2007; Birch 2007). This relationship has been empirically observed in multiple studies (Birch 2007; Simpser 2013). Simpser (2013) also found that federal systems, and, under some circumstances, parliamentary systems, have a positive relationship with electoral manipulation.

The most intuitive and prolific explanations for electoral manipulation and fraud have been found at the electoral level. In particular, many studies argue that it is deployed to help incumbents win tight races, and thus varies depending on the competition of the election. This type of reasoning is especially common when describing fraud and clientelism in democratic states (Argersinger 1985; Nyblade and Reed 2008), where such efforts are expected in especially competitive elections. Vote-buying and other extra-legal mobilization efforts have been associated with more competitive elections in Russia as well (Harvey 2016). Electoral fraud has also been argued to serve this instrumental purpose of ensuring victory in non-democratic, electoral authoritarian states. For example, both Magaloni (2006) and Greene (2007) have argued that fraud committed by the PRI political party in Mexico in the 1980s was just for this purpose; the party had suffered from an economic downturn and could therefore no longer rely on regime performance for voter support. Yet Harvey (2016) has found the opposite, where the falsification of results and ballot box stuffing were more associated with elections with lower competition. In general, elections with the largest margin of victory across the post-Soviet landscape, such as those in Kazakhstan, Belarus, Azerbaijan, and Russia, are also those where fraud has been the most rampant (Bader 2012). Fraud has also been positively associated with the presence of an opposition boycott, presumably to increase overall vote totals that have suffered from low voter participation (Schedler 2013). These perspectives instead suggest that ballot box stuffing and the falsification of election results are most common in the least competitive of elections.

Simpser (2013) presents an alternative view of electoral manipulation in electoral authoritarian regimes. He argues that the most dominant and confident incumbents should also be the ones who engage in the largest quantity of manipulation. For incumbents and regimes under these circumstances, the manipulation is not deployed to ensure victory, but instead to demonstrate power and dominance. By doing this, voters view the regime as inevitable and are more likely to reluctantly vote for the regime instead of "wasting" a vote on the opposition. Therefore, according to his argument, elections with less competition and greater incumbent dominance should see the most electoral manipulation, both before the actual voting and on the election day itself. This type of argument aligns with many other arguments on the informational power of electoral manipulation. Schedler (2013) found that the larger the previous margin of victory, the more likely incumbents were to exclude opposition actors from subsequent contests. In electoral authoritarian regimes, where competition is already low, the public actually expects manipulation. If a regime refrained from such behavior, it may actually appear weak and without confidence (Little 2015). This is especially the case within the Soviet successor states of Eastern Europe and Central Asia, where elections are significant public events or "electoral carnivals" (Birch 2011b). Similarly, state capacity may affect the usage of manipulation. Seeburg (2014) argues that outright fraud is more likely in elections with low state capacity as last-ditch efforts to remain in power. Conversely, states with high capacity have the resources needed to stay in power through subtler strategies of manipulation. Magaloni (2006) makes a similar argument about the usage of fraud versus the abuse of state resources. She asserts that when the Mexican PRI was at the height of its dominance, it did not engage in fraud because it did not need to, instead relying on state resource abuse. It was only when their continued dominance was challenged that they committed electoral fraud.

Hauser (2018) echoes this by demonstrating that instrumental varieties of manipulation are more likely to occur when the outcome is more uncertain, while the same was not true for informational manipulation.

This discussion has thus emphasized two potentially competing arguments. When elections are competitive, whether in democracies or electoral authoritarian regimes, fraud and some manipulation are expected to be used more, as they can help guarantee victory for a threatened incumbent, party, or regime. Conversely, when the regime is firmly in control and enjoys elections that are no longer competitive, whether through a dominant party, electoral hegemony, or high state capacity, then the regime is expected to refrain from electoral fraud. Instead they may focus their efforts on manipulation that can send a message. Here the authors have disagreed, however, in what best does this. While Simpser (2013) argues it is the quantity that matters, Seeberg (2014) instead emphasizes the subtlety of state resource abuse. Schedler (2013) also notes that candidate and party exclusion are more common in elections with low competition, but that competition had no relationship with repression, censorship or outright fraud.[13] Given the literature, manipulation is expected to both go up and down in the most and least competitive of elections.

Moreover, many of these studies have focused on multiple types of electoral manipulation, including those committed during the pre-election period as well as fraud and intimidation on the election day itself. Birch (2011a) performed one of the most detailed analyses of manipulation at every step of the election process. Her results found notable variations in the relationships between the hypothesized variables and the prevalence of the manipulation type, emphasizing the need to separate out different categories of manipulation. Similarly, Schedler (2013) investigated four types of incumbent manipulation: repression, censorship, exclusion, and fraud. He too reported mixed relationships among these types, with each having varied positive and negative associations with different explanatory variables. Finally, Hauser (2018) reported that the correlated factors for instrumental and informational manipulation types were vastly different and often in opposing directions, further demonstrating distinction within categories of manipulation. This suggests the need to disentangle the different findings on manipulation, as different strategies may serve different purposes. As this book distinguishes between instrumental and informational manipulation strategies, it aims to further the scholarship and conversation on electoral manipulation.

Previous Explanations for Opposition Pre-Election Coalitions

Opposition pre-election coalitions have been identified as one of the most successful strategies in unseating authoritarian incumbents in electoral authoritarian regimes. In the case of a legislative election, the coalition typi-cally means bringing together the combined resources of two or more parties, which, depending on the electoral rules in place, may produce a combined list of candidates or may agree to only field certain candidates in agreed-upon districts. An opposition pre-election coalition that forms prior to an executive election instead typically means that the actors or parties agree in advance to support just one candidate for the post from their combined roster. These coalitions were present in the notable 2004 Orange Revolution of Ukraine, where the opposition proved to be so successful that voters did not accept the election results when the incumbent announced victory. Similarly, after Geor-gia's 2003 and Kyrgyzstan's 2005 parliamentary elections, public discontent was so strong in the face of perceived manipulation that the opposition united after the election and refused to accept the outcome. The elections' results were discarded, new elections were held, and they were then victorious in all three of these cases.

The events of the Color Revolutions brought significant attention upon opposition unity. Most of these studies have focused on how the presence of a bloc makes opposition victory more likely, and can produce shifts toward democratization. However, no study has provided a comprehensive look at the factors that may affect the occurrence of such a bloc. Up until these events, explanations for pre-electoral coalitions came primarily from demo-cratic environments. These types of explanations focus on the institutional and societal attributes of the state. Thus, the electoral system in place (SMP versus PR), the ideological cleavages within society, and district magnitude have all been correlated with the emergence of pre-electoral coalitions (Cox 1997). However, these same relationships have not been observed in electoral authoritarian regimes, suggesting that the explanations vary between demo-cratic and non-democratic states (Wahman 2011; Gandhi and Reuter 2013).

One potential factor may be the dearth of truly competitive elections. The practice of elections in non-democratic, autocratic states may make such coalitions less likely to occur in general. This may be due to the fact that the opposition under such circumstances are "trapped" into participating in such contests which ultimately seek to benefit the non-democratic regime. Oppo-sition forces therefore are expending their resources on futile endeavors for victory when they actually have little chance of attaining power. To survive, some opposition forces may become loyal to the regime over time, while others may continue to oppose it genuinely (Gandhi and Przeworski 2007; Magaloni 2006). This scenario can make opposition coalitions less likely to emerge because the opposition may have fragmented or even been coopted by the regime through the process of elections. However, this explanation does not account for the actual observations of opposition pre-electoral coalitions.

Specifically, such coalitions have formed in electoral authoritarian regimes with varying degrees of incumbent dominance. Returning to the examples of the Color Revolutions, while Ukraine, heading into the 2004 presidential election, was considered to have low incumbent dominance in the state, the incumbent regimes in both Georgia and Kyrgyzstan prior to their notable elections were highly dominant. This is because the incumbent executives at the time had been reelected with at least 70% of the vote prior to the elections that would become the Color Revolutions. Given this, opposition coalitions can and do occur in states with varying levels of incumbent dominance. Donno (2013) argues that when it comes to success, opposition coalitions are more likely to positively influence democratization when incumbent dominance is low. She discusses some of the logic behind coalitions, agreeing that opposition actors may be more likely to become loyal to the incumbent regime when it maintains high dominance, making coalitions less likely.

The reversal of this argument holds that when opposition actors do not expect the incumbent regime to win, then they are more likely to band together and form a pre-election coalition. Therefore, the competitiveness of the election likely matters in explaining its usage. This is indirectly suggested by Donno (2013) and Bunce and Wolchik (2011). Bunce and Wolchik (2011) argue that while the track record for pre-election coalitions is compelling, opposition actors need more than simple unity to succeed. While they do not seek to explain why actors form coalitions, or under what circumstances opposition actors adopt the savvy, effective campaign strategies that Bunce and Wolchik (2011) argue are crucial, they do suggest that competitiveness of the election probably matters. Addressing the topic more explicitly, Wahman (2011) argues that poor economic conditions may make opposition actors more likely to coalesce before the election, as such circumstances make the public less likely to trust or reelect the incumbent regime; however, Gandhi and Reuter (2013) did not observe the same relationship.

Finally, some studies have identified opposition attributes that may influence the formation of pre-electoral coalitions. Gandhi and Reuter (2013) report that the higher the age of the largest opposition party, the more likely opposition actors are to form a pre-electoral coalition. The degree of policy differences between opposition and regime actors is also associated with the emergence of coalitions (Wahman 2011; Kellam 2015). Yet this argument seems to hinge upon a longer history of holding elections and political competition, as many argue that parties in newly democratizing states, as well as in electoral authoritarian ones, are typically underdeveloped and void of coherent policy platforms (Mansfield and Snyder 2002; Gandhi and Lust-Okar 2009). This argument, as will be discussed in chapter 2, is especially relevant within the post-Soviet context. Overall, most previous studies have emphasized the potential for democratic openings through the formation of a pre-electoral coalition, but have not produced a systematic explanation for their occurrence.

Previous Explanations of Opposition Boycotts

Opposition boycotts, or the strategic decision by at least some opposition actors to not participate in an election, have received the least amount of attention of these three categories of electoral strategies. Research on opposition boycotts has also produced the least conclusive findings. While scholars have disagreed over the factors that influence boycotts and the utility of such efforts, they have agreed that opposition boycotts do not produce any subsequent observable democratic improvements.

One set of explanations focuses on the international influences. As with electoral manipulation, the presence of international election monitors has been correlated with opposition boycotts. Beaulieu and Hyde (2009) have analyzed this association and concluded that boycotts are more likely due to the presence of monitors. They argue this is because opposition actors feel the need to protest the regime precisely when monitors are present. Regimes may alter their strategies of manipulation as a result of inviting monitors to observe, shifting their efforts in ways that make them less detectable. This may produce a positive conclusion from the international observers, which would grant the regime further legitimacy. Therefore, opposition actors who anticipate such actions may decide that the only way to contest such behavior is to not participate at all (Beaulieu and Hyde 2009). However, Kelley (2011) argues that this logic is flawed and reverses the direction of causality, contending that election monitors are expected to be deployed precisely to the states with the most flawed elections, so the correlation is misleading. Instead, she argues that opposition actors in many cases have changed course as a result of the monitors being present, deciding against the initial plan of an electoral boycott.

The domestic context and the nature of the opposition may also affect the occurrence of opposition election boycotts. Public access to information about the election is one factor argued to influence boycotts. More specifically, when the public has limited access to accurate information, especially in cases with low adult literacy rates, then opposition actors may be more likely to stage a boycott (Beaulieu 2014). Institutional limitations on the actions of incumbents may also influence the decision to participate in an election, or to instead boycott it entirely. Incumbents with less institutional restrictions that limit their power are better positioned to engage in electoral manipulation. Therefore, the lack of limitations on incumbent power is associated with an increase in the likelihood of an opposition electoral boycott (Beaulieu 2014). Economic development has also been associated with opposition boycotts. Lower GDP per capita and high income inequality are both associated with boycotts in electoral authoritarian regimes (Schedler 2013). Therefore, boycotts may stem from societal and economic frustration and a perceived lack of opportunities for improvement.

The context of the election may also figure into the decision to boycott an election by an opposition actor or actors. If an opposition party or actor fears they will lose big in an election or will underperform relative to expectations, then they may instead decide to boycott the contest entirely. This act of self-preservation aims to protect the party or actor from any further deleterious effects that could arise from a poor electoral performance (Bratton 1998). The preservation of resources also has been given as a reason to sit out an election. Boycotts by the Communist Party of the Russian Federation, typically seen as the most prominent systemic opposition party, have been associated with limited funds and campaign operations, rather than protest. As Turovsky (2015:130) notes, "strong actors have never boycotted elections in Russia." Conversely, if opposition actors perceive the elections to be conducted in a free and fair manner, or with minimal manipulation to sway the outcome of the election, then they are more likely to buy into the process and participate (Lindberg 2006a). These findings suggest that opposition parties are able to judge the size of a potential opening in an election, or its degree of competition, and act accordingly. Boycotts have also been observed more often in presidential elections rather than those for legislative contests (Schedler 2013). This suggests that opposition actors may view these contests as greater opportunities to signal frustration, explaining the higher likelihood. Alternatively, presidential elections, as winner-take-all contests, are more difficult to win, and therefore, some opposition actors are comfortable resigning themselves to defeat in a more difficult contest.

Boycotts have been mainly considered as a causal variable, noting the various potential outcomes associated with the act. One such outcome may be the unseating of the incumbent regime. An election with a major opposition boycott can reduce voter turnout, which can make the incumbent vulnerable to future criticisms and electoral challenges (Beaubieu 2014). This has been one of the main arguments behind opposition boycotts: that while they are defeatist in the short term, they may open up the electoral playing field further in the long term, allowing for future opposition victories. However, empirical analyses have not observed this relationship. In fact, an opposition boycott may actually reduce competition in subsequent elections (Schedler 2009a) and typically does not spur democratic improvements in the future (Smith 2014). Instead, when opposition actors participate in authoritarian elections, this decision actually makes democratization more likely than if some or all actors boycott the contest (Lindberg 2006a). Finally, the presence of a boycott may also have the unintended effect of increasing the likelihood of post-election violence (Lindberg 2006b), although this finding has been inconsistent (Beaulieu 2014).

SUMMARY

This chapter has introduced the puzzle and literature that fuel this book. It emphasized the different, but related dilemmas faced by both opposition and incumbent political actors in electoral authoritarian regimes, as well as the importance of considering their electoral strategies together in one study. The scholarship on the presence of incumbent and opposition strategies across the post-Soviet region reveal that these behaviors are often widely observed. Yet much of this work is limited to case-specific accounts or single-country analyses. This book aims to unify these observations with a cross-national approach while also including case study illustrations. Furthermore, the literature on previous explanations for the usage of pre-election strategies is quite mixed, producing in some cases conflicting and counterintuitive results. These studies demonstrate the importance of developing a unified theoretical approach in understanding incumbent and opposition behavior in electoral authoritarian regimes.

In addition, this book furthers the overall study of elections in non-democratic states. It asserts that, in contrast to fully authoritarian states, elections in electoral authoritarian states matter and deserve continued scholarly attention. They are not merely facades or routines carried out without thought. Instead, they witness serious strategic decision making by both incumbent and opposition actors, and still represent the main access to the political institutions of the state. It is through the control of these institutions that the authoritarian system can either be perpetuated and solidified, or dismantled and reformed. This reality demonstrates the importance of analyzing and explaining the strategies pursued by all political actors during elections in electoral authoritarian regimes.

PLAN OF BOOK

The remainder of this book analyzes the occurrence of incumbent and opposition electoral strategies in post-Soviet electoral authoritarian regimes. Chapter 2 establishes the theory and research design of this book. It discusses the presence of these different strategies in the post-Soviet region and also presents some general descriptive information on the explanatory variables under consideration. Chapter 2 also discusses the key indicators used in this book, namely the degree of competitiveness and incumbent dominance, addressing both their conceptualization and measurements. It displays the variation in these measures over time across the ten included states. Finally, it addresses the research design and sources of data more broadly, defending the usage of election observation reports from the Organization for Security and Cooperation in Europe as the source of electoral manipulation.

Chapters 3 through 6 present individual analyses of each electoral strategy. Chapter 3 considers incumbent instrumental manipulation, presenting the empirical evidence on the relationship between the conditions of the election and the selection of this strategy. The quantitative estimations examine three categories of instrumental manipulation—regulatory, financial, and enforcement resource abuse. These estimations find that combinations of these categories are positively associated with legislative elections as well as with elections that are more competitive. In other words, instrumental manipulation is more likely to occur in legislative elections and in elections with a greater degree of competitiveness. Chapter 3 then delves into case studies on Georgia's 2012 parliamentary election, Moldova's 2009 parliamentary elections, and Kazakhstan's 2016 parliamentary elections. The first two of these cases featured a high degree of competition, and as expected, featured many instances of instrumental manipulation. While the incumbents were unsuccessful electorally in Georgia, the pro-government parties initially were victorious in Moldova; however, they were unable to form a government and forced a new election two months later. That election also featured numerous examples of instrumental manipulation, and saw the pro-government party lose power. The third case on Kazakhstan instead explores a negative case study. The 2016 election featured very low competitiveness, and also no instrumental manipulation. Combined, these three cases help illustrate the broader relationships on instrumental manipulation that have been identified in the chapter.

Chapter 4 focuses on incumbent informational manipulation. This chapter focuses on institutional resource abuse as an example of informational manipulation, and introduces four types of such abuse. The ability of each type to interfere by sending a signal about the regime is discussed, demonstrating how each type is highly visible and able to serve this purpose. The statistical estimations in chapter 4 examine each individual type of informational manipulation, as well as collectively. These estimations reveal slightly different findings across models, but overall find support for the theoretical expectations. Informational manipulation is associated with high incumbent dominance, a low degree of competitiveness, and executive elections. That these findings are the opposite of those presented in chapter 3 demonstrates the distinctive roles that these strategies serve. Incumbents appear to view these strategies differently and select them according to the conditions of the election. Chapter 4 then turns to present three case studies, examining the many instances of informational manipulation in Azerbaijan's 2008 and Russia's 2008 elections, as well as the lack of such activities in Kyrgyzstan's 2015 election.

Chapters 5 and 6 then consider opposition strategies, examining the conditions for opposition pre-electoral coalitions and boycotts, respectively. Chapter 5 focuses on the formation of pre-election coalitions in electoral authoritarian regimes. It discusses in greater detail the role that this strategy can play for opposition forces and it explores short-term and long-term costs and benefits from this decision. The statistical estimation finds that such coalitions are more likely to be formed in legislative elections and in elections with low incumbent dominance; these two relationships support the theoretical expectations of this book. The chapter then presents three case studies on the 2012 parliamentary election in Georgia, the 2012 parliamentary election in Armenia, and the 2011 parliamentary election in Russia. The first of these two elections both featured opposition coalitions, one of which was successful (in Georgia) while the other was not (in Armenia). The third case, in contrast, did not feature an opposition pre-election coalition. These case studies then explore the diverging long-term effects from the adoption of this strategy.

Finally, opposition boycotts are explored in great detail in chapter 6. I consider the utility of selecting this protest strategy, and the short-term and long-term logic that typically is used to explain its selection. This chapter presents statistical estimations on the usage of boycotts, finding that it is more likely to be deployed in elections with a low degree of competitiveness, even when controlling for electoral manipulation in previous elections. I then examine two opposition boycotts from Armenia's 2013 presidential election and Belarus's 2012 parliamentary election. These two cases differ on the degree of incumbent dominance as well as the type of election, but both feature low competition and also opposition boycotts. Each case study concludes by discussing the long-term impacts following the deployment of boycotts, which reveal that it is not easy to point to improvements in democracy or damage to the legitimacy of the incumbent regime. The chapter ends with the consideration of Belarus's 2010 presidential election as a negative case that did not feature a boycott.

NOTES

1. "Russian Federation Presidential Election 4 March 2012." *OSCE/ODIHR Election Observation Mission Final Report*. Warsaw: 11 May 2012.

2. Twenty-four observed pre-election coalitions out of 88 total elections, author's data.

3. Schedler's (2013) analysis is one exception to this; another comes from Greene's (2007) study on Mexico.

4. As calculated from data made available by Hyde and Martinov (2011).

5. A more detailed discussion of the conceptualization of electoral authoritarian regimes will follow in chapter 2.

6. Sakwa (2005) recounts a different narrative where the Kremlin actually worked to help Yabloko gain representation, but that the electorate was so disengaged by the party's message that the efforts failed.

7. The candidacy of Ksenia Sobchak was the subject of much popular and political scrutiny. For an example, see Masha Gessen's February 12, 2018, article in *The New Yorker* entitled, "The Curious Case of the Television Star Running Against Vladimir Putin."

8. Steve Gutterman. "As Putin Cruises, Navalny and Sobchak Spar in Election-Day Standoff." *Radio Free Europe/Radio Liberty*. March 18, 2018.

9. The one exception to this is Russia's 2008 presidential election. The OSCE declined an invitation to monitor the election after many of their visas were denied and they were not granted sufficient time, access or resources to effectively carry out the mission. Opposition actors did not boycott this election.

10. Tom Balmforth. "Navalny Announced He Will Seek Russian Presidency." *Radio Free Europe/Radio Liberty*. December 13, 2016.

11. Tom Balmforth. "At Lease 350 Detained At Election Boycott Rallies in Russia." *Radio Free Europe/Radio Liberty*. January 29, 2018.

12. "Republic of Kazakhstan Early Presidential Election 3 April 2011" *OSCE/ODHIR Election Observation Mission Final Report Warsaw*: 16 June 2011.

13. Schedler (2013) did find that predicted competition does correlate with the types of manipulation strategies: higher predicted competition is associated with repression and fraud, while lower predicted competition is associated with exclusion.

Chapter Two

Theory, Design, and Methods

Chapter 1 established a) the need for a general theory of incumbent and opposition strategies in electoral authoritarian regimes and b) the relevance of election-level factors in explaining the variation in strategies. Elections in these non-democratic regimes still provide the bedrock of political maneuvering, even as it is clear that the elections themselves feature incumbent interference and manipulation. Due to this, opposition actors are often forced to react to the incumbent-influenced circumstances in which they operate, rather than having the freedom to shape the environment themselves. The vast abilities of incumbent and government actors to dictate the terms of elections gives them undue sway beyond simple incumbency advantage. It is this reality that necessitates the importance of a combined, comprehensive approach to understanding how and why both incumbent and opposition actors select the strategies that they do. This chapter aims to do just that. It begins by establishing the four electoral strategies that drive the theory and analysis of this book. It next dives into the development of a comprehensive theory based on Tsebelis's (1991) concept of nested games, and it presents concise, measurable propositions about under what conditions we should expect the different theories to be deployed. This chapter then shifts toward unpacking the relevant concepts and indicators that fuel this study, including the definition and operationalization of electoral authoritarianism. It subsequently shifts its attention toward the explanatory or independent variables to be used throughout the book. Finally, this chapter ends by describing the data sources used in the subsequent empirical chapters.

THEORY OF ELECTORAL STRATEGIES

As I begin the discussion on relative costs and benefits of the selected electoral strategies, I must re-emphasize that this book in no way attempts to consider or include a comprehensive analysis of all incumbent and opposition strategies. Instead, I focus on four strategies, two of which can be selected by incumbent political actors, and two of which apply to opposition actors. In selecting these strategies, I am cognizant of the temporal variation in many strategies, with some decisions being made at the start of an electoral campaign, while others instead are committed on the election day itself. For the sake of theoretical and analytical simplicity, I focus solely upon those strategies that are both *selected and carried out* during the pre-election campaign period. Otherwise, the selection of one strategy (e.g., obstruction of opposition campaigning) could influence the selection of another (e.g., ballot box stuffing). Given this, the four strategies included in this book are instrumental incumbent manipulation, informational incumbent manipulation, the formation of an opposition pre-electoral bloc, and opposition electoral boycotts.

Incumbent Strategies

For the incumbent side of the equation, I focus exclusively on strategies of manipulation. I make this decision for a few reasons. First, incumbent manipulation in elections has been one of the trademark behaviors observed in electoral authoritarian regimes. Its usage does not appear to be a regional, institutional, or cultural phenomenon, and has been observed in the vast majority of elections in post-Soviet space. Second, this behavior varies, with numerous different types of manipulation observed. In the pre-election period, on which I focus in this book, incumbents have a range of options to select, including vote-buying, the obstruction of opposition candidate registration, interference with opposition campaign events, and biases in state-run media. Finally, this behavior carries potential costs. Wide-spread and highly visible manipulation can spur public outcry and protests rejecting either the terms or the outcome of the election. I emphasize the existence of costs to reiterate the puzzling dynamic that faces both incumbent and opposition actors in electoral authoritarian regimes. In this case, incumbent actors want to win elections, and they can benefit from manipulation. However, they also wish to avoid spurring public outcry and frustration at their victory if it is perceived to rely too much upon manipulation.

Because incumbents can potentially select multiple, different manipulation strategies, I further disaggregate them into two categories: instrumental and informational manipulation strategies.[1] This distinction is not meant to suggest that these are the only two categorizations of incumbent manipulation. Indeed, other authors have noted additional types as well. Instead, I do this to acknowledge the different goals inherently contained within the different types of strategies. I argue that these two potential strategies are distinguished by their ability to directly interfere with the election, and their level of public visibility.

Instrumental Incumbent Manipulation

Instrumental manipulation refers to any practice or activity that seeks to directly manipulate the process of voting or the vote tabulation process. Its primary goal is to affect the process and outcome of the election. In particular, I argue that any manipulation that directly interferes with the behavior of voters, opposition parties and candidates, or the actual process of voting demonstrate instrumental incumbent manipulation. By directly manipulating either voter or candidate actions, this type of manipulation has the potential to explicitly interfere with the conduct of the election, and can enable an incumbent to win an unfair electoral contest. Examples of instrumental manipulation include voter suppression, obstruction of opposition campaign events, and public spending and gifts meant to sway voter opinions. One instance of this occurred in the Ukrainian 2010 presidential election, when pensioners received letters bearing the official seal of the incumbent prime minister Yuliya Tymoshenko, which noted that if she were elected to the position of president, pension payments would increase.[2] Another example took place in Georgia's 2003 parliamentary elections, where the Central Election Committee, containing many pro-incumbent actors, repeatedly avoided any clarification on the rules guarding against ballot box stuffing and improbable results, which was seen to benefit pro-incumbent parties.[3] The degree of public visibility is less important for instrumental manipulation; in fact, high visibility may actually detract from the goal of the manipulation itself, as it could produce public outcry and protests. Therefore, I assert that any type of manipulation that directly interferes with the actors and rules of the election, and with medium or low visibility can be considered an instrumental manipulation strategy.

Informational Incumbent Manipulation

In contrast, manipulation strategies that are highly visible and only indirectly interfere with the election are considered informational. For this type of manipulation, the overall goal is to simply send a large and broadly received message about the incumbent regime; the nature of this message can vary, but many have primarily focused on its ability to inform regime elites, opposition actors, and the broader public about the strength of the regime. In this regard, high visibility is crucial. Manipulation can only convey information if its usage is public enough to project the intended message. Yet informational manipulation does not directly interfere with the election process. Its usage absolutely affects the tone and fairness of any contest, but it does not directly manipulate the actions of voters, opposition actors, or the rules underlying the electoral process. Examples of informational manipulation include the presence of campaign offices and materials inside government buildings, public rallies in support of the incumbent regime filled with state employees, and biased state media coverage in favor of incumbent actors. During Azerbaijan's presidential election in 2013, for example, international election monitors observed massive rallies for the president where attendees reported being compelled to attend due to their state employment.[4] Another instance of informational manipulation was observed in Russia's 2012 presidential election, where the three state-run television networks aired biased coverage of the election strongly in favor of the regime candidate.[5] Therefore, informational incumbent manipulation includes highly visible strategies that indirectly interfere with the conduct of the election.

Measurement of Manipulation

Given these distinctions between instrumental and informational manipulation, I need to decide which specific types of behavior would qualify as one or the other. As noted in chapter 1, incumbent actors have a variety of pre-election strategies available to them. In order to clearly and consistently measure these concepts, I have identified four specific categories of manipulation that can firmly be placed in either the instrumental or informational column. Ohman's (2013) report provides four distinct and measurable varieties of state resource abuse that can and do occur in elections prior to the election day itself. These four categories are institutional resource abuse, financial resource abuse, regulatory resource abuse and enforcement resource abuse.[6] From these four, each category maintains multiple subtypes of abuse that fit within the designated category. Table 2.1 displays the four categories and relevant subtypes of manipulation. Based on the criteria discussed, financial resource abuse, regulatory resource abuse and enforcement resource abuse all qualify as instrumental manipulation due to their ability to directly interfere with either the voters, candidates or parties involved in the election. Conversely, I argue institutional resource abuse includes behaviors that are highly visible, but do not directly interfere with the conduct of the election. These distinctions will be covered in greater detail in chapters 3 and 4 on instrumental and informational manipulation, respectively.

Table 2.1.   Four Types of State Resource Abuse from Ohman (2013)

Category of Manipulation	Specific Types of Manipulation
Institutional State Resource Abuse	1. Use of state employees at official campaign events, 2. Use of state/ government property, buildings or organizations for campaign activities, 3. Campaigning by officials during official state activities, 4. Abuse of state-owned media.
Financial State Resource Abuse	1. Direct allocation of goods or financial support to voters, 2. State financial activity beneficial to incumbent candidates, 3. Announcements of unplanned increases in state spending on welfare and social services.
Regulatory State Resource Abuse	1. New regulations seen to hinder or obstruct opposition activities, 2. Politicized or biased activities by electoral commissions, 3. New campaign or political finance rules seen to benefit incumbents.
Enforcement State Resource Abuse	1. Security or police manipulation into activities of opposition, 2. Unbalanced usage of security details to candidates.

Opposition Strategies

As discussed in chapter 1, I also focus on two potential opposition strategies—pre-electoral blocs and election boycotts. In selecting these, I also follow the same guidelines used when selecting incumbent electoral strategies. First, the strategies need to be observed prior to the election day, which is the case for both of these options. Second, they must represent options available to any opposition actor no matter their degree of organization, their age or their access to resources. I argue that forming a pre-electoral coalition can be done by parties of different ages and with different resource assets. Moreover, forming a coalition represents the opportunity to pool resources and organizational structures, allowing actors to possibly overcome any weaknesses. Staging a boycott is unquestionably a tactic that any actor can select no matter how limited their resources. Finally, the strategies should reflect the electoral dilemma introduced earlier in the book. This dilemma especially comes across from the decision to boycott. By conceding any chance at victory, the actors take a huge risk in assuming that they can survive and maintain their voters in a future contest. Moreover, both strategies risk frustrating the incumbent regime if (or in the case of a boycott, when) they fail to succeed in the election, but in different ways. A pre-electoral coalition, as a strategy with a relatively proven track record, could intensify the contest and force the regime to exert greater effort. This could lead the regime to further suppress opposition actions in the future as punishment. However, an opposition boycott, especially if staged by multiple parties, could reduce the legitimacy of the election, and could detract from the meaningfulness of the incumbent regime's victory. This outcome could then lead to retribution in the future as well.

Opposition Pre-Electoral Coalitions

Opposition pre-electoral coalitions can potentially challenge a powerful incumbent regime whose dominance is exacerbated by the uneven nature of competition. The formation of a pre-electoral coalition can be useful to opposition actors in numerous ways. First, it can make it mathematically possible for a challenger to receive a plurality of votes when competing against an authoritarian incumbent, who may rely on a single party. Second, the formation of a coalition can convince voters that the opposition is actually viable and maintains a chance at victory; this can convince them to consider voting for the opposition bloc, when under different circumstances they may have thought that such an act would be pointless. Finally, a coalition can allow parties and factions to pool resources, supporters, and political knowledge, making the team more well-rounded, prepared, and capable of challenging an incumbent that has the tools of the state at their disposal. Pre-electoral coalitions can be useful in both legislative and executive contests. While the coalition can serve to gain the actors a majority in the legislature, it can also agree to submit a single candidate in an executive race.

Opposition Boycott

An opposition boycott is more self-evident. This strategy means that an opposition actor or party publicly announces their intention not to participate in an electoral contest. A boycott is by definition a protest strategy, seeking to signal displeasure with the status quo and the existing system. The party or parties typically offer some sort of explanation for their decision, which can refer to the unfair nature of the contest, any previous or ongoing pressure or suppression that they have received, frustration over the electoral process and rules, or all of the above. As with pre-electoral blocs, boycotts can be done by major or minor parties and actors, which can alter the severity of the strategy. By refusing to participate, boycotting actors and parties often seek to discredit the electoral process and signal to voters that they should not accept the current political process either.

PROPOSED THEORY OF ELECTORAL STRATEGIES

While the previous chapter considered the explanations for opposition and incumbent behavior separately, I now plan to unify those arguments and findings into a general theory of electoral strategies in electoral authoritarian regimes. As I seek to explain electoral strategies that may seem counterintuitive, such as boycotting an election, or manipulating an election that would be won anyway, I turn to the logic of political institutions as nested games (Tsebelis 1990). Tsebelis (1990) argued that this two-level approach can help observers understand perceived counterintuitive behavior and choices made by political actors. By acknowledging that political behavior and strategies are inherently goal-oriented, we can use the context of a situation (or game) to understand how a strategy may serve a particular goal. This approach argues that because of this reality, when we witness strategies that may not be interpreted immediately as serving a particular goal, we should consider the other relevant game arenas. While a strategy may appear self-defeating in one game, it may actually make perfect sense in another. Because "the actor perceives that the game is nested inside a bigger game that defines how the contextual factors influence his payoffs and other players," we can use this information to understand and predict the strategic behavior of political actors (Tsebelis 1990:8).

The nested game approach has more recently been applied to describe incumbent or opposition strategies in electoral authoritarian regimes (Schedler 2006, 2013; Smith 2014). According to Schedler (2013), elections and electoral institutions can be visualized as two-level games within electoral authoritarian regimes. At the game level we can observe electoral competition, where actors compete to win votes. Above the game of electoral competition lies the meta-game level of institutional rules. Within electoral authoritarian regimes, these rules represent the real prize, as they can help perpetuate an authoritarian incumbent regime, or they can be altered to promote democratization. What is crucial in the study of electoral authoritarian regimes is that the games are by definition asymmetrical, due to the fluidity of the rules and the dynamics of power. Schedler (2013) has focused on incumbent strategies of manipulation and opposition strategies of protest as engaged in the meta-game rather than the game level of the election. I instead argue that incumbent strategies of manipulation can function at both levels, with short-term goals prevailing at the election level while long-term goals are deemed more important at the institutional level. Due to this contrast, the actual types of manipulation strategies should vary depending on the context of the election. Similarly, opposition strategies of forming an electoral bloc and boycotting an election, I contend, also operate at different levels, with short-term goals at the election levels potentially superseding any long-term goals at the level of the political institutions. In the following pages, I apply the principles of nested games to the selection of electoral strategies, isolating the levels where the optimal expected outcomes of each strategy, based on the benefits and costs, are likely to lie.

Instrumental Incumbent Manipulation

This book asserts that some strategies of incumbent manipulation function primarily in an instrumental fashion. This means that the strategies are most useful in nudging the incumbent candidate or party over the top toward victory, and are perpetrated to directly influence (or more accurately, interfere with) the behavior of voters, candidates, and parties. So how does this strategy fit within the framework of nested games? As I have stated earlier, within electoral authoritarian regimes, the game level represents the electoral contest (the election level) and the meta-game level represents control over the political institutions (the institution level). To determine at which level the optimal expected outcome lies, I compare the potential short-term and long-term costs and benefits associated with the usage of instrumental electoral manipulation.

In order to properly examine the options available to incumbents, I must consider the costs and benefits of both selecting and *not selecting* instrumental manipulation strategies. Given that the premise of this book is that incumbents pick and choose not just when and what types of manipulation to use, but whether to use it at all, the costs and benefits of using or not using the strategy merit attention. Thus table 2.2 displays the expected costs and benefits of either selecting or not selecting instrumental manipulation, broken down by the election and the institution level.

Instrumental manipulation contains both short- and long-term benefits. At the election level, the benefit is clear: incumbents can use such manipulation to ensure victory by interfering with the behavior of voters and opposition actors. Manipulation strategies of this sort, including the provision of goods and community items in exchange for votes, as well as harsh law enforcement treatment toward opposition candidates, can work to assist an embattled authoritarian incumbent win reelection. This translates into clear short-term benefits of winning the election, along with the clear costs of needing to expend energy and resources to make it happen. At the institutional level, the incumbent (or incumbent-supported candidate) then gains or (maintains) access to the political institutions, allowing them to potentially adjust the laws and rules of the state in their favor. However, this same strategy carries with it costs for the future. Since this kind of manipulation directly interferes with the actions of parties and voters, it can cause lasting damage to the reputation and legitimacy of the incumbent. The perception of altering an election's outcome through the direct manipulation of candidates and votes has indeed spurred post-electoral protests and reduced confidence in some regimes. This long-term cost of reduced legitimacy, I argue, means that their subsequent control over the political institutions is lessened. Any attempts to alter the institutions for the benefit of the incumbent regime may be met with frustration or even public outcry. Therefore, I argue that within the level of the political institutions, the strategy of instrumental incumbent manipulation carries more profound costs. Due to the trade-off between the expected outcomes in election and institutional levels, I argue that the expected optimum payoff would lie primarily within the former. This suggests that electoral level factors may better predict the usage of instrumental manipulation.

The avoidance of instrumental manipulation also can bring certain benefits at the election and institutional levels. The absence of such blatant interference with voters and opposition candidates and parties can potentially lower the risks of public frustration with the regime, and with that, lower the chances of pre- or post-election protests and demonstrations. This is clearly of value to incumbents, as such events have led to the nullification of elections or the toppling of regimes. This benefit is likely to be tempting, given the landscape of post-Soviet states and the successes of anti-regime protests, but it remains an intangible gain. The benefit is the absence of an event, rather than a more readily perceptible benefit like winning the election. The long term benefit is even less tangible: incumbents and regimes that win without using instrumental manipulation can govern with a reputation of integrity and honesty. This can serve them well among pro-democracy supporters both at home and abroad, potentially increasing their status and respectability. Unfortunately, these benefits may seem too abstract to incumbent actors who already have certain powers and access, and they also come with expected costs. At the election level, the party or candidate may fail to garner sufficient support for victory, thus ending their access to the institutional level. And if victorious, long-term costs could loom as well. Regime insiders and elites may be more willing to criticize or dissent against an incumbent who follows the letter of the law. More credibility may not translate into greater policy successes at the institutional level, which could spur insiders to be more likely to defect from the regime or to undermine the government. Normatively, the benefits of a transparent victory are preferable to a marred and anti-democratic one, but given the nature of electoral authoritarianism, elections have not always served as normative tools. Instead, incumbents and regimes in the post-Soviet region may prefer to take the short-term election level benefits of using instrumental manipulation, rather than risking a loss or insider pressure.

Table 2.2.   **Instrumental Incumbent Manipulation Expectations**

Strategy: *Instrumental Manipulation*	*Level: Electoral Competition*	*Level Political Institutions*
Yes	*Short-term Benefit:* Win Election *Short-term Cost:* Expended Resources **Optimal Expected Outcome**	*Long-term Benefit:* Access to Institutions *Long-term Cost:* Public Discontent, Reduced Legitimacy to Control Institutions
No	*Short-term Benefit* Reduce chances of post-election protest *Short-term Cost:* Election outcome uncertain	*Long-term Benefit:* Victory is more credible and transparent Long-Term Cost: May fuel internal dissent and defections, could reduce ability to control institutions

Informational Incumbent Manipulation

The second variety of incumbent manipulation concerns strategies that seek to provide information about the incumbent's strength and power. These strategies do not directly interfere with the casting of ballots or the campaigns of opposition candidates; instead, they manipulate the election indirectly, and in a highly public manner. Examples of informational manipulation include maintaining incumbent campaign offices in state buildings and regime bias in the state-run media. These tactics clearly skew the election in a different way, I argue, then what we expect from instrumental strategies, because they do not directly interfere in the actions of voters and opposition actors.

When we consider the potential short-term and long-term costs and benefits for informational manipulation, I observe the opposite pattern from instrumental manipulation. Within the arena of electoral competition, I assert that the potential benefits are limited. These types of manipulation send clear messages about incumbent strength, power, and inevitability; as such, they are less capable of ensuring any sort of victory for the incumbent or regime-supported actors. Yet they require vast amounts of resources and coordination to conduct, meaning that they bear certain economic and resource costs to the incumbent regime. Within the game of electoral competition, I conclude that there is no clear optimal benefit to achieve through the usage of informational electoral competition. Since Tsebelis (1990) argues that if clear benefits cannot be found within the game level, we should shift our attention toward the meta-game, or in this case, control over political institutions. By signaling power and strength throughout the election, incumbents stand to gain greater dominance over the political landscape. Informational manipulation can demotivate political opponents within the state to push back on new legislation, or it can encourage opposition actors to join the incumbent's party or group of supporters. It can also demoralize the public and convince them that the incumbent regime is firmly in control, making any resistance less likely (Simpser 2013).

Yet informational manipulation is still a choice, thus incumbents and regime-supported candidates likely consider whether to pursue such a strategy at all. As with the benefits posited with the absence of instrumental manipulation, incumbents may receive a clean, honest victory in the short term. This type of benefit also serves an informational purpose as it informs voters, opposition actors, and international observers that the regime values transparency and honesty over the abuse of state resources. This can be valuable in the short term in the wake of an election, but it serves a much less notable long-term benefit. Ideally, this can improve the standing of the regime in the eyes of pro-democracy actors and advocates, but this benefit may not substantially help at the level of the political institutions. Levitsky and Way (2010) remind us that in many states in the former Soviet Union, linkages to the West are typically low, so Western observers from the US and the EU are more likely to devote the most attention to elections; they refer to this as 'electoralist' pressure. This kind of intermittent pressure, as they describe it, means that any benefits gained from an honest victory may disappear in the months after the event. Furthermore, the costs of avoiding informational manipulation also are more likely to be felt at the institutional level. The manipulation is unlikely to determine the outcome of the election in the short term, but in the long term, incumbents may suffer from a perception of domestic weakness.

I argue that when viewed within the framework of nested games, we see clear expected benefits at the institutional level stemming from the usage of informational manipulation. Incumbents can optimally expect few challenges from those within the elite, from opponents, and from the public. This means that there are few long-term costs for the incumbent regime.[7] Unlike what we see with instrumental manipulation, I consider informational strategies to produce considerable benefits in the control over the political institutions, meaning that the optimal expected outcome is found at this level. This suggests that incumbents may select this strategy based on the certainty of the electoral contest. Again, this is absolutely against the normative ideal of what we would expect from elections and proper conduct. But much of the recent literature on electoral authoritarianism has reminded us that these regimes are not democratizing or even necessarily moving toward democracy; they are often quite sustained in authoritarianism through biased and unfair elections.

Table 2.3.   Informational Incumbent Manipulation Expectations

Strategy: Informational Manipulation	Level: Electoral Competition	Level: Political Institutions
Yes	*Short-term Benefit:* Win the Election *Short-term Cost:* Usage of resources and organizational capacity	*Long-term Benefit:* Enhanced Dominance over Institutions *Long-term Cost:* Increases Perception as Undemocratic **Optimal expected Outcome**
No	*Short-term Benefit:* Clean, honest victory *Short-term Cost:* Could produce close result	*Long-term Benefit:* Gives regime enhanced reputation and standing *Long-term Cost:* Dominance may be challenged

This provides the context for such behaviors and the weighing of the perceived costs and benefits behind such a strategy. Table 2.3 presents these short-term and long-term benefits and costs for either selecting or not selecting informational manipulation.

Opposition Pre-Electoral Blocs

Turning my attention to the political opposition, I argue that we can also categorize the strategic logic of forming a pre-election bloc among several opposition actors or parties. As noted earlier, this strategy has been associated with opposition victories and democratic openings in many electoral authoritarian states. By forming an alliance prior to the election, opposition actors hope to effectively challenge and ultimately defeat an authoritarian incumbent actor or party's dominance in the legislature. In the short term, this is the obvious expected benefit. Opposition actors can pool their resources, energy, and organizational power together to collectively challenge the regime. This also sends a signal to voters that they are more viable, and potentially worthy of a vote. Few short-term costs are associated with this strategy, given that resources may be used more efficiently by one bloc or alliance rather than individually. The main concession that must be made within the game of electoral competition is the decision of which actor should head an executive ticket or a parliamentary party list, so that the voters and opposition actors know who will take power upon victory.

Turning to the long-term calculus, if this bloc is victorious, then they gain access to the political institutions in the state. This is a clear long-term benefit, as it can allow the actors to move the state in a more democratic direction. However, I observe multiple long-term costs associated with pre-electoral blocs. These costs may arise either if the opposition wins or loses. With victory, the alliance or bloc must shift away from campaigning and instead learn to govern together. Given that the alliances are formed primarily for the election, this means that the parties or candidates may hold different ideologies and preferences on the rules and institutions governing the state. Such dynamics have indeed proved challenging, as the case of Ukraine following the 2004 Orange Revolution demonstrates. The electoral alliance between Victor Yushchenko and Yuliya Tymoshenko was short-lived, as the two disagreed on the political direction and the power dynamics in Ukraine following their victory. In this case, the two ultimately severed any connections between the two factions of the pre-electoral bloc, and transformed into enduring political rivals. Thus, even with victory, control over the political institutions may be tenuous at best, and impossible to maintain at worst. Long-term costs are also to be expected if the bloc fails to achieve victory in the game of electoral competition. An electoral loss even with an opposition bloc can potentially be extremely demoralizing to the voters and supporters of the alliance. This may cement incumbent dominance into the attitudes of both voters and opposition actors, leading to apathy and the atrophy of voter support. In comparing the potential costs and benefits associated with this strategy, I argue that the optimal expected outcome lies within the game arena of electoral competition.

With these costs in mind, opposition actors may prefer to go it alone and not join a pre-election coalition at all. This strategy has the short-term benefit of complete control over candidate, campaign, and issue decisions, rather than needing to establish some consensus on these areas. Additionally, the rejection of a coalition may actually deemphasize the threat that opposition actors may pose to the regime, who might be less likely to scrutinize or pressure them. In the long term, opposition actors who forgo a coalition can also retain policy control and internal consistency as a movement. Yet the decision against the formation of a coalition carries costs, including the alienation of voters in an election. Voters may feel that the actors are behaving in a self-defeating manner by refusing to join forces with other actors. In the long term, opposition actors may risk exclusion from the political process and may face sustained marginalization. In comparing the potential costs and benefits associated with this strategy, presented in Table 2.4, I argue that the optimal expected outcome lies at the level of electoral competition.

Table 2.4.   **Opposition Pre-Electoral Coalition Expectations**

Strategy: Opposition Pre-Electoral Coalition	*Level:* Electoral Competition	*Level:* Political Institutions
Yes	*Short-term Benefit:* Win the Election, pool resources and voters *Short-term Cost:* Need to compromise on campaign decisions ***Optimal expected Outcome***	*Long-term Benefit:* Gain access to Political Institutions *Long-term Cost:* (If victorious) Challenges of governing as a bloc and maintaining a majority; (If defeated) Increased voter apathy and organizational atrophy
No	*Short-term Benefit:* Greater control over election strategy, less scrutiny from regime *Short-term Cost:* Voters may view vote as wasted, less access to resources	*Long-term Benefit:* Greater policy freedom and internal consistency for institutions *Long-term Cost:* Excluded from institutions, risk further marginalization

Opposition Boycotts

Finally, I consider the costs and benefits at both levels of political competition for the opposition strategy of an election boycott. As discussed earlier, this strategy may be counterintuitive, as it guarantees defeat. However, by examining it through the lens of nested games, we can better understand the strategic logic underlying this opposition tactic. Within the game of electoral competition, we can clearly identify the costs and benefits for any political actors that stage a boycott. Any short-term benefits to this strategy are difficult to locate; as victory is not an option in this scenario. A potentially cash-strapped party may conserve its resources and energy for future contests, but beyond this, benefits are scarce. The short-term cost is clear: the boycotting actor(s) or party(ies) have forfeited any possibility of winning the election. For a political actor, this is a potentially devastating outcome, as it sacrifices the main avenue through which power and influence are attained. However, opposition actors would not boycott an election unless they saw a future outcome that held promise. In other words, we should expect to find potential long-term benefits to boycotting an election.

This is indeed what has been argued previously; boycotts, especially in electoral authoritarian regimes, are intended to produce long-term gains for opposition actors. An opposition boycott, especially if conducted by multiple actors, can produce a large incumbent victory within the electoral competition. This can frustrate voters, framing the elected parties or candidates as illegitimate, and can lead voters to view the political system as fundamentally flawed. Opposition actors hope that this discontent lasts long enough so that in subsequent elections voters reject incumbent actors and parties. Ideally, opposition actors receive electoral gains in these future contests, even potentially winning power. For an opposition boycott, the potential benefit is indeed in the long term, and is contingent upon multiple factors working to their favor. However, a potential long-term cost of an electoral boycott is the increasing marginalization of a party within the authoritarian system, which could lead to further decline and electoral losses. This strategy thus carries with it striking costs in both levels of political competition, but we can clearly place the optimal expected outcome within the meta-game of control over the political institutions.

The empirical research on the effectiveness of boycotts was discussed in chapter 1, and overall it tells us that this strategy does not yield these long-term benefits. As a self-defeating strategy, opposition actors likely consider whether this is the most productive option available, which brings us to the benefits and costs of not pursuing an opposition boycott. The decision to not boycott features the short-term benefit of actual electoral participation, which holds the theoretical option of victory and access to the political institutions. Furthermore, if an opposition actor participates while many others boycott, they may actually benefit from the reduced electoral landscape. Voters who turn out but oppose the regime have fewer options available and this can reward any opposition candidates and parties that refused to join a boycott movement. By fielding candidates, the opposition actor may benefit over the long term from sustained electoral participation. By engaging with voters and adjusting or evolving their campaign strategies, they may gain future insights for electoral competition. This participation has an alternate view; voters and supporters of boycotting candidates and parties may decry the participating actors as spoilers meant to legitimize the unfair contest. This could also pose long-term costs to opposition actors, as they may lose credibility with the anti-regime forces, which could marginalize them even when they did not boycott the election. Table 2.5 summarizes these points.

SO WHAT EXPLAINS
THE USAGE OF ELECTORAL STRATEGIES?

By viewing electoral strategies as actions within a two-level game, one that potentially has short-term and long-term costs and benefits, I argue that we

Table 2.5.   Opposition Boycotts Expectations

Strategy: *Opposition Electoral Boycott*	*Level: Electoral Competition*	*Level: Political Institutions*
Yes	*Short-term Benefit:* Conserve Resources *Short-term Cost:* Guaranteed Electoral Defeat	*Long-term Benefit:* Potential for future victory to gain access to Political Institutions *Long-term Cost:* Further political marginalization ***Optimal expected Outcome***
No	*Short-term Benefit:* Compete in election May capitalize on reduced competition *Short-term Cost:* May be perceived as spoiler or part of system	*Long-term Benefit:* Maintain consistent political involvement *Long-term Cost:* May contribute to regime consolidation

can better identify the factors that influence the selection of strategies. This framework puts the focus in particular on electoral explanations, rather than domestic conditions or international factors, as they are the most likely to affect and alter the game-level of the electoral contest. As I have outlined, each strategy encounters an optimal and a suboptimal outcome in either the level of the electoral contest or of the political institutions. This does not mean that actors would be expected to select that strategy in every situation. On the contrary, it merely indicates that when the conditions are right, that would be the most optimal strategy that yields the best ratio of costs and benefits. Thus I argue that both incumbent and opposition actors are more likely to base their strategic behavior on the attainability of either level. Therefore, in understanding the factors that lead opposition and incumbent actors to select certain strategies, we should focus on any strategies that affect the attainability of the election level and the level of political institutions. Given this, I focus on the three previously identified electoral explanations: the competitiveness of the election, incumbent dominance, and the type of election.

Competitiveness

Competition and the competitiveness of the election directly alter the electoral contest. As discussed earlier, many previous studies have hinted at the importance of competition in influencing the selection of strategies. Yet, these studies have produced different conclusions, with some authors arguing that high competition increases the occurrence of manipulation and fraud, while others argue that manipulation is more likely in uncompetitive elections. Using the nested-game approach, we can better disentangle these conflicting theories and findings. A highly competitive election typically means that results may be quite close, and that incumbents may not be guaranteed victory. When the outcome of an election is uncertain, this directly alters the attainability of the game. Therefore, we can expect that both incumbent and opposition actors would be more likely to select a strategy that yields them greater benefits in the game arena. The previous section established that the optimal expected outcomes for two strategies lie within the level of the electoral contest, rather than the level of the political institutions. Given this, we should expect opposition and incumbent actors to prioritize these strategies when faced with a highly competitive election. *More specifically, we should expect incumbents to be more likely to focus on instrumental manipulation, and we should expect opposition actors to be more likely to form pre-electoral blocs in highly competitive elections.*

These relationships make intuitive sense as well. As discussed earlier, instrumental manipulation includes strategies that directly interfere with the conduct of an election so as to influence the outcome. Moreover, the short-term benefits of electoral victory clearly override the potential long-term cost of reduced or hindered control over the political institutions, since instrumental manipulation strategies directly affect voters, candidates, and the electoral process. The perceived costs should make incumbents wary of these types of manipulation unless they genuinely fear losing power, as would be the case in a competitive election.

The same logic holds true for opposition pre-electoral coalitions. This strategy has the most assured benefit or payoff in the short term at the game arena of the electoral contest. By creating the ability for a larger winning coalition to challenge the incumbent's hold on power, opposition actors may see a pre-electoral bloc as the only pathway to victory, and to removing the authoritarian incumbent from power. The short-term benefit of winning the election far outweighs the costs of time, resources, and energy, but this short-term cost is not negligible. Therefore, we should expect opposition actors to strategically deploy a pre-electoral coalition only in circumstances in which the game is actually attainable, as is the case in a competitive election.

Finally, when an election is more competitive, we should not expect incumbent or opposition actors to select strategies *without* an optimal payoff in the election level. An election in which incumbents and opposition actors genuinely feel that the outcome is unknown would not be the prime circumstances for focusing solely on benefits in the long term. Therefore, informational manipulation and an opposition boycott would be less likely in a competitive election.

If the competitiveness of the election is low, however, then this likely has the opposite effect on the attainability of games. Low competitiveness means that the results of the election should be quite predictable and that the incumbent faces little risk of losing power. In the language of two-level games, this means the attainability of game is quite certain. With this being the case, incumbent and opposition actors should be better positioned to consider optimal outcomes at the level of political institutions. As the previous section established, informational manipulation strategies can provide the long-term benefit of enhancing incumbent dominance over the political institutions at the meta-game level. *When there is no question about the attainability of the game level due to an uncompetitive election, incumbents may therefore be more likely to utilize informational manipulation strategies.* Concerning the opposition, the same logic applies. If the election is uncompetitive, then the opposition likely are certain that they will not win and the electoral contest is unattainable. Therefore, they too may instead pay attention to any potential long-term benefits that they can achieve in the meta-game of the political institutions. *An uncompetitive election may make opposition actors more likely to decide to boycott the election altogether.* Doing this, they are instead setting their sights on the potential long-term benefit of undermining the legitimacy of the regime.

Similarly, an uncompetitive election would provide a suboptimal setting for instrumental manipulation or for an opposition pre-election coalition. Instrumental manipulation serves primarily the short-term goal of directly affecting the conduct of the election, but carries fewer benefits and greater costs for the long term. Likewise, a coalition would require significant coordination and resources in the short term for the almost certain lack of a payoff. Opposition actors would therefore be less likely to opt for such a strategy when the election is less competitive.

Incumbent Dominance

In keeping with the focus on factors that can alter the attainability of the election or the political institutions, incumbent dominance presents a second feature deserving attention. Incumbent dominance typically refers to the degree of control held by the existing regime within an electoral authoritarian state. Incumbent dominance can increase through the presence of a dominant political party, reliance on natural resource exports, or dependence on significant electoral victories.[8] When dominance is high, scholars argue that space for organizing and the potential for support among voters is reduced for opposition actors. With this in mind, I argue that in states with low incumbent dominance, incumbents and opposition actors may be more focused on the electoral contest, rather than on control over the political institution. The incumbent cannot rely on the benefits of significant dominance and control to win elections or remain in power. *Therefore, they may be more likely to utilize instrumental manipulation when they maintain low incumbent dominance.* Instrumental manipulation can work toward the short-term benefit in winning the election, which may eventually lead to the long-term benefit of maintaining access to the political institutions. Similarly, by increasing the attainability of the election, opposition actors may focus on forming pre-electoral blocs when incumbent dominance is low. Low incumbent dominance means that the playing field of electoral competition has not been further reduced to severely limit or exclude opposition participation. Therefore, under these circumstances, opposition actors may view a coalition as a realistic and pragmatic strategy seeking to prevent any future gains made by the incumbent regime. *Elections in states with low incumbent dominance are more attainable than those with high dominance, making opposition actors more likely to form pre-election coalitions.*

When incumbents already have a dominant presence in the state, then this should have the opposite effect on the attainability of the electoral contest and the political institutions. The space for organizing and winning voter support is heavily skewed in favor of the authoritarian incumbent regime. Moreover, incumbent actors with high dominance typically possess features that can maintain electoral control and facilitate victory without the usage of instrumental manipulation strategies. *Given this, incumbents may be more likely to instead pursue informational manipulation efforts under conditions of high incumbent dominance, hoping to demonstrate their power and further legitimize their rule.* This would serve the optimal outcome of enhanced domestic legitimacy and control over the political institutions, a potential long-term benefit. When faced with high incumbent dominance, opposition actors may instead view few options and pathways for electoral victory in the short term. With a reduced space for organizing and a diminished pool of voter support, they may look beyond short-term benefits and shift their attention toward potential long-term options. In the short term, victory in the electoral contest may be unlikely anyway, persuading opposition actors to shift their focus to long-term prospects. This scenario may make an electoral boycott more likely. A boycott can have the potential long-term effect of presenting the election as a sham, thereby reducing the legitimacy of an incumbent victory. *Therefore, high incumbent dominance may make opposition actors more likely to select the strategy of an electoral boycott.*

Type of Election

Finally, the type of election being held can also alter the attainability of the game and meta-game. With the exception of Moldova, all other states in the post-Soviet region have had directly elected presidents in either presidential or semi-presidential systems.[9] This means that they maintain separate elections for the executive and the legislature, and that the elected president is a more prominent political figure than in pure parliamentary regimes. As discussed earlier, the type of election has been observed in some instances to have a relationship with incumbent and opposition behavior. This can be better understood using the framework of nested games. Factors that influence the attainability of the level of the electoral contest or the level of political institutions can be expected to influence the selection of electoral strategies. In particular, I argue that a legislative election alters the attainability of the electoral contest level. Electoral representation is more attainable during legislative elections by simple virtue of the number of seats available. *Given this, incumbent actors may be more likely to utilize instrumental manipulation strategies during legislative elections in the hopes of increasing their own vote share, and reducing support for opposition actors. Similarly, opposition actors may see legislative contests as particularly attainable games, encouraging the formation of pre-election coalitions.* A pre-election coalition can allow opposition actors to potentially gain a plurality of seats in the legislature. This can serve both the short-term goal of winning the election, but also can provide the coalition actors with a realistic check within the government to work toward the long-term benefit of limiting incumbent control over the meta-game of the political institutions.

Conversely, executive contests, particularly within the electoral authoritarian universe of states, can be especially uphill battles. While the other two factors outlined above, competitiveness and incumbent dominance, can definitely influence the attainability of elections on its own, an executive contest within an electoral authoritarian regime is likely to be tightly held and guarded by authoritarian incumbents. Therefore, this type of contest is less able to alter the attainability of the election itself. Instead, it can offer both incumbents and opposition actors the opportunity to focus on long-term goals that lie within the level of the political institutions. Executive elections, as singular political contests, are more visible to the public, which means that they may be especially suited for certain incumbent and opposition strategies. Incumbents may be more likely to view executive elections as attractive contests for informational manipulation. While this strategy is less able to directly influence the outcome of the election, it can work toward the long-term benefit of increased control over the political institutions governing the state through its high visibility. Informational manipulation itself refers to strategies that are highly visible but that indirectly affect the election, so an executive contest can actually augment the degree of visibility. *Therefore, incumbent actors may be more likely to select informational manipulation strategies in executive elections.* As for opposition actors, executive elections can also present highly visible opportunities to publicly dissent against the incumbent regime. While these contests, other factors withstanding, may be less attainable at the game level, they can serve potential long-term benefits at the meta-game stage. *This may make opposition actors more likely to boycott an executive election, to work toward the potential long-term benefit of reducing incumbent legitimacy.*

CONCLUSION

The previous sections introduced the three primary explanatory conditions that are expected to influence the selection of incumbent and opposition strategies. The competitiveness of the election, the degree of incumbent dominance, and the type of election all present particular influences on the attainability of the election or of control over the political institutions. Accordingly, I have postulated that depending on each factor, incumbent and opposition actors are more likely to opt for strategies that correspond with the attainability of the level. We would be more likely to see instrumental incumbent manipulation in competitive elections, in elections with low incumbent dominance, or in legislative elections than we would be in uncompetitive elections, those with high incumbent dominance, or in executive elections. This produces a clear set of propositions about the occurrence of each of the four strategies. Table 2.6 presents a summary of these expectations.

Table 2.6. Summary of Theoretical Expectations

Electoral Strategy	Optimal Conditions
Incumbent Instrumental Manipulation	High Competitiveness, Low Incumbent Dominance, Legislative Election
Incumbent Informational Manipulation	Low Competitiveness, High Incumbent Dominance, Executive Election
Opposition Pre-Electoral Coalition	High Competitiveness, Low Incumbent Dominance, Legislative Election
Opposition Boycott	Low Competitiveness, High Incumbent Dominance, Executive Election

CONCEPTS AND OPERATIONALIZATION

The premise of this book lies on the conduct of elections in electoral authoritarian regimes, while the theory relies on a precise and consistent understanding of what factors affect the conditions of the elections themselves. While this chapter has previously discussed the meanings of the four primary incumbent and opposition strategies under consideration, it has yet to explicitly do the same for these other crucial terms. We cannot begin to investigate these expectations without first establishing the definitions and indicators of these foundational concepts. The next few sections do just that. They identify the defining characteristics of these concepts, explaining in detail how they are measured. Moreover, these sections present descriptive statistics on the observations of these indicators among the universe of post-Soviet elections.

Defining Electoral Authoritarianism

While I have discussed electoral authoritarian states and the practice of elections within such political regimes, I have not yet provided a clear operationalization of the concept. Electoral authoritarian regimes must contain elections that are meaningful and allow opposition parties to exist; without such legitimate competition, states would instead be considered fully authoritarian regimes. To ensure that I capture the existence of genuine elections, I follow Hyde and Martinov's (2011) three distinctions of electoral from non-electoral competition to determine whether a state meets this criteria: whether the opposition is allowed to formally organize, whether the law allows multiple political parties to legally exist and contest elections, and whether more than one political party or candidate actually takes part in the elections. I also agree with Schedler's (2013) distinction that electoral authoritarian regimes must contain elections for the highest executive decision-making office; this serves to avoid the inclusion of fully authoritarian states that hold either legislative or subnational elections but not elections for the top decision-making officials.

Yet for such regimes to be considered electoral authoritarian regimes, they must therefore contain factors that prevent them from being classified as full-fledged democracies. Incumbent manipulation in elections is not only a common features of the political landscape in electoral authoritarian regimes, it is often put forward as a definitional aspect of the regimes themselves. Of course, such activities can be witnessed in democratic regimes as well[10], making its existence far from demonstrative of a regime that is not democratic. Moreover, if I define my sample of states based on the existence of electoral manipulation and then seek to test what affects electoral manipulation, the analysis would be tautological. Therefore, instead of focusing on the electoral playing field, I follow the framework presented by Gilbert and Mohseni (2011) in their conceptualization of illiberal hybrid regimes by classifying states as such based on the existence of restrictions on civil liberties. They categorized states on this factor depending on whether they were coded as free, partly free or not free by Freedom House's annual civil liberties scores, and considered states illiberal if they fit into either of the latter two categories.

With this in mind, I present the previous factors for all twelve post-soviet states to determine which fit the criteria stipulated. The factors for these states are presented in Table 2.7. To ease the presentation of the data, state averages are presented for each factor. The civil liberties scores come from Freedom House, which gives states yearly scores from a scale of one to seven: scores of 1–2 are considered free, 3–5 partly free and 6–7 not free. The corruption scale comes from Transparency International and measures corruption on a scale from zero to ten, with ten being completely clean while zero is completely corrupt. Table 2.7 shows that of the states included, there is some variation. All of the states, with the exception Turkmenistan and Uzbekistan, fit the minimal criteria for inclusion. These ten states all legally allow for a political opposition to exist and for multiple political parties to organize. Moreover, during actual elections, multiple parties compete and the executive of the state is elected from a popular vote. This means that an analysis of elections is appropriate for ten of the twelve states. All states maintain civil liberties that are coded as either partly free (3–5) or not free (6–7), and also maintain fairly high corruption scores. This provides support that while these states do maintain genuine open and multiple elections, the political conditions face limitations that prevent the states from being fully democratic. Thus I maintain that the inclusion of these ten states in this analysis as electoral authoritarian regimes is appropriate.

Electoral Factors

This book argues that electoral factors are essential correlates of incumbent and opposition strategies. This is due to the two-level game approach used, which argues that strategies should be influenced by the level where they have the optimal benefit available. If the optimum benefit occurs in the level of the electoral contest, then I would expect any electoral factor that makes the election more attainable to be important. Conversely, when the optimum benefit is found in the meta-game level of the political institutions, electoral factors demonstrating the security of the game level should instead influence the selection of this strategy. As established, this book focuses specifically on three electoral factors—the degree of competitiveness, the level of incumbent

Table 2.7. Case Selection of all post-Soviet States from 1992-present

State	Is Opposition legally allowed? From NELDA	Are multiple political parties legal? From NELDA	Does more than one party/candidate compete in elections? From NELDA	Is the Executive elected? From NELDA	Average Civil Liberties score (1993-present) From Freedom House	Average corruption score (1995-present) From Transparency International
Armenia	Yes	Yes	Yes	Yes	3.9	3.0
Azerbaijan	Yes	Yes	Yes	Yes	5.0	2.2
Belarus	Yes	Yes	Yes	Yes	5.6	2.9
Georgia	Yes	Yes	Yes	Yes	3.9	3.4
Kazakhstan	Yes	Yes	Yes	Yes	4.9	2.6
Kyrgyzstan	Yes	Yes	Yes	Yes	4.4	2.2
Moldova	Yes	Yes	Yes	Yes	3.9	2.9
Russia	Yes	Yes	Yes	Yes	4.7	2.1
Tajikistan	Yes	Yes	Yes	Yes	5.7	2.1
Turkmenistan	No	No	Yes	Yes	6.9	1.8
Ukraine	Yes	Yes	Yes	Yes	3.3	2.3
Uzbekistan	No	Yes[1]	Yes	Yes	6.5	2.0

1. While multiple parties or candidates have competed in Uzbekistan's most recent elections, they were all overtly supportive of the incumbent

dominance, and the type of election. In the following sections, I explain the operationalization and measurement strategies of these factors.

Electoral Competitiveness

The degree of competitiveness seeks to capture how competitive the election is, or how uncertain the outcome of the election is. While competition or contestation is an oft-discussed factor in the comparative politics literature, attractive measures of it have been wanting. One typical measure is a retrospective one that measures the difference between the winner and the first runner-up in the election (Eifert, Miguel, and Posner 2010). However, this measure leaves much to be desired as it captures the contestation of an election by looking at the election's results and then applying it retroactively to the pre-election period. Moreover, this measure would be empirically problematic in statistical analyses, as the measure would be an independent variable that occurred after the timeframe of the dependent variable (in this case, the selection of a pre-election strategy). Schedler (2009a; 2013) addresses this by using a similar measure that notes the difference between the winner and the runner-up in the most recent previous electoral contest. This is an improvement, but the time between elections can be years, during which many circumstances can change. While one party or candidate may have won a resounding victory, such a result may not accurately capture the degree of competition in an election two or four years later. Finally, other measures are regionally specific and therefore not always generalizable. For example, in analyzing the effect of political competition on anti-American sentiment, Blaydes and Linzer (2012) created an original measure for elite competition within Muslim-majority states, including the percentage of religious individuals within the state and the variation in religiosity.

As the margin of victory from a previous election has been one of the main accepted measures of competitiveness, I will include the difference between the first- and second-place candidates or parties in this book. Conventionally, this indicator would suggest that the larger the number, the less competitive the election, as it is based on the difference or margin of victory. However, for this book I opted to invert these figures by subtracting them from 100.[11] I do this so that the larger the number, the higher the degree of competitiveness would be. In applying these figures to subsequent elections, I also followed the type of election, so I used the previous inverted margin of victory from a parliamentary election for the subsequent parliamentary, and similarly for presidential contests. I argue that the size of the difference between winners and runners-up varies between executive and legislative elections, especially in electoral authoritarian regimes. A small margin of victory in a parliamentary election may not necessarily mean that a subsequent presidential election may be similarly competitive. In this book, this inverted margin of victory indicator is referred to as *previous competitiveness*.

Nonetheless, I opt to create an additional measure that captures the conditions of an election that may make a contest more or less competitive. The *previous competitiveness* indicator accurately captures the outcomes of prior contests, but it tells us little about what has transpired in the months or years since that election took place. To address this, I have created an index based on multiple factors theorized to affect the degree of competition, especially within electoral authoritarian regimes. The first two indicators refer to a state's economic conditions, and in particular, when a state faces economic problems. Under such conditions, the opposition is more likely to see regime change as a possibility and thus to attempt to pose a serious challenge to incumbents (Case 2006), or it may compel party member or regime insiders to defect (Reuter and Gandhi 2011). This is related to the idea that democratic transitions can emerge from serious economic crises by either exhausting elite resources (Bratton and Van de Walle 1997; Bueno de Mesquita et al. 2003), by upsetting the balance of power between elites within the government (Boix and Svolik 2013), or by diminishing regime legitimacy based on economic performance (Gasiorowski 1995). Moreover, voters are more likely to abandon an autocratic leader when faced with a prolonged economic crisis or a serious economic downturn; during prosperous times, the regime could build support based on its performance, but once this is absent, then voters are willing to consider an alternative (Magaloni 2006). To capture this, I include measures for both whether the economy is said to be doing poorly and whether it is in crisis. These indicators come from the National Executive and Legislative elections across Democracy and Autocracy or NELDA dataset (Hyde and Martinov 2012), which includes dichotomous measures for both.[12]

I also include a measure that captures incumbent confidence of victory. This measure also comes from the NELDA dataset and captures whether an incumbent candidate or party is publicly confident of victory during the electoral campaign. I argue that incumbent confidence provides evidence of low electoral competition, while the lack of confidence can reveal some genuine uncertainty over the outcome of the election. With these three factors, I have produced an index of *perceived electoral competitiveness* that ranges from zero to three. A score of three would indicate a positive on all three factors, and would represent a very high degree of competitiveness. A zero, on the other hand, would signify that the degree of competitiveness is very low. I contend that this index of perceived competitiveness is appropriate for this analysis and is preferable to previously used measures. It is appropriate because it includes factors that all can reveal, both logically and based on the literature, how competitive a given election is. Moreover, it is preferable to previous measures due to its reliance on factors more representative of the actual electoral campaign. It avoids using retrospective or prospective measures based on electoral results.

Table 2.8 presents the rates of competitiveness over time in the ten post-Soviet states included in this book. The index ranges from 0 to 3, with three representing an election with the highest degree of competitiveness, while

Table 2.8. Degree of Perceived Competitiveness by Election over time

Perceived Degree of Competitiveness	*0*	*1*	*2*	*3*
Legislative Elections	Azerbaijan 2010	Armenia 2007	Armenia 1999; 2003; 2012	Moldova 2001; 2009b
	Belarus 2008; 2012	Azerbaijan 2000; 2005	Azerbaijan 1995	
	Kazakhstan 2004; 2007; 2012	Belarus 2004; 2016	Georgia 2008; 2012; 2016	
	Kyrgyzstan 2005	Georgia 1999; 2003; 2004	Kyrgyzstan 2007; 2010; 2015	
	Moldova 2005	Kazakhstan 1999; 2016	Moldova 1998; 2009a; 2010; 2014	
	Russia 2003	Kyrgyzstan 2000	Russia 1999; 2011; 2016	
	Tajikistan 2015	Russia 2007	Ukraine 1998; 2012; 2014	
	Ukraine 2002	Tajikistan 2000; 2005; 2010		
		Ukraine 2006; 2007		
Executive Elections	Azerbaijan 2008	Armenia 2003; 2013	Armenia 1998; 2008	Armenia 1996
	Belarus 2006	Azerbaijan 1998; 2013	Azerbaijan 2003	Ukraine 2010; 2014
	Kazakhstan 2005; 2011	Belarus 2001; 2010; 2015	Georgia 2008; 2013	
	Kyrgyzstan 2000; 2005	Georgia 2000; 2004	Kyrgyzstan 2009; 2011	
	Moldova 1996	Kazakhstan 1999; 2015	Ukraine 1999	
	Russia 2000; 2004; 2008	Russia 1996; 2012		
	Ukraine 2004a	Tajikistan 2006; 2013		
		Ukraine 2004b		

a zero conversely captures an election with very low competitiveness. This table demonstrates that there is indeed variation in this index both within and between cases.

Incumbent Dominance

Next, I turn to the second explanatory variable, incumbent dominance. This variable has a straightforward and commonly utilized operationalization. One main distinction between low and high incumbent dominance has been the differentiation between competitive and hegemonic authoritarian regimes, respectively. Previous studies have coded a state as hegemonic if its executive is reelected with at least 70% of the vote (Brownlee 2009a; Roessler and Howard 2009; Donno 2013). Such a vote share demonstrates that the incumbent executive is highly dominant enough to be supported by more than two-thirds of the electorate. This measure is prospective, by using election results from a previous contest and applying them to future ones. Yet in this case, I find this prospective approach more appropriate. First, it takes into consideration multiple contests, by looking at the reelection of an incumbent. This ensures that the contest is more representative of the political situation and is not an aberration or a one-off event. It takes the long-term trend of incumbent dominance into account. Second, it looks specifically at the executive, which is often the seat of imbalanced power within electoral authoritarian regimes, especially among those in the post-Soviet region (Schedler 2006). Finally, it is parsimonious enough to clearly capture change in incumbent dominance. If an incumbent or an incumbent-endorsed candidate fails to wins at least 70% of the vote, then the classification would also shift from hegemonic to competitive authoritarian.

I also include a second factor in the measurement of incumbent dominance, the export of natural resources. When such exports comprise a sizable percentage of total Gross Domestic Product, the revenue can provide incumbents with significant resources to be used for political ends. As natural resources have been commonly argued to either derail or deter democratization (Ross 2001; Alaksen 2010, although see Haber and Menaldo 2011 for a contrarian take on this), many have also argued that this is due to the revenue from such resources insulating the regime from external pressures to democratize (Levitsky and Way 2010; Boix and Svolik 2013). Similarly, natural resource revenues can be used by a regime to repress opposition challenges (Ross 2001), can potentially serve as sources of revenue for patronage to maintain support (Ross 2001; Miller 2015), or their presence combined with low state capacity may ultimately contribute to the persistence of non-democracy (Haber, Razo, and Maurer 2003). Most of these arguments have still argued that more is better, and have not alluded to a threshold effect. One exception is Boix and Svolik (2013), who suggest that when a state's economy receives at least a third of its total GDP from the export of a single natural resource, it gives regimes strength to maintain their power through the various causal mechanisms discussed above. Given this, I also treat any election year where the export of natural resources represents at least a 33% of the state's total GDP as an indicator of incumbent dominance. I use these two measures together to create an index that ranges from 0 to 2, with a 2 suggesting very high incumbent dominance.

Table 2.9 displays the rates of incumbent dominance over time in the ten post-Soviet states. This demonstrates that incumbent dominance is not a

Table 2.9. Incumbent Dominance by Election over time

Incumbent Dominance	0	1	2
Legislative Election	Armenia 1999; 2003; 2007; 2012 Georgia 1999; 2004; 2008; 2012; 2016 Kyrgyzstan 2007; 2010; 2015 Moldova 1998; 2001; 2005; 2009a; 2009b; 2010; 2014 Russia 1999; 2003; 2016 Tajikistan 2000; 2005 Ukraine 1998; 2002; 2006; 2007; 2012; 2014	Azerbaijan 1995 Belarus 2004; 2008; 2012; 2016 Georgia 2003 Kazakhstan 1999; 2016 Kyrgyzstan 2000; 2005 Russia 2011 Tajikistan 2010; 2015	Azerbaijan 2000; 2005; 2010 Kazakhstan 2004; 2007; 2012 Russia 2007
Executive Election	Armenia 1996; 1998; 2003; 2008; 2013 Georgia 2000; 2004; 2008; 2013 Kyrgyzstan 2005; 2009; 2011 Moldova 1996 Russia 1996; 2000 Ukraine 1999; 2004a; 2004b; 2010; 2014	Belarus 2001; 2006; 2010; 2015 Kazakhstan 1999; 2015 Kyrgyzstan 2000 Russia 2004; 2008 Tajikistan 2006; 2013	Azerbaijan 1998; 2003; 2008; 2013 Kazakhstan 2005; 2011

static measure, but instead can and does change from one election to the next. No state remains entirely at the maximum level throughout every election; the three states that all reach this level at one point or another, Azerbaijan, Kazakhstan, and Russia, all either began below this point or have since seen incumbent dominance, as it is measured here, decrease. It does reveal three states that have remained at a zero for incumbent dominance throughout these elections: Armenia, Moldova, and Ukraine. In each of these states, incumbent executives have never been reelected with at least 70% of the vote, and the share of the state's GDP from natural resource exports has never been a third of the total GDP.

These three indicators, perceived competitiveness, previous competitiveness, and incumbent dominance, all bear some similarity. This is particularly true when considering the latter two, previous competitiveness and incumbent dominance, because both look retrospectively at previous elections. This raises the prospect of multicollinearity and whether the different variables may absorb statistical relevance from one another. The highest correlation of the three is between perceived competitiveness and incumbent dominance at -48%. This negative correlation follows the theoretical expectations, as it shows that as perceived competitiveness rises, the degree of incumbent dominance decreases. Next, previous competitiveness has a negative correlation with incumbent dominance at -43%. The directions of these two correlations provide confirmation that the measures used accurately operationalize the desired indicators. They also suggest that multicollinearity remains a concern. The lowest correlation of the three is between perceived competitiveness and previous competitiveness, which is measured at 25.8%. To account for these three correlations, the quantitative estimates in chapters 3–6 will take multicollinearity into account.

RESEARCH DESIGN AND METHODS

As explained earlier in this chapter, this book covers ten post-Soviet states that can be classified as electoral authoritarian regimes. These ten states provide diversity within the region, including states from Eastern Europe (Moldova, Ukraine, Belarus), the Caucasus (Armenia, Georgia, Azerbaijan), Central Asia (Kazakhstan, Kyrgyzstan, and Tajikistan), and Russia. Yet they all share a common starting point for such political development, having gained independence after the disintegration of the USSR. This shared past means that none have had any substantial experience with competitive elections or political party development outside the Communist Party of the Soviet Union. Additionally, these states also share previous histories of patrimonial politics even prior to the creation of the Soviet Union, a legacy that remains important across the region (Hale 2015; 2016). Moreover, these states have all faced the challenge of corruption, a factor linked in particular to electoral interference. Many studies of electoral authoritarian regimes remarked upon the former Soviet Union as a region with a high concentration of such states (Levitsky and Way 2010; Gilbert and Mohseni 2011), which I argue makes it a useful setting to test the theoretical expectations put forward in this book.

This book follows a mixed-methods approach to tackling the questions and propositions of incumbent and opposition strategies in electoral authoritarian regimes. Each of the four empirical chapters contains both quantitative statistical estimations as well as qualitative case study considerations. The quantitative portions help establish general patterns and relationships among the data using the entire universe of observations for guidance in this. This kind of analysis allows me to evaluate the theoretical expectations broadly and to draw general conclusions about the relationships between electoral factors and incumbent and opposition strategies. Meanwhile, each chapter also contains three case study considerations of individual elections. The elections have been selected based on the presence or absence of key explanatory factors (the degree of competitiveness, incumbent dominance, and type of election) based on the findings from the quantitative analyses. The case studies then describe what we would expect to take place based on the conditions of the election and reports to what degree the expected relationship is indeed present or absent. These qualitative case studies provide greater depth into and detail on the elections, noting the political context for each case as well as bringing in any additional case-specific factors that may be of importance. An added benefit of the case studies is that they allow for a long term perspective into the effects of the strategies well after the elections themselves have concluded.

The case studies also provide valuable insights into more recent elections in the post-Soviet region. While the Color Revolutions have received enormous attention, as have many of the elections that took place in their wake, the elections selected for the case studies are more recent and have been featured far less in relevant scholarship. The elections selected for case studies are Georgia's 2012 parliamentary election, Moldova's 2009 parliamentary elections, Kazakhstan's 2016 parliamentary election, Azerbaijan's 2008 presidential election, Russia's 2008 presidential election, Kyrgyzstan's 2015 presidential election, Armenia's 2012 parliamentary election, Russia's 2011 presidential election, Armenia's 2013 presidential election, Belarus's 2012 parliamentary election, and Belarus's 2010 presidential election. Moreover, while the elections are more recent, they have also taken place with enough distance to allow for the consideration of the long-term effects from the election strategies.

The data in this book comes from a few different sources. First, the data on electoral manipulation come from an original coding of election observation reports from the Organization for Security and Cooperation in Europe (OSCE). Each final report issued by the OSCE at the conclusion of their election observation missions was read and used in the coding of the presence or absence of the different types of electoral manipulation. The final reports represent the accumulation of their findings and conclusions from throughout their mission in the country. As such, they contain reports and observations from both long-term and short-term observers. Long-term observers (LTOs) typically arrive before the actual election campaign begins and remain in country for the duration of the campaign which, depending on the state, can be a few weeks or a few months. LTOs are better positioned to witness specific instances of manipulation and are also more likely to have developed contacts with domestic election monitors and civil society groups that may report violations or other instances of interference (Hyde 2009). The final reports also include conclusions from short-term observers (STO) who typically are only present in the final days of the campaign, for the election day itself, and the subsequent vote count procedures. The reports offer specific examples of manipulation, typically citing the location where it occurred as well as the source of the information.

The primary data analyzed in this book were compiled by the author through a detailed reading of these reports and subsequent recording of whether a specific type of manipulation occurred or not. This book asks how electoral conditions affect the selection of particular strategies, and as such it is primarily concerned with the presence or absence of a strategy. Therefore, the OSCE reports allow me to effectively establish whether a particular type of manipulation occurred within a specific election. The book is not concerned with the quantity of such manipulation or whether a certain type was committed multiple times or just once. This approach on the simple presence or absence of a type of manipulation is amenable to the contents of the OSCE reports.

I regard these reports as sufficiently valid and reliable as data sources for several reasons. First, they have served as the source of data for other comparable studies of electoral manipulation (Birch 2011a; Simpser 2013). The OSCE is a well-regarded organization operating without a partisan ideology. It also provides the endeavors of election monitoring with consistency, as they regularly observe elections not just within the former Soviet Union but also across Europe and in parts of Asia. Their established practices mean that missions are carried out in a systematic fashion by professionals who often bring regional expertise to the process. Second, the content of the reports has been examined and scrutinized in a recent study by Kelley (2012). She sought to examine and compare the reports to other election observation organizations, and to judge whether they accurately captured the dynamics of the election. Kelley (2012) concluded that one disadvantage to these reports is that in some cases, the executive summary may offer a fairly neutral or even a somewhat positive evaluation of the election as a whole, while the details of the report may paint a more negative picture of the electoral processes. This disconnect, she posited, could be due to the political dynamics at work between the OSCE and the recipient states who invite and welcome such international observers into their domestic elections. This criticism is important, as it suggests that the OSCE may sometimes seek to water down their overall conclusions to maintain sufficient access to the proceedings. However, she does note that the bodies of the reports are typically much more explicit in their characterizations of events and are more honest in their conclusions. This disconnect could also be due to the input from STOs, who may not have witnessed as much manipulation (Hyde 2009). Nonetheless, Kelley (2012) concludes that the reports overall reported manipulation regardless of the evaluation given in the executive summary. For this book, the details of the reports provided the basis for the evidence of specific types of manipulation, rather than the executive summaries. Therefore, I do not expect the data to have been influenced by this trend. Finally, it is very possible, given the sometimes limited scopes of election observation missions, that the OSCE reports are actually conservative estimates of manipulation. Observers cannot be everywhere at once, and more manipulation may occur precisely in locations without observers. This means that the data on manipulation may in fact be underestimating its occurrence. I consider this to be an acceptable limitation, as it means that any relationships that I do find have been observed despite the conservative estimates used.

The data on opposition pre-election coalitions came from Donno's (2013) data on the topic. I extended her data to 2016 by reading about elections on the Inter-Parliamentary Union database of elections, as well as from discussions of coalitions from the OSCE and from election summaries published in Electoral Studies. I also used OSCE reports as a source for instances of opposition boycotts. Economic indicators used in the quantitative analysis come from the World Bank World Development Indicators. The measure for the Rule of Law, lagged by one year, was from the World Bank World Governance Indicators. This indicator was more comprehensive in its time span than a similar measure from Transparency International.

The data for the qualitative case studies came from multiple sources. First, I relied on the preliminary reports and findings published by the OSCE in addition to the final reports. The preliminary reports provide further detail into the election and are almost exclusively written by LTOs. The combination of the preliminary reports with the final reports provide a more complete picture of the conduct of the election. I also utilized any summaries of the election written by scholars in the journal *Electoral Studies*, which regularly solicits and publishes five- to ten-page overviews of elections written by a specialist on the country. I included relevant coverage from Radio Free Europe/Radio Liberty's archives. As an international news agency, they provide more re-gion-specific coverage of political developments in the former Soviet Union than most other Western sources. Finally, I also sometimes turned to certain domestic news coverage that has been previously used by other scholars in their own publications on the region.[13] Together, these different news sources provide contemporaneous coverage of the elections as they were happening and allow me to flesh out the strategies that were observed.

CONCLUSION

This chapter provides the theoretical underpinnings to this book. It estab-lishes clear expectations and electoral conditions that are more and less conducive to each electoral strategy. Furthermore, this chapter specified the concepts necessary to this study. In particular, it has defined and measured electoral authoritarianism, which serves as the blanket concept of this book. It has then explored the coverage and consideration of the different varieties of incumbent manipulation strategies, as well as opposition electoral strate-gies within the post-Soviet universe of electoral authoritarian states. This section demonstrates the insights as well as the remaining questions on these strategies, particularly in this region. I assert that the lack of a comprehensive approach to these strategies in this region merits the scope of this book and its mixed methods approach to triangulating how the conditions of elections may influence the selection of certain strategies.

NOTES

1. This book builds upon the distinction between informational and instrumental manipulation established by Hauser (2018).
2. "Ukraine Presidential Elections 17 January and 7 February 2010" *OSCE/ODIHR Election Observation Mission Final Report.* Warsaw: 28 April 2010.
3. "Final Report: Georgia Parliamentary Elections 2 November 2003" *OSCE/ODIHR Election Observation Mission Final Report.* Warsaw: 28 January 2004.
4. "Republic of Azerbaijan Presidential Election 9 October 2013" *OSCE/ODIHR Election Observation Mission Final Report.* Warsaw: 24 December 2013.

5. "Russian Federation Presidential Election 4 March 2012" *OSCE/ODIHR Election Observation Mission Final Report.* Warsaw: 11 May 2012.

6. I argue that the distinctions offered by Ohman (2013) are superior for a few reasons. First, unlike other studies on electoral manipulation (Simpser 2013), these distinctions focus on different types, as opposed to cumulative manipulation. Second, Ohman's distinctions are fairly similar to those made by Birch (2011), who included the manipulation of the legal framework, vote choice, and the electoral administration. These factors are all covered by Ohman (2013) and I argue that his divisions are more apt to capture the varying goals of incumbents discussed in this dissertation. I also contend that Ohman's four types are more straightforward in allowing for the direct measurement needed for hypothesis testing.

7. Of course we can rightly observe clear costs to political competition and the potential for democracy due to informational incumbent manipulation.

8. Many scholars (Schedler 2006; Brownlee 2009a; Donno 2013) maintain that regimes where the incumbent executive is reelected with at least 70% of the vote are considered hegemonic authoritarian regimes, while states that do not meet this criterion are labeled competitive authoritarian regimes. In the former, opposition activities are typically more limited, while they may be more open in the latter. In this book, I will follow this classification based on vote share, but will not use the terms "competitive" and "hegemonic" authoritarian regimes, to avoid confusion with the previous explanatory concept, competitiveness.

9. Moldova maintains a parliamentary system. Following the 1996 presidential election, Moldova shifted to indirect elections of the president, the head of state, held within the parliament. However, since 2016, Moldova has reintroduced the direct election of the president. In 2010, Kyrgyzstan adopted what it terms a semi-parliamentary system that still maintains a directly elected president.

10. Examples include clientelism and vote-buying in Latin America (e.g., Stokes 2005) as well as voter outreach in Japan by the Liberal Democratic Party, which often includes patronage, incentives, and gifts aimed at persuading voters (Nyblade and Reed 2008).

11. For example, in the 2012 presidential election in Russia, Vladimir Putin won 63.6% of the vote, while in second place, Gennady Zyuganov won 17.2%. The difference between these two indicators is 46.4. I then invert this figure by subtracting it from 100. Thus the previous margin of victory for the next Russian presidential election, according to this study, is 53.6. Similarly, in Georgia's 2012 parliamentary election, the inverted margin of victory between the Georgian Dream coalition, which received 54.97% of the vote, and the United National Movement, which received 40.34%, would be 85.37. In this case, the degree competitiveness for Georgia's subsequent parliamentary election in 2016 is higher than the figure for Russia's next presidential election.

12. Technically, NELDA includes a measure for whether the economy is said to be doing well; I used the reverse of this to indicate that the economy is not doing well.

13. These include the *Moscow Times* and *Civil Georgia*, both of which have been relied upon by Levitsky and Way (2010) and Hale (2015), among others.

Chapter Three

Explaining Incumbent Instrumental Manipulation

Instrumental electoral manipulation refers to interference that serves the purpose of helping a candidate or party secure enough votes to win. Governments and parties interfere because they are worried that in a fully honest and fair contest, they would lose. Therefore, they engage in manipulation to *directly influence* the main actors in the election so as to ensure, or at least tip the scales in favor of, incumbent victory. In doing so, the manipulation serves an instrumental role in producing a particular outcome that may not have been as attainable without such manipulation. Given this, I have argued that instrumental manipulation produces the clearest benefits in the short term at the election level of analysis. This suggests that any factors that affect the attainability of the election are likely to influence the selection of this strategy. As such, this chapter examines the relationship between instrumental incumbent manipulation and electoral factors. I assert that higher competition, lower incumbent dominance, and an election for the legislature all can affect the attainability of the election. This chapter presents an overview and analysis of this relationship. First, it briefly discusses the measures of instrumental manipulation used in this chapter, and demonstrates their ability to directly influence the behavior of candidates, parties, and voters. Next, it presents the descriptive statistics of instrumental manipulation, noting the frequency of the three categories across the universe of cases in the post-Soviet region. It then examines and discusses the results of statistical analyses as to whether electoral factors influence the odds that an incumbent party or candidate will select instrumental manipulation strategies. I subsequently explore these findings with three case illustrations: Georgia's 2012 parliamentary elections, Moldova's 2009 parliamentary elections, and Kazakhstan's 2016 parliamentary elections. The first two cases are elections with higher degree competitiveness, and, as expected, witnessed several instances of instrumental manipulation. The third case contained low competitiveness and subsequently was absent of instrumental manipulation.

CATEGORIES OF INSTRUMENTAL MANIPULATION

To serve in an instrumental purpose, manipulation strategies must directly influence the main actors taking part in an election, meaning candidates, parties, and voters. Since instrumental manipulation is an incumbent electoral strategy, I am especially interested in behaviors that directly a) help pro-government candidates or b) seek to curtail the efforts of opposition parties and candidates during the pre-election campaign period. Direct influence is crucial for instrumental manipulation; strategies that only indirectly engage with campaign activities or voter behavior are less reliable in seeking to produce the intended outcome. As already established, this book focuses exclusively on manipulation committed before the election itself. Therefore, this chapter examines three different categories of electoral manipulation that directly interfere with the primary actors of an election: regulatory resource abuse, financial resource abuse, and enforcement resource abuse.

Direct support for the Incumbent Regime

Regulatory, financial, and enforcement resource abuse all directly interfere with candidates, parties, and voters. First of all, these categories can work to help the efforts of pro-government and incumbent candidates and parties. In all elections, incumbents enjoy a clear and observable advantage when it comes to reelection. While this kind of advantage is typically an unavoidable element of democratic elections, the exploitation of an election and its components in service of the incumbent regime is counter to the ideals of democratic competition. Organizations such as the OSCE and other election observation groups suggest that electoral regulations be drafted and implemented in as neutral or nonpartisan a manner as possible, that a government refrain from using its influence over social and economic policy in financially advantageous ways, and that law enforcement and other security services, as organs of the state, avoid any pro-regime or partisan behavior during the election. Yet these principles are often weakly observed or ignored, which paves the way for financial, regulatory, or enforcement resources to be manipulated in favor of the incumbent regime. These categories of electoral manipulation can assist pro-government and incumbent candidates and parties through financial activities and regulations, election and campaign regulations on registration or operations, or the biased provision of security forces.

Regulatory Resource Abuse

The manipulation of election regulations directly alters the electoral playing field, and is able to provide the incumbent regime with an additional advantage. Regulatory resource abuse occurs most commonly at the level of the election administration, which includes different levels of the electoral commission. These bodies typically address complaints or appeals submitted during the election regarding improper or questionable electoral conduct. This role provides commissions with the opportunity to rule disproportionately in favor of pro-government parties. As Jarabinsky (2015:90) notes, "the Electoral Commission has a direct influence on election results: if any actor wished to directly manipulate Russian elections, they would have to do so through the EC." As the descriptive tables will show, all ten states were the site of regulatory manipulation in more than three or more elections. Thus this is a common occurrence across the former Soviet Union, but it has received limited scholarly attention. Some exceptions have provided extensive coverage on regulatory manipulation in Russia and Ukraine. Jarabinsky (2015:98) describes the effects on Russia's 2011 parliamentary election, "the observed results thus tend to confirm the assumption that the behavior of the Russian EC [Electoral Commission] clearly favour the party UR [United Russia] and harm the JR [Just Russia], and probably the CPRF [Communist Party of the Russian Federation] as well." Similarly, in Ukraine, Boyko and Herron (2015:33) note how having affiliations with members of the administration helps certain parties, "we found that both Batkicshchyna and Party of Regions experienced enhanced election outcomes when technical parties had officers in PECs [Precinct Electoral Commissions], and that the magnitude of effect was greater for the Party of Regions." Therefore, partisanship and the manipulation of election administrations and electoral commissions can directly affect political parties' abilities to field and submit candidates.

Financial Resource Abuse

Incumbent regimes in electoral authoritarian states have used their privileged position and their access to state resources to coopt the opposition and provide benefits to loyal partisans (Bueno de Mesquita et al. 2003; Magaloni 2006; Gandhi and Przeworski 2006). Patronage and the disbursement of resources to pro-government supporters and parties, even if they do not belong to the main political party, can maintain loyalty and discourage dissent and criticism. In this way, financial resource abuse is a transparent example of seeking to directly influence and alter the behavior of voters in their election day decisions as well as the ability for opposition parties and candidates to compete on a level playing field. This is especially notable in places with dominant or hegemonic parties, as observed in Azerbaijan (Radnitz 2012) and Russia (Remington 2008; Reuter 2013). In the case of Russia, patronage and resources are often employed most successfully in connection with supportive regional officials. Reuter (2013:120–121) remarks that, "hegemonic parties win elections by larger margins when the regional elites who support the party resources, machines and/or authority dependably generate popular support for the party." Overall, such government-aligned parties and actors can directly benefit from access to such resources and support, giving them a crucial advantage.

Enforcement Resource Abuse

Security forces and law enforcement officers can directly interfere in elections in service of the incumbent by demonstrating a clear alliance and support for the regime. When incumbent candidates receive explicit support for the regime from security services, this provides an additional boost to the regime during an election campaign. For example, when police in Armenia's 2008 presidential election displayed flags in support of the incumbent president's political party on their cars and gave out such flags while in uniform, this further tilts the electoral playing field in favor of the incumbent, as it demonstrates that law enforcement officers are partisan, rather than nonpartisan, officials.[1] Moreover, this behavior politicizes the day-to-day work of the law enforcement officers and security personnel, providing an advantage to the incumbent regime.

Direct Obstruction of Opposition Candidates

Second, these three categories are all able to curtail or limit the campaign activities of opposition candidates. Regulatory, financial, and enforcement resource abuse can all be deployed in ways that directly interfere with opposition campaign and election behavior, thereby explicitly tipping the scales against opposition victory. In the subsequent paragraphs, I outline specifically how each category can directly manipulate opposition parties and candidates.

Regulatory Resource Abuse

Electoral regulations can be manipulated to directly obstruct the campaign activities of opposition parties and candidates. One of the most common ways that electoral regulations can hinder opposition activity is through the denial of candidate registration. Electoral commissions have been observed disqualifying some opposition candidates from officially registering in the first place. This type of manipulation can be facilitated by lax or vague election regulations that provide commissioners with a great deal of latitude in ruling on candidate registration, using stringent signature verification as the reasoning for disqualification. Election regulations may be designed to limit candidate registration. Members of the electoral commission may also decide to disqualify certain candidates in a politicized manner based on unreasonable or unstated criteria. Birch (2011a:75) notes that these kinds of manipulation "are blatantly undemocratic in that they hinder contestation, completion or the equality of electoral subjects before the law." Delegation to regional and precinct levels can also serve this purpose; one or both of these methods have been observed in recent elections in Russia (Baekken 2015) and Azerbaijan (LaPorte 2015). LaPorte (2015:349) describes this process in Azerbaijan, explaining that

> while opposition candidates are legally permitted to field candidates for elected office, the government employs a number of informal and legalistic measures that make it difficult to do so in practice. For example, opposition candidates have been refused registration at a significantly higher rate than pro-government politicians.

Baekken (2015:69) argues that "the Russian registration system is indeed prone to abuse. The combination of ambiguous laws, formalistic enforcement, and incumbent control over the legal and administrative actors responsible for implementing the election laws makes it possible to establish and conduct political filtering of candidates." The common thread among these reports is the unequal implementation of electoral regulations so that harsh rules are applied with greater pressure on opposition candidates and regime outsiders than on those belonging to pro-government parties and groups.

Financial Resource Abuse

Opportunities for campaign finance, or the lack thereof, can be devastating to opposition parties. Financial regulations can restrict the availability of resources and campaign finance, so much so that opposition candidates and parties operate with a barebones staff and campaign operations. In Azerbaijan, opposition parties have experienced difficulty in securing office space or receiving permits for political rallies due to government pressure on real estate figures and developers (LaPorte 2015). Similar pressure was put on opposition offices in Belarus following the Orange Revolution in neighboring Ukraine.

> New housing regulations have given the regime a pretext for closing down local branches of the leading opposition parties registered at residential apartments. Opposition and civil society groups are no longer allowed to rent state-

owned property, so many party conferences and NGO meetings take place in restaurants, Western embassies, private apartments, and even forests. (Silitski 2005:94).

Access to Western financial assistance has been linked to the opposition victories in the Color Revolutions; this has contributed to the diffusion of new financial regulations that often seek to reduce or eliminate foreign support for opposition political actors and non-governmental organizations that criticize the regime. These restrictions have emerged in multiple post-Soviet states, including Belarus, Russia, Kazakhstan, and Azerbaijan (Silitski 2005; Carothers and Brechenmacher 2014; Ziegler 2016). Moreover, these kinds of restrictions can be especially detrimental if the economy is still relatively state-controlled, which eliminates other private sources of financial support (Radnitz 2010). In Belarus, elections must be entirely publicly financed, while "private donations can only be made to the State budget, to be equally distributed between candidates" (Ohman 2013: 178). These kinds of restrictions directly and disproportionately limit opposition candidates' and parties' abilities to build and finance a robust, competitive campaign.

Enforcement Resource Abuse

Opposition parties and candidates need opportunities to campaign and disseminate their message to the voters. Yet in many instances, opposition campaign events, offices, and rallies have been disrupted or canceled by police or security interference. This directly interferes with opposition parties and candidates' abilities to campaign fairly alongside pro-government actors. Police disruption of opposition campaign events and demonstrations have taken place in Belarus (Silitski 2005), Armenia (Hess 2010), and Azerbaijan (Bunce and Wolchik 2011). The actual deployment of enforcement resource abuse varies, from police confiscating opposition campaign literature from public places (Azerbaijan) to the beating and detainment of opposition supporters and demonstrators (Silitski 2005). Security forces may go further by preventing rallies or campaign events from occurring at all. In Belarus, "local authorities and the police used the provisions of the Law on Mass Events to prevent the holding of opposition election-related gatherings, including meetings of campaign activists held in residences. This curtailed the freedoms of association and public assembly" (OSCE 2006: 14). Conversely, one of the components that helped the opposition succeed in Ukraine's 2004 presidential election was the neutrality of the security forces, and their unwillingness to intimidate and disrupt opposition campaign events (Bunce and Wolchik 2011).

Direct Interference with Voter Behavior

Finally, these categories directly engage with voters and vote choices made on election day. Financial and enforcement resource abuse can target voters directly through the provision of goods, new social spending, or through harassment for attending opposition campaign rallies. Birch (2011a: 90) echoes this in noting that "rewards can be used to lure voters into ignoring their true preferences when they vote. On the other hand, tactics of intimidation can be used either to get voters to vote a certain way or to make them abstain altogether."

Regulatory Resource Abuse

Electoral regulations can be used to directly interfere with the behavior of voters themselves. One way this can be accomplished is through military voting. This practice creates new polling locations for active duty military officials on military bases, rather than allowing them to vote based on their permanent residence. On-base voting can allow superior officers and other actors to subtly (or not so subtly) influence the vote choices of active duty military officers, typically in a pro-regime direction. Lax or problematic regulations on military voting have been observed in Belarus, Kazakhstan, Tajikistan, Georgia, and Armenia (Bader 2014). Additionally, new voter registration regulations can be implemented that can have the effect of significantly augmenting or restricting the voter base. New regulations that enlarge the total voter rolls at a rate disproportionate to population growth or other factors facilitate double voting, fake ballots, and electoral fraud, while those that limit participation instead may exclude certain elements of the population from voting at all. Additionally, voters, especially those in public sector occupations, can be pressured to change their location of registration, which can be subtle or not so subtle pressure on voters to turn out for a certain candidate. In Kyrgyzstan's most recent presidential election, "(s)everal interlocutors, mainly from civil society, shared credible information with the ODIHR EOM about cases of university students, civil servants, and employees of state-owned companies being pressured to request temporary voting addresses and to vote for Mr. Jeenbekov" (Sooronbay Jeenbekov was the favored pro-government candidate) (OSCE 2018a: 9). Finally, voters who register from abroad in a system with single member districts may be registered in particular districts; in Russia's 2016 parliamentary elections, "voters residing abroad were arbitrarily assigned to 75 out of 225 SMCs, even though they had no connection with the constituency. This solution was criticized by many OSCE/ODIHR interlocutors for potentially skewing the vote in SMCs" (OSCE 2016b: 10).

In all of these instances, these regulatory manipulations directly interfere with the voters' capacity to cast free and unencumbered votes.

Financial Resource Abuse

Incumbent candidates and parties can seek to influence or alter voter behavior through manipulation of state financial resources. One of the most well-known strategies of this is the exchange of money, goods, and services for political support, or vote-buying. In the post-Soviet region, vote-buying can take place both at the individual level as well as at the community level. In the case of the latter, new infrastructure or public goods, such as parks or public buses may be installed or provided in coordination with a pro-government campaign rally. Yet this strategy is risky, as voters may accept the reward and vote how they choose anyway, and costly for regimes to carry out. Such practices nonetheless persist under certain circumstances in Russia (Harvey 2016). Officials may also increase pre-election spending on social services in a strategy to increase public support. This type of behavior is especially unfair and partisan when the new spending is unannounced, or even tied to political support. Revenue from the export of oil and other natural resources has been found to facilitate this kind of behavior in Azerbaijan and Kazakhstan (Kendall-Taylor 2012). Finally, public sector employees are often especially vulnerable to intimidation. Such employees may have their future employment threatened, being either encouraged to vote for the incumbent, or threatened for attending any opposition campaign events. This behavior directly affects voters through financial pressures; if voters worry that their jobs are at stake, they may be compelled to vote in a particular way, or to not vote at all. These types of interactions between employers and employees has emerged as an additional form of machine politics or clientelism in use in Russia, as well as other post-Soviet states (Golosov 2011).

Enforcement Resource Abuse

Members of the varied security forces have the ability to put pressure on individuals to encourage, or more accurately, intimidate them to support the incumbent regime. Another way that such pressure manifests is through the criminal justice system. The families of individuals serving prison sentences, for example, may be informed that the sentence could be reduced in exchange for a commitment to vote for the incumbent or pro-government candidate. Such behavior was indeed witnessed in Georgia's 2008 parliamentary election by election monitors. These interactions clearly demonstrate the intention to directly influence and interfere with the choices and behavior of voters.

OCCURRENCES AND ESTIMATES OF
INSTRUMENTAL INCUMBENT MANIPULATION

As discussed in chapter 2, there are perceived costs and benefits to the act of instrumental incumbent manipulation, and these costs and benefits occur both in the short term at the game level of the election as well as in the long term at the institutional level. I contend that, due to the long-term risk of reduced legitimacy associated with the direct manipulation of an election, the largest benefits lie in the election contest itself. Given this, I assert that factors that alter the attainability of the election should influence the choice to engage in instrumental manipulation. In particular, I expect incumbents to be more likely to abuse financial, regulatory, and enforcement resources a) when the election has higher competitiveness, b) when the election occurs with low incumbent dominance, and/or c) during legislative elections. However, first I will present the frequency of instrumental manipulation over the course of the 88 elections which comprise the data of this book. I will then present the rates at which these categories have been observed across the universe of cases. After that, I will present quantitative analyses that examine these relationships.

Table 3.1 presents the frequency of each type of instrumental manipulation. As the table shows, each type was observed in at least one of the 88 elections surveyed for this book, although some types were more frequently observed than others. Manipulation by police or security authorities proved to be the most frequent type of abuse, observed in one-third of all elections included. Next, politicized actions and decisions made by electoral commissions were observed in just over 30% of all elections contained within this study. Finally, in 18.2% of cases, election monitors observed the direct allocation of goods and/or financial compensation to voters. Overall, this tells us that individual types of instrumental manipulation vary in their selection. Moreover, it confirms that while elections in the post-Soviet region regularly feature irregularities and unfair conditions, instrumental manipulation is by no means a constant occurrence. This supports the presumption that it represents a choice for incumbents and government-supported actors during electoral campaigns, one that they choose to avoid in the majority of cases.

As discussed in the previous paragraph, instrumental manipulation is not observed in every election, demonstrating that this is not simply behavior that occurs in any and every contest, regardless of the context. I next examine whether it is witnessed through the ten states included in this study. One possible assumption about instrumental manipulation is that this might be confined to a few "bad apples," or that one or two post-Soviet states might represent the bulk of the observations. As Table 3.2 shows, this is not the

Table 3.1. Frequency of Instrumental Manipulation by Type

Type of Instrumental Resource	Zero instances reported during election	One or more instance reported during election	Percentage of Occurrence
Direct allocation of goods or financial support to voters	72	16	18.2%
State financial activity beneficial to incumbent candidates	80	8	9.1%
Announcements of unplanned increases in state spending on welfare and social services	86	2	2.3%
New regulations seen to hinder or obstruct opposition activities	76	12	13.6%
Politicized or biased activities by electoral commissions	61	27	30.7%
New campaign or political finance rules seen to benefit incumbents	86	2	2.3%
Security or police manipulation into activities of opposition	60	29	33%
Unbalanced usage of security details to candidates	84	4	4.5%

Table 3.2. Number of Elections Featuring Instrumental Manipulation, by State

State	Financial Resource Abuse	Regulatory Resource Abuse	Enforcement Resource Abuse
Armenia	4 out of 9	3 out of 9	3 out of 9
Azerbaijan	1 out of 8	5 out of 8	7 out of 8
Belarus	2 out of 8	7 out of 8	4 out of 8
Georgia	3 out of 10	4 out of 10	8 out of 10
Kazakhstan	1 out of 9	4 out of 9	3 out of 9
Kyrgyzstan	5 out of 9	4 out of 9	4 out of 9
Moldova	1 out of 8	3 out of 8	3 out of 8
Russia	4 out of 10	6 out of 10	3 out of 10
Tajikistan	0 out of 6	3 out of 6	4 out of 6
Ukraine	5 out of 11	4 out of 11	5 out of 11

case. Every single state has witnessed at least one category of instrumental manipulation in at least one election; in fact, every single state, with the exception of Tajikistan, has been the site of all three categories in at least one electoral contest. Moreover, elections in most states have contained more than one of such resource abuses. The median number of elections per state with financial resource abuse is 3.5, while the median numbers for regulatory and enforcement resource abuse are 4 and 4, respectively. That all three categories are observed across the universe of cases helps ensure that the data are not driven by extreme country-specific outliers. Instead, instrumental manipulation has generally been observed in more than one election in every single state included.

Next, I examine the frequency of manipulation by category. Table 3.3 captures the rates at which elections feature zero, one, two, or, for financial and regulatory manipulation, all three types of abuse. For each category, zero types were observed in at least half of the elections examined; for financial resource abuse, this was true for just over 70% of cases. One type of regulatory or enforcement abuse was reported in over 40% of elections, while for

Table 3.3. Observations of Instrumental Manipulation Frequencies

Types of Instrumental Manipulation	Frequency in Election	Percentage of Occurrence
Financial Resource Abuse		
Zero Types Observed	62	70.5%
One Type Observed	21	23.9%
Two Types Observed	5	5.6%
All Three Types Observed	0	0%
Total	88	100%
Regulatory Resource Abuse		
Zero Types Observed	44	50%
One Type Observed	37	42.1%
Two Types Observed	6	6.8%
All Three Types Observed	1	1.1%
Total	88	
Enforcement Resource Abuse		
Zero Types Observed	44	50%
One Type Observed	43	48.9%
Two Types Observed	1	1.1%
Total	88	

financial resource abuse, this percentage falls to under a quarter. Once again, this table supports the assertion that these strategies of interference are not universally used or selected in electoral authoritarian regimes. They remain infrequent, though not rare, events and further suggest that governments and incumbents vary their behavior from one contest to the next.

Finally, I also present the data as combinations of the three categories. The overarching hypothesis of this chapter is that instrumental manipulation methods are more likely to be selected under circumstances that alter the attainability of the election. This means that such strategies may be combined with one another, rather than chosen in insolation from the other types. Thus financial resource abuse may be selected in the same election that regulatory resource abuse is used. Moreover, an election that features multiple categories of instrumental resource abuse may demonstrate a case where the regime was especially motivated (or desperate) to directly interfere with the behavior of incumbents, opposition actors, and voters and to influence the outcome. Table 3.4 displays the number of elections in which one or more types of financial, enforcement, and regulatory resource abuse coincide with one another. This shows that while elections with instances of both financial and regulatory abuse as well as financial and enforcement resource abuse occur in less than 20% of elections, the presence of both regulatory and enforcement resource abuse is observed in just under a third of cases. Finally, the presence of at least two different categories of instrumental resource abuse is observed in about 45% of elections included in this study. These descriptive statistics suggest that these combinations are not rare, and there are indeed situations where multiple categories are deployed in a given contest.

I next seek to examine the descriptive statistics on the occurrence of instrumental manipulation depending on the conditions of the election. Tables 3.5, 3.6, and 3.7 display the rates of financial, regulatory, and enforcement resource abuse based on these conditions. Looking at the frequency of these

Table 3.4.   Combined Instrumental Manipulation Categories

Categories of Instrumental Manipulation	Frequency in Elections	Percentage of Occurrence
One or more types of both Financial and Regulatory Abuse	13	14.8%
One or more types of both Financial and Enforcement Abuse	15	17%
One or more types of both Enforcement and Regulatory Abuse	28	31.8%
One or more types of Enforcement, Regulatory, or Financial Abuse	40	45.5%

Table 3.5. Instrumental Manipulation by Election Type

Type of Financial Resource	Legislative Election	Executive Election
Direct allocation of goods or financial support to voters	17	4
State financial activity beneficial to incumbent candidates	4	4
Announcements of unplanned increases in state spending on welfare and social services	2	1
Total instances of financial resource abuse	23	9
New regulations seen to hinder or obstruct opposition activities	11	2
Politicized or biased activities by electoral commissions	27	10
New campaign or political finance rules seen to benefit incumbents	3	0
Total instances of regulatory resource abuse	41	12
Security or police manipulation of activities of opposition	26	15
Unbalanced usage of security details to candidates	1	4
Total instances of enforcement resource abuse	27	19
Total instances of all instrumental manipulation	91	40

Table 3.6. Instrumental Manipulation by Degree of Competitiveness

Type of Financial Resource	0 out of 3	1 out of 3	2 out of 3	3 out of 3
Direct allocation of goods or financial support to voters	2	6	11	2
State financial activity beneficial to incumbent candidates	1	4	2	1
Announcements of unplanned increases in state spending on welfare and social services	0	2	1	0
Total instances of financial resource abuse	3	12	14	3
New regulations seen to hinder or obstruct opposition activities	4	4	4	1
Politicized or biased activities by electoral commissions	9	14	13	1
New campaign or political finance rules seen to benefit incumbents	0	2	1	0
Total instances of regulatory resource abuse	13	20	18	2
Security or police manipulation of activities of opposition	11	16	13	1
Unbalanced usage of security details to candidates	1	3	1	0
Total instances of enforcement resource abuse	12	19	14	1
Total instances of all instrumental manipulation	28	51	46	6

Table 3.7.   Instrumental Manipulation by Incumbent Dominance

Type of Financial Resource	0 out of 2	1 out of 2	2 out of 2
Direct allocation of goods or financial support to voters	15	5	1
State financial activity beneficial to incumbent candidates	5	2	1
Announcements of unplanned increases in state spending on welfare and social services	1	0	2
Total instances of financial resource abuse	21	7	4
New regulations seen to hinder or obstruct opposition activities	8	5	0
Politicized or biased activities by electoral commissions	16	13	8
New campaign or political finance rules seen to benefit incumbents	2	1	0
Total instances of regulatory resource abuse	26	19	8
Security or police manipulation of activities of opposition	21	10	10
Unbalanced usage of security details to candidates	4	1	0
Total instances of enforcement resource abuse	25	11	10
Total instances of all instrumental manipulation	72	37	22

three categories, instances of abuse are observed far more often in cases with some degree of competitiveness, when compared to cases that scored a zero on competitiveness. Conversely, the frequency of financial, regulatory, and enforcement resource abuse declines as the degree of dominance increases. Finally, these descriptive statistics demonstrate that, based on the universe of data, more types of instrumental manipulation have been reported in legislative elections than in executive contests.

I now turn to the statistical estimations on the relationship between instrumental incumbent manipulation and electoral factors that alter the attainability of the election. This data is not linear, as it instead captures whether or not a particular type of manipulation was present or absent from an individual election; therefore, linear regression would be an inappropriate mode of analysis for this data. Instead, I dichotomize each category based on whether one or more types of manipulation were present in a given election. This fits the data presented in Table 3.3, which shows that elections with just one type of manipulation present were the most frequent, while those with two or more occurred far less often. Table 3.8 presents the results of probit regression estimations, examining each category on its own.[2] These results report some support for the theorized relationships, particularly in terms of the competitiveness of the election and the type of election. A higher degree of competitiveness, measured with either the index of perceived competitiveness created, or the previous level of competition, is positively associated with the abuse of financial and enforcement resource abuse. Similarly, legislative elections contain a positive relationship with the abuse of regulatory and financial resources. What's more, a higher GDP per capita is associated with the abuse of financial resources, which is actually counter-intuitive. One might expect such financial manipulation to be less compelling or powerful as the average incomes rise; however, this relationship could instead demonstrate that a larger economy facilitates the abuse of financial resources. Finally, experience with elections is negatively associated with financial resource abuse.

I next examine these relationships by combining the categories of manipulation. As I assert that these categories all serve the instrumental, optimal benefit of winning the election, it seems very possible that incumbents would combine these categories. The first model in Table 3.9 presents the combined probit regression estimation on whether two or more types of financial, regulatory and enforcement resource abuse were present.[3] The second model instead captures a count of all types of instrumental manipulation observed, with values that range from 0 to 5. Higher competitiveness is clearly associated with the abuse of two or more of these categories of instrumental manipulation in the first model, using either one or both of the indicators of competitiveness. Similarly, the count model also found a positive relationship between perceived competition and the increase in the quantity of instrumental manipulation. Both models also observed that instrumental manipulation is more likely to be observed in legislative, rather than executive, elections. However, as in the previous estimations, incumbent dominance is not statistically significant in its relationship to instrumental manipulation in either model.[4] Additionally, experience with elections, as measured by a count of elections that have been held in the state, has a negative association; this implies that as states hold more elections, instrumental manipulation may decrease in likelihood. Finally, the rule of law has a positive relationship in the first model, suggesting that a higher score on a state's rule of law may increase the likelihood of instrumental manipulation.

The final model looks at whether instrumental or informational manipulation alters the outcome of an election. This is crucial, as the primary distinction between the two lies in the ability for instrumental manipulation to directly influence the election itself. This model features a dichotomous variable that

Table 3.8. Standard Errors in Parentheses, p-value * <0.10, **<0.05, ***<0.01, ****<0.001

	Regulatory Manipulation	Enforcement Manipulation	Financial Manipulation
Perceived	0.178	−0.017	1.227***
Competitiveness	(0.261)	(0.259)	(0.387)
Previous Competitiveness	−0.004	0.016*	0.01
(Previous Margin of Victory, Inverted)	(0.008)	(0.009)	(0.011)
Incumbent Dominance	0.022	0.263	0.549
	(0.449)	(0.478)	(0.633)
Executive Election	−1.285***	0.038	−1.095**
	(0.389)	(0.367)	(0.444)
Proportional Representation	−0.719	−0.856	−1.136
	(0.802)	(0.875)	(1.141)
Mixed Electoral System	−0.58	0.251	−0.205
	(0.784)	(0.838)	(1.134)
GDP per capita, logged (lagged one year)	−2.493	−0.589	10.671***
	(2.585)	(2.638)	(3.439)
GDP % growth (lagged one year)	0.026	0.008	0.01
	(0.035)	(0.034)	(0.042)
Experience with Elections	−0.02	−0.091	−0.547***
	(0.153)	(0.152)	(0.204)
Rule of Law (lagged one year)	0.952	0.604	1.318
	(0.775)	(0.806)	(0.999)
Armenia	−0.948	−0.53	−0.226
	(0.809)	(0.766)	(0.915)
Azerbaijan	0.522	1.649	−2.196
	(1.204)	(1.377)	(1.785)
Belarus	1.672	0.894	−3.906**
	(1.351)	(1.359)	(1.843)
Georgia	−0.56	0.865	−1.226
	(0.788)	(0.827)	(1.122)
Kazakhstan	1.121	0.495	−5.662***
	(1.43)	(1.509)	(1.964)
Kyrgyzstan	−1.141	0.739	6.17***
	(1.473)	(1.499)	(2.042)
Moldova	−1.639	0.443	−0.23
	(1.069)	(1.1)	(1.217)
Russia	2.263	0.241	−4.951***
	(1.467)	(1.489)	(1.893)
Tajikistan	−1.964	0.543	−1.024
	(1.566)	(1.639)	(3622.604)
Ukraine	reference	reference	Reference
Constant	10.259	1.457	−33.801***
	(8.525)	(8.549)	(10.995)
N (countries)	10	10	10
N (total)	88	88	88
Wald Chi 2	20.05	24.77	21.61

captures whether the incumbent officeholder or party lost the election, while instrumental and informational manipulation are included as independent variables. The results confirm the theorized differences between these two types of manipulation. Incumbent election losses are negatively associated with instrumental manipulation, while they bear no statistically significant relationship with informational manipulation. This suggests that when the number of types of instrumental manipulation increases by one, incumbents are less likely to lose the election, thereby having a direct effect on the outcome of the election. Finally, previous competitiveness has a positive relationship in this model. This logically follows what we would expect about a more competitive election: that the incumbent would be more likely to lose in one.

PARLIAMENTARY ELECTION CASE STUDIES

As the quantitative estimates presented earlier have demonstrated, incumbent manipulation that serves an instrumental purpose is statistically associated with higher competitiveness and with legislative, rather than executive, elections. Given this, I will next examine how this relationship can be observed in particular elections that meet these conditions. This section presents case studies on Georgia's 2012 parliamentary election, and Moldova's two parliamentary elections held in 2009. While both cases contained a high degree of competitiveness, they are differentiated by the outcome. In Georgia's case, the opposition was victorious despite the efforts of instrumental manipulation observed. However, in Moldova, the incumbent political party was victorious in the first election, but lost power as a result of the second. This section then presents a third negative case, Kazakhstan's 2016 parliamentary election. As an election it featured very low competiveness, and it also did not feature instrumental manipulation. This third case presents a contrast to the others by illustrating how electoral factors, in particular competitiveness, may influence the selection of strategies in electoral authoritarian regimes. One caveat is that these case studies do not explicitly present intentionality behind the decision making of incumbent and pro-government actors. Instead, they merely offer a detailed look at the conditions of each election, and how those conditions may have produced a conducive environment for instrumental manipulation.

Georgia's 2012 Parliamentary Election

Georgia has received much scholarly attention since its 2003 parliamentary elections and the subsequent post-election demonstrations and protests of the announced results. Georgians witnessed and perceived widespread fraud

Table 3.9.   Statistical Estimations of Instrumental Manipulation

	Two or more types of Financial, Regulatory and/or Enforcement[1]	Count of total types of Financial, Regulatory and Enforcement Abuse[2]	Incumbent Loses Election[1]
Instrumental Manipulation	—	—	-0.615*
			(0.34)
Informational Manipulation	—	—	0.192
			(0.31)
Perceived Competitiveness	0.666**	0.315*	0.212
	(0.296)	(0.168)	(0.417)
Previous Competitiveness	0.03***	0.005	0.027*
	(0.011)	(0.005)	(0.015)
Incumbent Dominance	0.855	0.003	−7.922
	(0.585)	(0.271)	(10457.41)
Executive Election	−1.076**	−0.52**	0.768
	(0.424)	(0.216)	(0.732)
Proportional Representation	−0.375	−0.565	7.591
	(1.165)	(0.482)	(1666.31)
Mixed Electoral System	1.195	−0.251	8.048
	(1.163)	(0.441)	(1666.31)
GDP per capita, logged (lagged one year)	4.522	1.551	−2.266
	(2.934)	(1.473)	(3.863)
GDP % growth (lagged one year)	0.028	0.006	0.034
	(0.039)	(0.019)	(0.058)
Experience with Elections	−0.457**	−0.15*	0.011
	(0.181)	(0.087)	(0.189)
Rule of Law (lagged one year)	1.895**	0.535	3.589
	(0.893)	(0.435)	(2.391)
Armenia	−0.874	−1.321	−8.028
	(0.832)	(0.877)	(2817.95
Azerbaijan	0.901	−0.61	6.716
	(1.468)	(0.905)	(10910.61)
Belarus	0.853	−1.151	9.862
	(1.645)	(1.213)	(20046.95)
Georgia	−0.52	−0.928	−1.313
	(0.883)	(0.885)	(1.572)
Kazakhstan	−2.612	−1.752	3.153
	(1.871)	(1.45)	(10989.24)
Kyrgyzstan	3.896*	−0.025	1.294
	(1.827)	(0.494)	(1.955)
Moldova	0.405	−1.382	−0.768
	(1.18)	(0.888)	(2.1)

Russia	−1.727	−1.453	1.731
	(1.689)	(1.551)	(2.56)
Tajikistan	2.776	Reference	dropped
	(1.707)		
Ukraine	Reference	−1.007	Reference
		(0.931)	
Constant	15.176	−2.978	0.106
	(9.552)	(4.152)	(16666.31)
N (countries)	10	10	10
N (total)	88	88	88
Wald Chi 2	25.04	24.97*	9.71

Standard Errors in Parentheses, p-value * <0.10, **<0.05, ***<0.01, ****<0.001
1 Models estimated using probit regression function.
2 Model estimated using negative binomial regression function.

and unfairness in the results, and demanded new elections be held. The public protests were successful and led to the demise of the regime headed by Eduard Shevardnadze, who had been in power since 1993. These events have since come to be known as the Rose Revolution, due to the roses that many protestors carried and held along with their signs and banners. The Rose Revolution did produce new elections that marked the victory of opposition figure Mikhail Saakashvili and his political party, the United National Movement (UNM). These events signified a remarkable defeat for a previously authoritarian government, and led many Western observers to believe that Georgia was unambiguously moving toward democracy. Indeed, since the Rose Revolution, competition has increased in Georgia's subsequent elections, and a third turnover power occurred following the 2012 and 2013 elections. Yet scholars and election monitors have also continued to note ongoing challenges and setbacks in Georgia since 2003. The Polity IV measure of democracy did increase after 2003, reaching a high of an 8 from 2004 to 2007, but then lowered its ranking to a 6 until 2012; this still met Polity's minimum threshold for electoral democracy (Marshall and Jaggers 2015). However, Freedom House maintained Georgia's Partly Free ranking in the years following the Rose Revolution, and additionally noted some declines in political rights and civil liberties during Saakashvili's final years in office. Saakashvili and his party, the UNM, were reelected in 2008; however, OSCE monitors reported continued instances of electoral manipulation in these contests. Saakashvili was observed to have created a new system of patronage and loyalty in the wake of Shevardnadze's downfall (Hale 2015). Yet this does not mean Saakashvili succeeded in solidifying power in Georgia; he faced growing opposition and some criticism that he and his party were engaging in authoritarian behavior themselves. These events provide the backdrop for Georgia's 2012 parliamentary elections.

The degree of competition was moderate in Georgia's 2012 election. In the months leading up to this election, held on October 1, 2012, multiple factors increased the competitiveness of the election. This can be observed in multiple ways. First, according to the perceived competitiveness index developed, this election scores a 2 out of 3. The ruling UNM party was not confident in their ability to win a majority of votes. However, on their behalf, President Saakashvili initially stated that the party should aim to win by a large majority, so as to demonstrate strength.[5] Interestingly, the opposition leader Bidzina Ivanishvili also publicly asserted that his coalition the Georgian Dream should ideally win by a large margin.[6] This demonstrates clear competition in the election and signals that both sides believed they could win.

Moreover, economic conditions in Georgia were perceived to be bad. While the Georgian economy had already begun recovering from the 2008-2009 Global Financial Crisis[7], surveys revealed that Georgians were still very concerned about economic prospects, and perceived the economy to be in poor shape.[8] Second, popular opinion of the incumbent president Mikhail Saakashvili and his party, the UNM, had deteriorated since the previous elections held in 2008. After the 2008 election, the UNM held almost 80% of the seats in the Georgian Parliament, while the United Opposition earned 17.73% of the vote, but secured a lower percentage of seats. In pre-election polls taken earlier in 2012, the percentage of respondents who were planning to vote for the UNM decreased, from 47% in February to 36% in June. The primary opposition bloc, who competed under the label Georgian Dream in 2012, instead saw their appeal grow, with 18% of respondents reporting that they intended to vote for them in June; this rate was higher than the 10% recorded in February.[9] Most strikingly, evidence of human rights abuses in Georgian prisons emerged in late September 2012. Footage of abuses and the rapes of multiple prisoners were released to the public on national television less than a month before the election. The revelation of these abuses spurred significant public outrage and led many to call for the resignation of the official in charge of Georgia's penitentiary system, which ultimately occurred on September 19, 2012.[10] In addition, Saakashvili and his regime were perceived to not be taking the footage and public outcry seriously; Saakashvili at one point suggested that the recordings were produced by the political opposition to tarnish his regime. Their muted response prompted confidence in the pro-presidential party, the UNM, to fall even further in the days leading up to the election (Mueller 2013).

Given this, the stakes of the election were extremely high in the weeks and months before the 2012 parliamentary election. Incumbent dominance was low in this contest. Saakashvili was reelected in 2008 with 53.7% of the vote, which is below the 70% threshold that signals high incumbent dominance in electoral authoritarian regimes. Furthermore, the Georgian economy was not reliant on the export of natural resources; energy exports represented only 1.16% of total Georgian GDP in 2011. According to the logic of two-level games, incumbents would be primarily motivated by the short-term goal of winning the election. Based on this, I would expect incumbents and their supporters to be more likely to deploy instrumental electoral manipulation in this election. This was indeed the case in this election. This book has focused on three categories of instrumental manipulation—regulatory, enforcement, and financial state resource abuse. In the Georgian case, two types of both regulatory and enforcement manipulation were observed by election monitors.

The manipulation of electoral regulations was noted by observers from the OSCE.[11] One type of such manipulation that the monitors witnessed pertained to new electoral and campaign finance regulations; the OSCE expressed concerns that the new regulations were designed to benefit the incumbent UNM party. Less than a year before the election, a new Election Code was introduced in December of 2011; Georgian officials then continued to alter and amend the Election Code until as late as June of 2012, less than six months before the election date.[12] OSCE observers reported that this code contained vague language on the disqualification of candidates after the election, and that the criteria for such disqualifications was contrary to the democratic nature of elections. Moreover, monitors documented concerns about the election districts presented in the Election Code, noting severe disparities in the district magnitude, with the sizes ranging from 6,000 to 140,000 people. Many of these districts were holdovers from the previous election, which saw huge vote gains for the incumbent UNM party. Furthermore, the new Election Code also established new campaign finance rules that banned donations from corporate entities, reduced the total possible amount that individuals can donate, and forced donors to register as "persons with electoral goals." Donations received from corporations prior to the passage of the new regulations would either need to be returned to the donor within three days of its enactment, or be seized by the state.[13] Furthermore, there was confusion over whether the new laws would be enforced retroactively or not; the version originally published at the time of passage stated this, but a later version seemed to reverse this.[14] The OSCE considered these new regulations to be crafted so as to benefit the incumbent regime, and hinder the campaign finance activities of the GD. Many of the new laws and regulations of the Election Code were perceived to be targeted at Bidniza Ivanishvili, the ultra-rich Georgian oligarch who help establish the Georgian Dream coalition. The new laws would severely limit the ability of the GD to utilize funds given to the coalition by Ivanishvili, and would force donations to either be returned or seized by the state. At the time of the Election Code's passage, the affiliated parties in the GD had received a total of GEL 4.1 million in donations, and it was initially unclear whether those funds would be affected by the new regulations.[15] The fact that these laws were pushed through in the months after Ivanishvili announced his political ambitions struck OSCE observers as problematic. Combined, these three aspects of the newly introduced Election Code represent new campaign regulations that are perceived to be beneficial to the incumbent regime.

Additionally, the OSCE observed a different dimension of campaign regulation abuse prior to the 2012 election. Monitors reported that the certain campaign finance regulations were applied to candidates from the GD at disproportionate rates.[16] Such regulations are implemented by the State Audit Office (SAO), a body that the OSCE noted was not impartial, as it was run by two serving members of parliament from the UNM. The OSCE observed the SAO as disproportionately investigating and ultimately fining donors of the GD more than those of the UNM. In one instance, 100 GD donors were investigated and 68 received fines, while the numbers for UNM donors were 10 and 8, respectively. Moreover, the grounds upon which the SAO based their decisions were often impartially applied or were based upon criteria not established within the Election Code. Given this, the OSCE considered the actions the SAO to be political and done to hinder the campaign finance activities of the GD.

Election monitors also reported two types of enforcement resource abuse. The first type was the explicit intimidation and arrests of GD candidates and supporters during the pre-election campaign.[17] In one instance, the OSCE reported that at least 44 or as many as 60 GD supporters were either detained, fined or both in the final week prior to the election day. Less than a week before the election, law enforcement officers were warned to use greater discretion when issuing detentions or fines of individuals attending campaign events. Additionally, state employees, nongovernmental organizations (NGOs) and many recipients of social welfare programs reported feeling pressured or intimidated to not support the GD or other opposition candidates. The second type of enforcement resource abuse reported in the 2012 election pertained to military voting. In many cases, military voting precincts were established for active duty members of the Georgian military.[18] The locations of some of these voting stations shifted more voters into single mandate districts where GD candidates reportedly posed significant challenges to UNM incumbents. Moreover, other non-active duty employees at some bases were also requested to vote in the military voting stations. This combination presents the potential for a pro-government bias the voting behavior of military personnel.

While the OSCE did not include any abuses of financial resources in their final reports, other election observation organizations raised such concerns.

The Georgian group This Affects You Too was formed earlier in 2012 to serve as a non-partisan organization dedicated to protecting the conduct of the elections and to strengthening Georgia's democratic institutions. It noted multiple complaints of vote-buying by UNM party officials beginning in August of 2012, and voiced concern over the lack of response from the government or the State Audit Office about such accusations.[19] Transparency International's Georgia division also noted that vote-buying had been witnessed in the election, stating that both the UNM and the opposition Georgian Dream had engaged in such activities.[20] Such manipulation represents financial resource abuse that directly interferes with the behavior of voters. These reports represent an additional type of instrumental resource abuse observed during this election.

Overall, this case presents an election with a high degree of perceived competitiveness that also witnessed the usage of many instrumental strategies of manipulation. Since the incumbent governing party was voted out of power, I am unable to easily evaluate whether the regime suffered any losses to their legitimacy. However, we can examine the electoral performances of the UNM in subsequent elections. One year after the 2012 parliamentary elections, Georgia held a presidential contest. The incumbent, Saakashvili of the UNM party, was constitutionally unable to run for a third term. The 2013 election saw the main competition between Giorgi Margvelashvili, representing the Georgian Dream coalition, and David Bakradze of the UNM. The UNM was soundly defeated in this contest, with Bakradze winning just 21.7% of the total vote. More recently, parliamentary elections were held on October 8, 2016. At this point, the UNM had been fully in the opposition for the last three years. Coming into the election, the UNM held 65 seats in the legislature. However, they saw their vote share drop to 27 as a result of the 2016 election. Using vote share and turnover in power as indicators, the UNM did indeed suffer long-term repercussions after the usage of highly visible instrumental manipulation strategies.

Following the most recent elections in 2016, the UNM split into two parliamentary factions. One group continues to operate under the same name, while the other faction refers to itself as European Georgia. Members of the new faction attribute their decision to split to former president Saakashvili and his questionable political legacy in Georgia. He had since moved to Ukraine, where he was appointed governor of Odessa in 2015, and from which he resigned in 2016. The governing Georgian Dream revoked Saakashvili's citizenship due to this move, and also have charged him with criminal offenses related to his tenure as president.[21] Also, another leader of the UNM and the former mayor of the capital, Tbilisi, Gigi Ugulava, was found guilty of misconduct for the usage of public funds in the 2012 parliamentary elections and served almost 16 months in prison.[22] The poor handling of these post-2012 events by the UNM have been suggested as a main reason for their electoral marginalization.[23] These events further demonstrate the potential for long-term political consequences from the usage of instrumental electoral manipulations.

Moldova's 2009 Parliamentary Elections: April and July

Prior to 2009, Moldova had not been home to a Color Revolution, in contrast with Georgia. Nonetheless, politics in post-Soviet Moldova had been quite contentious. The main political divide concerned the role of communism in post-Soviet governments. The Party of Communists of the Republic of Moldova (PCRM) was the ruling party heading into the 2009 elections, and had held a majority in parliament since 2001. The main opposition parties in this election instead opposed the Communists and the role of communism in Moldova more generally. While the main opposition parties competed separately, they were united in their frustration with the PCRM and were prepared to form a post-election parliamentary coalition together.[24] The Communists had also been known to abuse their power and engage in electoral manipulation, as noted by the OSCE. They also had become increasingly cohesive and dominant in the Moldovan state overall (Way 2015). As Moldova is a parliamentary republic, these elections would produce the future legislature and executive. Moreover, this system of government requires that coalitions be formed if a single party does not win a majority of seats in the legislature. While coalition governments had ruled in the past, the Communists were solely in power as the pre-election campaign began for the April 5th contest in February of 2009.

Competition in this election was high. According to the competitiveness index, all three indicators were present in Moldova. First, the incumbent Communist party was not publicly confident of victory prior to the election. While support for the Communists was significant, voters were increasingly demonstrating their favorability toward the anti-Communist parties (Senyuva 2010). A pre-election poll revealed that 36.2% of respondents reported that they intended to vote for the PCMR. Moreover, the Communists had suffered vote losses in the 2005 parliamentary election and in local elections held in 2007. Second, not only were economic conditions bad in Moldova prior to this election, but they were actually perceived to be in crisis. In 2009, Moldova's GDP contracted by 5.8% and its GDP per capita also dropped to $3647.[25] Combined, these three indicators of competitiveness suggest that the election was highly competitive. Moreover, as in Georgia, incumbent dominance was low in Moldova. While the PCMR had been in power for the majority of the decade, their share of the vote was below the 70% threshold.

Furthermore, Moldova does not rely on the export of natural resources or fossil fuels to drive its economic output. This demonstrates that the incumbent regime was not dominant. I would therefore expect the incumbent regime led by the PCMR to be likely to engage in instrumental manipulation.

First, regulatory resource abuse was observed during this election. New election regulations, implemented prior to the election, caused concern that they would benefit the incumbent regime. The new regulations pertained to the process of generating the complete lists of eligible and registered voters. Election monitors observed that the process used to generate these voter rolls was inconsistent and problematic. More specifically, when the CEC first reported the total number of registered voters, the figure was 10% higher than the number reported in the previous 2005 election. This significant increase was not explained. Moreover, the Central Election Committee (CEC) continued to revise the total number of registered voters two additional times during the pre-election period. These frequent changes, which lacked a consistent or comprehensible explanation, fueled speculation that voters were registered in multiple places or that the conditions facilitated fraud.[26]

Second, financial resource abuse was witnessed during the campaign. Public employees were often subject to intimidation during the campaign, and their job was suggested to be contingent upon support of the incumbent PCRM. Many public workers reported explicit threats to their continued employment were they to attend campaign rallies in favor of opposition candidates. These behaviors put pressure on the financial viability of the electorate, and encouraged state employees to actively suppress any pro-opposition political attitudes.[27]

Third, monitors from the OSCE observed enforcement resource abuse during the 2009 pre-election campaign. In particular, the activities of opposition candidates and supporters were disrupted on numerous occasions. People who attended rallies in support of some opposition parties reported receiving police intimidation or threats. On multiple occasions, vehicles or buses transporting supporters to campaign events held by opposition parties were stopped by police, and prevented from arriving at their intended destinations. These acts represented quite overt obstruction of candidate and voter activities by security forces. Additionally, multiple opposition parties and events received targeted harassment or obstruction, including the vandalism of campaign offices and violence against rally attendees. These acts were not tied to the police or security personnel, but nonetheless hindered the campaign environment.[28]

The second type of enforcement resource abuse, biased pro-government behavior by security actors, was also observed. The OSCE reported that police and/or security services initiated multiple investigations against prominent opposition figures. These investigations included allegations of criminal acts and tax fraud. Overall, multiple types of instrumental resource abuse were observed in this election, as expected given the conditions of the election.[29]

The official results of the election gave the Communists 49.5% of the total vote, 60 out of 101 seats, which was an increase from the 2005 election. However, multiple opposition parties failed to recognize the results of the election, citing a lack of public confidence in the election process and the perceived manipulation of the process. Post-election protests formed two days after election day in the capital of Chisinau, with a reported 30,000 people in attendance; the protests voiced frustration with the conduct of the election and demanded that new elections be held. Some of the demonstrations took a violent turn, with some government buildings being set on fire, and both the parliamentary building and the office of the president were stormed by protesters.[30] These violent protests were subsequently broken up by the police and hundreds of people were arrested.[31] The PCRM won 60 seats in the 101-seat parliament, which was one seat short of the necessary number needed to officially form the new government.[32] No party or independent representative would join with the PCRM, which ultimately dissolved the parliament and triggered new elections, which were scheduled for July 29, 2009.[33]

The backdrop of the first election provided much of the context for this second and new election. The degree of competition remained high, as the political and economic conditions had not changed between April and July. Moreover, prominent frustration and mistrust of the first election by multiple opposition parties fostered a heightened sense of importance and urgency in regard to the outcome of this new election. In fact, the Communists were in an increasingly precarious situation, marked particularly by the defection of Marian Lupu from the PCRM to the opposition Democratic Party of Moldova (PDM). Lupu was widely expected to be the top candidate for the post of prime minister, so his defection was striking.[34] Given that the attainability of the election was once again in question, I would expect the incumbent regime, still represented by the PCRM, to be likely to select strategies of instrumental manipulation.

Regulatory resource abuse was once again witnessed in this contest. This abuse once again concerned the registration of voters. The composition of the voter rolls became an especially salient criticism of the April elections, and was cited by protesters and opposition party representatives that the election was conducted with the absence of transparency. The CEC introduced amendments to this procedure to delegate all authority on the voters' lists to the precinct level, and to increase transparency in the process. However, the revised procedures continued to spark discontent and mistrust. The newly calculated total voter roll added 6% more voters than the roll produced for the election in April. Multiple political and nongovernmental actors voiced that the process continued to be inconsistent and questionable. Additionally, the OSCE observed that prior to the July elections, accommodations were not made for university students who were on break and often residing away from their registered polling locations. Despite complaints from multiple parties that temporary accommodations be granted, the procedures remained unchanged.[35]

Second, financial resource abuse was observed during this second election. More specifically, the direct allocation of goods or services was observed in connection with PCRM campaign events. OSCE observers reported that a campaign rally in favor of the Communists also distributed medicines free of charge to attendees. At a different PCRM event, a local public kindergarten received new funding to revitalize its infrastructure. These interactions demonstrate the particularistic exchange of basic goods and necessities, as well as promises of more desirable public goods to be enjoyed at the community level.[36]

Finally, enforcement resource abuse occurred in this election, as it did in the April contest. Opposition campaign activities were once again hindered and obstructed on numerous occasions. More specifically, "[s]everal cases of intimidation of voters and candidates were confirmed by the OSCE/ODIHR EOM, such as the disruption of opposition party rallies by provacateurs in at least four locations, a case of a PDM supporter having been questioned by the mayor in the presence of the police after placing a campaign poster, and . . . a fire at the entrance of the PL office in Orhei" (OSCE 2009: 9–10). OSCE observers reported that in these cases, the perpetrators of such obstructions were either directly connected with the Communists, or were law enforcement officials.

Like in Georgia, the 2009 parliamentary elections in Moldova presented a case with a high degree of competition and incumbent instrumental manipulation. This relationship was observed in both the April and July elections. Moreover, it also demonstrates some support for the notion that instrumental manipulation may produce long-term consequences for the incumbents that use it. After the April election, the PCRM was unable to add just one additional vote needed to their parliamentary coalition to election a new president; this event ultimately triggered the July special elections. The results of this second election saw the PCRM lose seats, while two anti-Communist parties, the Our Moldova Alliance and the Democratic Party of Moldova, gained seats. Together with two other anti-Communist parties, they formed a new governing coalition. In subsequent elections held in 2010 and 2014, the PCRM continued to lose votes and seats; they currently maintain twenty-one, down from the all-time high of 71 seats won in the 2001 election. Moreover, the OSCE has remarked that since the departure of the Communists, the Central Election Committee behaved in a more impartial manner.

Negative Case: Kazakhstan's 2016 Parliamentary Election

The previous two cases have illustrated elections that featured competitive legislative elections where widespread electoral manipulation was observed. Both illustrate the preferred conditions in which we would expect incumbent and pro-government actors to be driven by short-term concerns about winning the election at all. Thus they are willing to risk the potential long-term consequences of abusing state resources that directly interfere with the conduct of the election. However, this logic only makes sense when the election's outcome is generally unexpected, and presupposes that incumbent actors will bypass such manipulation when faced with more predictable conditions. This final case study therefore examines a third parliamentary election, but one that features a very low degree of competitiveness. Under these conditions, incumbents are not expected to resort to such manipulation because it serves few long-term goals; the political institutions may be already largely under control, so there is no risk of losing access to the machinations behind the regime. If anything, the usage of instrumental manipulation requires the deployment of resources in the short term, and may even reduce the regime's legitimacy at home by appearing desperate. Kazakhstan's 2016 parliamentary election presents just such a case, and as expected, this election features zero observations of instrumental incumbent manipulation.

Since its independence from the Soviet Union in 1991, Kazakhstan has been ruled by one president, Nursultan Nazarbayev, a former top Communist Party official. While Kazakhstan's constitution initially limited presidents to two terms, an amendment was passed in 2007 that removed all term limits, thus allowing presidents to serve for life (Isaacs 2008). Nazarbayev has been supported in parliament by the political party Nur Otan, or Fatherland, since its creation for the 1999 parliamentary elections. Since then, Nur Otan has seen its share of the seats dramatically increase from just under a third in 1999 to just over 80% of the seats following the 2012 election. Additionally, both of the other two parties that held seats in Kazakhstan's parliament, the Mazhilis, heading into the 2016 election, the Ak Zol Democratic Party and the Communist People's Party of Kazakhstan (CPPK) were considered to be pro-presidential parties due to their lack of criticism of Nazarbayev, and for their general support for his legislative agenda. Nazarbayev was reelected for a fifth term in early elections held in 2015.[37] The 2016 elections were then called early by Nazarbayev after the parliament issued a statement requesting snap elections in January of that year.[38] These events set the stage for the August 2016 contest.

Heading into this election, both the perceived competitiveness and the previous competitiveness were very low. In the previous parliamentary election, the margin of victory between Nur Otan and the party to win the next largest amount of seats, Ak Zol, was an extraordinary 73.52 points.[39] Furthermore, the three indicators of perceived competitiveness confirm that this election featured a very certain outcome. First, there seemed to be little doubt from the ruling party Nur Otan that it would win the most seats and maintain its supermajority in the Mazhilis. The second and third indicators concern perceptions about the economy. Kazakhstan's economy is highly reliant on the export of natural resources, with oil often making up almost 60% of its overall exports. The global price of oil fell rapidly in 2014, which had a negative effect on Kazakhstan's economy. Its overall GDP continued to grow during this time, but at a slower rate: while it grew 6% in 2013, by 2015 it only expanded by 1.2%.[40] Meanwhile, its GDP per capita fell between these two years from $13,890 to $10,510.[41] Finally, Kazakhstan's currency had suffered in these years, seeing its exchange rate with the US Dollar more than double from 2013 to 2016. While it was absolutely clear that Kazakhstan's economy was not in crisis, public frustration with the economic conditions had been on the rise. This in large part contributed to the decision for Kazakhstan to hold not just early parliamentary elections, but pre-term presidential elections in 2015 as well (Smagulov, Adilova, and Kambarova 2016). Due to clear public perceptions that the economy was doing poorly, this election scores a 1 out of 3 on the index of perceived competitiveness. This is only one point lower than both Moldova's 2009 and Georgia's 2012 elections. The second, and possibly more important, difference, is the degree of incumbent dominance.

As mentioned earlier, Kazakhstan's president has ruled the state since 1991. He is currently the longest-serving president in the post-Soviet region, and as president, he enjoys wide-ranging powers with little to no oversight from other branches of government, including the parliament (Kanapyanov 2018). This reality is also captured by his incumbent dominance in the state. Despite the deteriorating economic conditions leading to the 2015 presidential election, Nazarbayev was reelected with an astounding 97.75% of the vote. This alone meets one of the two criteria of incumbent dominance used in this book. Additionally, in the years leading up to this election, it was clear that the government had taken steps to further marginalize the already weak political opposition. This included the deregistration of the Communist Party of Kazakhstan and the arrests of leaders associated with other small non-systemic opposition parties (Smagulov et al. 2016). All of this had been accomplished well before 2015, so that Nazarbayev faced only two competitors in his fifth reelection, one of whom belonged to the pro-presidential CPPK. As the OSCE noted in their report of the election, "The two latter candidates did not address political or economic issues concerning Kazakhstan and openly lauded the President for the country's achievements" (OSCE 2015: 11–12). The second feature concerns the share of energy exports as a percentage of the state's overall economy. As mentioned earlier, oil is the dominant economic driver in Kazakhstan, and is often thought to represent over half of its total exports. Yet the decline in oil prices globally affected Kazakhstan so much so that by 2015, energy exports comprised just 9.2% of its overall GDP. This is a significant decline, as it was measured at 36.9% in 2011.[42] Combined, Kazakhstan measures a 1 out of 2 on the incumbent dominance index; this is one point higher than the degree of incumbent dominance observed in Georgia's 2012 and Moldova's 2009 elections.

With low perceived competitiveness and medium incumbent dominance, we would not expect regime actors to engage in instrumental manipulation. Based on the OSCE's final election observation mission report, Kazakhstan's 2016 parliamentary election did not feature any of the 3 categories of state resource abuse covered in this chapter.[43] This is not to say that the election was conducted in a free and fair manner; on the contrary, the OSCE noted many problematic aspects to the election and its campaign. However, none of these met the conditions of directly interfering with the conduct of the candidates, parties, and voters. I will therefore outline these deficiencies for each of the three categories—regulatory, financial, and enforcement resource abuse.

Regulatory resource abuse can easily affect the ability of candidates and parties to register, while also putting undue influence on voter decision making. The OSCE explicitly noted their concern about the makeup of Kazakhstan's Central Election Commission, saying,

> the de facto over-representation of Nur Otan in election commissions is at odds with the aim of the Election Law, which entitles each party to one seat on lower-level election commissions, and raises concerns regarding the impartiality and integrity of commissions provided for by international standards. A perceived lack of impartiality negatively affected the confidence of stakeholders in the election administration. (OSCE 2015: 7)

Despite the clear partisan nature of the Central Election Commission, the OSCE did not observe any new regulations introduced into this election that would hurt the opposition, nor did they note any new rules that would provide an advantage to incumbents. On the possibility of any biased activities by the electoral commission, such as the politicized denial of candidate registration, the OSCE noted, "[c]andidate registration, notwithstanding restrictions within the current legal framework, was inclusive" (OSCE 2015: 11).

Financial resource abuse has a long reputation for seeking to sway elections in favor of incumbent and regime actors. However, the OSCE did not report any instances that would qualify as any of the three types of financial resource abuse covered in this chapter. These issues received very limited attention in their report, although they did note that this election was the first to feature obligatory campaign finance disclosures twice monthly prior to the election.[44] Finally, the 2016 Kazakh parliamentary elections did not feature any instances of enforcement state resource abuse. This type of behavior can be the most explicit in its attempts to disrupt the ability for opposition actors to campaign and reach out to voters. On the contrary, "[t]he OSCE/ODIHR EOM did not receive any reports of interference in campaign activities," and further, "[a]ll parties had access to the places designated for posting materials" (OSCE 2015: 11–12). They did emphasize the low degree of competition in the election, stating that "the parties' campaign platforms and rhetoric were complementary rather than competitive and aligned with the President's long-term strategies" (OSCE 2015: 12).

Summary of Case Studies

Table 3.10 presents a summary of the findings from the three case study comparisons presented in this chapter. As seen, the Kazakh case presents a clear contrast with the more competitive elections held in Moldova in 2009 and in Georgia in 2012, and it also featured a decidedly different result. Nur Otan, the pro-presidential party that has dominated Kazakh politics for almost twenty years, won an even greater share of the seats, 82.2%, which translated into one additional seat in the Mazhilis. The other two parliamentary parties also retained their representation, albeit with one less seat than before.[45] It also clearly illustrates that authoritarian governments can and do demonstrate restraint in their manipulation activities. The 2016 election was the site of highly visible informational manipulation, but it did not feature any observations of instrumental manipulation that would directly interfere with the behavior of candidates, parties, and voters. As argued, this follows the logic that there was little benefit to be gained in the long term from instrumental manipulation, given that the outcome of the election was not in question.

CONCLUSION

This chapter has established instrumental electoral interference as any behavior that directly interferes with the actions of candidates, parties, and voters during the pre-election campaign. As described, these manipulation strategies work to either directly benefit incumbents, hinder opposition actors, put undue influence on voter behavior prior to election day, or any combination of the three. Yet because of the direct and overt nature of such behaviors, it

Table 3.10. Summary of Case Study Comparisons

Indicators	Georgia, 2012	Moldova, 2009a	Moldova, 2009b	Kazakhstan, 2016
Type of Election	Parliamentary	Parliamentary	Parliamentary	Parliamentary
Perceived Competitiveness	2 out of 3	2 out of 3	3 out of 3	1 out of 3
Degree of Incumbent Dominance	0 out of 2	0 out of 2	0 out of 2	1 out of 2
Instrumental Manipulation?	Yes	Yes	Yes	No
Financial Regulatory Abuse	0 out of 3 types	1 out of 3 types	1 out of 3 types	0 out of 3 types
Regulatory Resource Abuse	2 out of 3 types	1 out of 3 types	1 out of 3 types	0 out of 3 types
Enforcement Resource Abuse	2 out of 2 types	2 out of 2 types	1 out of 2 types	0 out of 3 types

is inherently risky. Police breaking up rallies or candidates denied registration by a biased Electoral Commission are decentralized actions that may not always seem connected to the regime itself. But to those affected, the intention is clear: the regime and its supporters are seeking to abuse certain state resources to help ensure victory. Such behaviors risk blowback and a further dampening of trust in the regime. It is not something that incumbents or their supporters would want to rely on regularly or consistently.

Given this, instrumental manipulation can be most worth the cost when the outcome of the election is uncertain. I have argued that instrumental manipulation is associated with a particular set of electoral conditions: a higher degree of competitiveness and elections for legislative offices. The empirical findings demonstrate support for these relationships, confirming that such manipulation does not occur at random. Financial resource abuse, regulatory resource abuse, and enforcement resource abuse, the three categories of instrumental manipulation survey, are positively associated in elections perceived to be more competitive, in elections with a higher degree of previous competition, and in elections for the legislature. As this is the case, the chapter then presents two cases that illustrate how a competitive election facilitates the deployment of instrumental electoral interference strategies. In both Georgia and Moldova, the examples cited revealed how instrumental manipulation is observed when the fate of the regime supporters is unknown. It then features a negative case from Kazakhstan's 2016 election, which featured lower competition and no instrumental manipulation.

The findings of this chapter contain several implications for the study of electoral manipulation. First, incumbents often combine multiple instrumental strategies in their goal to directly interfere with the election, rather than pursuing one single category, such as regulatory resource abuse. This finding builds upon a previous similar finding by Birch (2011a), who notes that regimes often engage in electoral malpractice at multiple stages of the election. What is different about the results in this chapter is that the manipulation strategies selected all occur prior to the voting day itself, in the preceding electoral campaign. It demonstrates that incumbents are aware of the electoral risk they face, and act accordingly weeks or even months before any voting takes place. The decision to combine strategies is likely not an easy one, as the actors involved in the manipulation of regulatory, financial, and enforcement resources are different. With the acts of manipulation being carried out by different actors in different contexts, the manipulation is more diffuse and potentially more difficult to prevent or root out.

Second, the case studies of elections in Georgia and Moldova also illustrate that instrumental manipulation is not always successful in its intended goal. In these cases, the incumbent parties both ultimately lost power; although this did not officially occur in Moldova until the second election held in July of 2009. While instrumental strategies were deployed in these competitive contests, they did not ensure victory. This demonstrates that while manipulation has the ability to directly interfere with the actions of candidates, parties, and voters, the outcome of the election is still unknown. Furthermore, in both of these cases, the incumbent party in question faced long-term consequences beyond defeat in the electoral contest. As discussed in chapter 1, elections represent the game level, while control over the political institutions denotes the meta-game level. Instrumental electoral manipulation risks both long-term benefits and costs at the level of the political institutions. If victorious, the party or actor may face reduced legitimacy, which could hinder their ability to shape the institutions, and if unsuccessful, then it risks relegating the party to a reduced status in subsequent elections as well. This latter scenario was observed in both Georgia and Moldova. Subsequent elections have produced further electoral losses for the UNM and the PCRM, respectively, in the wake of these elections, which contained many types of instrumental manipulation. While these parties clearly prioritized the short-term importance of winning an election through instrumental manipulation, they now are faced with the long-term consequences of these actions. Conversely, Kazakhstan's political system remains as stable and authoritarian as ever following its instrumental manipulation-free 2016 election.

Additionally, the case studies in this chapter reveal that electoral manipulation is an all-purpose tactic that knows no ideological barriers. The two incumbent parties discussed in the positive case studies, the United National Movement in Georgia and the Communist Party of the Republic of Moldova, are quite distinct in terms of their political programs and ideologies. This is noticeable despite the common observation that parties in the post-Soviet landscape are often underdeveloped or rely upon broad or vague policy positions. The UNM had positioned itself as a pro-European and pro-democracy party that supported greater political and economic openness. It also was staunchly anti-Russian in its foreign policy orientation. Conversely, the PCRM was a descendant, in both spirit and in policy, of the Communist Party of the Soviet Union, and thus opposes economic liberalization and free-market reforms, and promises greater state interventions in the economy. The PCRM was also far more pragmatic in its approach to Russia, and maintained fairly friendly relations with the regional hegemon. Yet despite these clear ideological differences, both parties selected instrumental electoral manipulation strategies in this election in service of their overarching goal of electoral victory and political survival.

Finally, this chapter reveals important relationships that may be of use to election monitors and practioners of democracy promotion. By demonstrating that certain types of electoral manipulation are more likely to be used in competitive and legislative elections, it can help these organizations anticipate these types of behaviors. Monitors and democracy promoters can advise voters and opposition candidates on the proper procedures surrounding the reporting and official complaint process for such behavior. By knowing the types of behavior that are expected in competitive elections, they can prioritize information campaigns designed to alert average citizens on what to look for, and what to do if instances of electoral manipulation are witnessed. This can lead to a more efficient use of resources and greater preparedness for both domestic and international election monitoring organizations. This also demonstrates the continued need for pre-election monitoring. As recent studies have confirmed, manipulation during the pre-election period is a growing phenomenon, possibly in part due to the emphasis put on proper election day procedures by international election monitors (Donno and Roussias 2012). Instrumental manipulation that takes place in the weeks and even months before an election can still directly interfere with the election's outcome. Thus election observers would do well to increase their presence and scrutiny during the pre-election period, allowing for more robust data on these practices. Even if ineffective, instrumental manipulation inflicts considerable harm on the norms of competitive elections and can hamper the development of democracy in both the short and long term. Thus it deserves not only continued attention but more precise measurements of its usage and effects.

NOTES

1. "Republic of Armenia Presidential Election 19 February 2008." *OSCE/ODIHR Election Observation Mission Report.* Warsaw: 30 May 2008.

2. Each category was dichotomized, where a 1 was coded if at least one type of abuse occurred in the election. This eased the interpretation of the data.

3. This measure is coded as a 1 if the election features at least one type from at least two different categories (i.e., one type of financial resource abuse and one type of regulatory resource abuse). It would be coded as a zero if an election contained two types of financial resource abuse but none from the other two categories.

4. This holds true even when the estimations are run without the two measures of competitiveness, so as to control for multicollinearity.

5. "Saakashvili: 'We Should Win Very Decisively,'" *Civil Georgia*, August 21, 2012.

6. "Ivanishvili: 'We Should Win by Very Large Margin,'" *Civil Georgia*, August 29, 2012.

7. According to three economic indicators, Georgia's economy had begun improving. First, GDP growth had increased from 2010 to 2011 (from 6.25% to 7.22%). Second, Georgia's GDP per capita rose to $3725 USD in 2011, making it the highest

GDP per capita in Georgia's post-Soviet history at that point. Finally, the unemployment rate decreased from 16.3% to 15.1% (Data from the World Bank, accessed on March 30, 2017).

8. A survey conducted by the International Republican Institute reported that 51% and 8% of Georgian respondents reported that unemployment and the general economic situation were their number one concern, respectively. This meant that these two issues received the most and the third most mentions, respectively. http://www.iri.org/resource/iri-poll-economic-and-healthcare-reforms-should-be-top-priorities-georgian-government.

9. "NDI poll indicates two way race in October Elections in Georgia." *Caucasus Elections Watch.* July 16, 2012. https://electionswatch.org/2012/07/16/ndi-poll-indicates-two-way-race-in-october-elections-in-georgia/#comments.

10. "Georgian Prisons Minister Steps Down in Wake of Abuse Video." *Radio Free Europe/Radio Liberty.* September 19, 2012.

11. "Georgia Parliamentary Elections 1 October 2012." *OSCE/ODIHR Election Observation Mission Final Report.* Warsaw: December 2012.

12. "Election Code to Be Amended," *Civil Georgia*, June 11, 2012.

13. "New Funding Regulations Target Parties' Savings," *Civil Georgia*, December 28, 2011.

14. "Senior MPs: Party Funding Rules not Retroactive," *Civil Georgia*, December 30, 2011.

15. Ibid.

16. "Georgia Parliamentary Elections 1 October 2012." *OSCE/ODIHR Election Observation Mission Final Report.* Warsaw: December 2012.

17. Ibid.

18. Ibid.

19. "Campaign Group Slams 'Uneven Playing Field' Ahead of Polls," *Civil Georgia*, August 11, 2012.

20. "New Report: Pre-Election Period Monitoring Results," *Transparency International Georgia*, September 28, 2012.

21. "Saakashvili's Party Splits in Georgia, Ex-President Blamed," *Radio Free Europe/Radio Liberty*, January 12, 2017.

22. "Gigi Ugulava Released from Prison," *Civil Georgia*, January 6, 2017.

23. Liz Fuller, "Can Georgia's Former Ruling Party Reinvent Itself?," *Radio Free Europe/Radio Liberty*, November 16, 2016.

24. In fact, the Election Code of Moldova bans the formation of pre-election coalitions.

25. According to World Bank World Development Indicators

26. "Republic of Moldova Parliamentary Elections 5 April 2009." *OSCE/ODIHR Election Observation Mission Final Report.* Warsaw: 16 June 2009.

27. Ibid.

28. Ibid.

29. Ibid.

30. "Moldovan president accuses Romania of being behind protests," *Radio Free Europe/Radio Liberty.* April 9, 2009.

31. "European Fact-Finders Cite 'Horrible Violence' Against Moldova Protesters," *Radio Free Europe/Radio Liberty* April 30, 2009.

32. In the case of Moldova, this means voting for the President and Prime Minister, both of which require 61 votes in favor.

33. "Moldova's Political Standoff Moves to Presidential Vote," *Radio Free Europe/Radio Liberty* May 20, 2009.

34. "Communist Leadership Splits Ahead of Moldova's Presidential Showdown," *Radio Free Europe/Radio Liberty* June 3, 2009.

35. "Republic of Moldova Early Parliamentary Elections 29 July 2009." *OSCE/ODIHR Election Observation Mission Final Report*. Warsaw: 14 October 2009.

36. Ibid.

37. Kazakhstan's presidents serve five-year terms, and since Nazarbayev was last reelected in 2011, he was not due for reelection until 2016.

38. https://strategy2050.kz/en/news/30435.

39. http://www.electionguide.org/elections/id/513/.

40. World Bank: GDP growth (annual %) from the World Development Indicators.

41. World Bank: GDP per capita (current US$) from the World Development Indicators.

42. Both figures come from the World Bank World Development Indicators.

43. It did, however, contain all four types of informational manipulation, as would be expected by the theory put forward in this book. Informational manipulation will be the focus of chapter 4.

44. Ibid.

45. http://www.electionguide.org/elections/id/2904/.

Chapter Four

The Usage of
Informational Manipulation

Informational electoral manipulation represents a departure from the manipulation practices covered in chapter 3. It refers to strategies that intend to signal incumbent power during the election, rather than to overtly change or influence the outcome of the election. This echoes the observation made in the electoral authoritarian literature that sometimes we see manipulation in elections that *the incumbent would comfortably win anyway*. Magaloni (2006) detailed how for much of the Institutional Revolutionary Party's (PRI) history in Mexico, it engaged in manipulation, even though it was confident of victory. Simpser (2013) observes that we often see the most blatant manipulation and fraud in the most predictable of elections. Schedler (2013) reminds us that even the most hegemonic regimes still manipulate elections, but that they are motivated by different assumptions and different priorities than actors in more competitive environments. These realities frame the puzzle behind informational manipulation: why engage in manipulation if it is not even intended to directly affect the electoral contest itself?

As I have argued in chapter 2, informational manipulation aims to project dominance to fellow elites, opposition actors, voters, and the citizenry at large; this distinguishes it from instrumental manipulation, which seeks to have a direct impact on electoral behavior. Given this purpose, informational manipulation should be *highly visible*. Without visibility, it cannot signal anything concrete, and would be relatively useless. Therefore, this is the most important feature of informational manipulation. Informational manipulation can contribute to the perception of inevitability of authoritarian regimes, which can encourage opposition cooptation, and can also discourage voters from supporting the opposition; this can have the effect of further marginalization of any anti-regime forces within the state.

With this being considered, I have argued the greatest benefits of informational manipulation occur not during the election itself, since it does not seek to alter the outcome of the election or to directly interfere with the actions of the primary actors. Instead, the optimal benefits are likely to be enjoyed at the level of the political institutions. Given this, I assert that informational manipulation is most likely to be selected in contests where it can have the greatest impact in enhancing the legitimacy of the regime through the demonstration of power and strength. I argue that this is most likely in elections where the attainability is not in question; in other words, I do not expect informational manipulation to be used in contests with a high degree of competition. Instead, I expect one or more of the following to influence the usage of informational manipulation: low competition, high incumbent dominance, and contests for the executive. Moreover, I expect that informational strategies should yield long-term benefits for incumbent regimes that should produce greater access and influence over the political institutions of the state.

This chapter demonstrates that the particular types of information manipulation are highly visible, as can be seen through elections across the post-Soviet region, but that they do not directly interfere with the behavior of candidates, parties, and voters. Second, it presents the frequency of such strategies across the universe of cases included within this study. I then turn to the empirical evidence for this relationship using quantitative statistical analysis, which indeed reveals that the usage of informational manipulation follows different patterns from instrumental manipulation. Next, I present three case study examples to demonstrate the relationship between incumbent dominance, competitiveness, and informational manipulation. The first two cases of Azerbaijan's 2008 presidential election and Russia's 2008 presidential election are examples of informational manipulation in action. The final case features a negative illustration from Kyrgyzstan's 2015 election as a contrast. Finally, I discuss the overall findings and implications of these relationships.

TYPES OF INFORMATIONAL MANIPULATION

Much of the recent scholarship on electoral authoritarian regimes and their political conduct emphasizes the evolution of authoritarian behavior. Incumbents often seek to avoid overt repression and the consolidation of power through fear. Instead, authoritarian regimes regularly prefer to maintain some general popularity and legitimacy among the population so that they can govern (or rule) without significant opposition or daily repression. Under these conditions, incumbents presumably enjoy some genuine support and thus may not be worried about losing elections. Schedler (2013) refers to this kind of manipulation as a demand-side restriction of unfairness.

When authoritarian incumbents go out to face the voting public and get its electoral seal of approval, they often confront emerging opposition parties under conditions of radical unfairness. In case after case, the unfairness of electoral competition derives from inequalities in access to money and mass media. Electoral autocrats usually enjoy ample access to public funds and favorable public exposure. The whole apparatus of the state—often including government-run media—is at their beck and call, and they often harass or intimidate privately owned media organs into ignoring opposition candidates. (Schedler 2013:93)

In this sense, the manipulation is public and highly visible, altering the conditions of the election indirectly rather than in a direct way.

Next, I further hone in on specific, measurable types of manipulation that are highly visible but that indirectly affect the election. Ohman's (2013) categorization of institutional resource abuse fits this description. He defines institutional resources as "material and personnel resources pertaining to public office. Material resources of the State range from vehicles to offices, to office equipment and other infrastructure, which may be used by incumbent political forces to provide themselves with advantages vis-à-vis non-incumbents." (Ohman 2013: 160). This category of state resource abuse then identifies four types, all of which fit the criteria of highly visible. These are the usage of public employees at pro-incumbent campaign events, the usage of public property for pro-incumbent campaign purposes, campaigning by an incumbent or state worker while performing official duties, or biased, pro-incumbent coverage on state-run television news. I will next discuss each of the four types of institutional resource abuse used to measure informational manipulation and explain how they are publicly visible while also indirectly interfering with the election.

The Usage of Public Employees for Campaign Events

The first type of institutional resource abuse concerns the usage of public employees for campaign events and functions. One common variant of this manipulation is when state employees that work for the incumbent regime in an official capacity also work as campaign surrogates and engage directly in the campaign efforts. A more common instance of this manipulation occurs when state employees attend campaign rallies for the incumbent candidate or party, often during work hours and at the urging of their bosses. Many reports of state workers being bused to large, televised rallies have come out of elections in the post-Soviet region. Large, well-attended political rallies, especially those filled with state employees, serve as highly visible activities. They publicly demonstrate significant organization and coordination among the incumbent's regime to the attendees themselves as well as to the consumers of media that cover such events (Geddes 2006).

The Usage of Public Infrastructure for Electoral Campaigns

A second strategy of informational manipulation concerns the treatment of state property during electoral campaigns in support of the incumbent regime. Such state property is often used for partisan purposes, sometimes in subtle ways, but typically in an explicit manner that reveals a lack of separation between the provision of government services and political activities performed during a campaign. One way in which this abuse occurs is the placement of campaign offices for incumbent candidates or parties in government buildings. Additionally, pro-incumbent campaign posters and materials can be placed in very public state buildings, including post offices, schools, and public clinics. The usage of goods, buildings, and other resources for campaign purposes provides a very public and visible connection between the incumbent regime and other state functions. While this type of manipulation does not directly interfere with voter behavior or opposition activities, it nonetheless indirectly skews perceptions about the power and control enjoyed by the incumbent regime.

The Combination of Campaign and Official Duties

Candidates for public office that are also currently incumbents are expected to explicitly separate their campaign behavior from their official duties as a public official. The expectation of such a distinction remains one of the fundamental principles of democratic elections, where incumbents are expected not to abuse their power while seeking reelection or a new position. Yet as the electoral playing field is fundamentally unfair in electoral authoritarian regimes, this separation is often violated during the pre-election campaign. The lack of such a distinction between official and campaign roles is indeed quite common in post-Soviet states. One especially common observance of such a manipulation concerns official visits during the electoral campaign. Instead of holding overt political rallies, such incumbents may publicly and frequently visit businesses, state institutions, and parks or recreational facilities in the guise of official behavior. But while at such destinations, the incumbent candidate often speaks of their accomplishments and their desire to continue with such policies and successes, seemingly imploring voters to reelect them based on such achievements. The unusual frequency of such visits when compared to the rest of their term also suggests that such "official" visits are in fact campaign appearances and appeals for voter support. This lack of distinction between official and campaign behavior provides a public and highly visible act, while still refraining from directly interfering with the behavior of voters and opposition candidates.

Biased State Media Coverage

Election coverage on state-owned media outlets represent the fourth institutional resource that can abused for an informational purpose. Under the most ideal democratic circumstances, the political coverage of an election on state-controlled media entities should avoid any sort of partisan leaning or political allegiance; such impartiality is less expected from private news organizations that often reveal a political position. Conversely, in electoral authoritarian regimes, state-run media often broadcast clearly biased coverage during the electoral campaign. Biased coverage includes news that presents a uniformly favorable image of the incumbent regime as well as the disproportionate amount of such positive coverage. Moreover, it also includes negative or critical coverage of opposition candidates and parties. In some cases, opposition candidates receive so little coverage at all that they seem entirely disconnected from the election (La Porte 2015). In Russia's 2018 presidential election, state media refused to even utter the name of Alexei Navalny, the anti-corruption opposition actor who was denied registration as a candidate; he later supported a total boycott. Yet state-run media did publicize the campaign of Ksenia Sobchak, who many viewed as a spoiler candidate allowed to run so as to increase perceptions of a legitimate, competitive election. Some also considered her pro-Western and pro-liberal program, which also failed to explicitly criticize Putin, as a way for the state media to convince voters that opposition candidates represent values that are too outside the mainstream.[1] The vast majority of such state-media bias occurs on state-run television networks, which still remain the primary source of information for populations in post-Soviet countries. This demonstrates the significant degree of high visibility that results from state media bias. While it does not directly interfere with voter behavior, it plays a significant indirect role by shaping political attitudes and the information climate of an election.

Summary: Institutional Resource Abuse as Informational Manipulation

As these previous sections have demonstrated, each type serves as an observable instance of electoral manipulation, all of which I argue serve an informational purpose, rather than an instrumental one. For the eighty-eight elections included in the data that support this book, the OSCE election monitoring reports were read and coded based on whether the type of manipulation was observed. This coding was dichotomous, as it was for the data used in chapter 3; if the OSCE observers reported the type of manipulation, then it was coded as a one in the dataset; if the report is absent of any statement or observation consistent with the type, then it was coded as a zero. As in chapter 3, these data by no means provide a comprehensive picture of electoral manipulation in the particular election. First, OSCE monitors are only able to report on what either they witnessed or on reports from different electoral actors and domestic groups that can be verified. Second, the OSCE will often make general statements on the abuse of state resources or on manipulations that have been witnessed. For example, the OSCE reports in its final report on Russia's 2018 election[2], "he [Putin] travelled throughout the country in his official capacity as president, enjoying unparalleled visibility and opportunities to address the electorate" (OSCE 2018b: 13). This type of statement would warrant a positive observation for type 3, incumbent campaigning while performing official duties. However, it does not give a total number of trips or a comprehensive list of appearances. Therefore, the data are unable to produce a sum or count of the number of times the type of manipulation occurred.

QUANTITATIVE EVIDENCE OF INFORMATIONAL MANIPULATION

I now turn to the quantitative analysis of informational manipulation. As with instrumental manipulation, there are both short-term and long-term benefits associated with informational electoral manipulation. In chapter 2, I argued that the short-term benefits for informational manipulation were few due to its high visibility, rather than its ability to directly influence an election. This distinction means that, in relation to instrumental manipulation, I actually expect it to follow the opposite pattern: I expect such strategies to be selected in elections with less competition, more incumbent dominance, and in executive contests.

Before examining the statistical relationships between these factors, I first present descriptive statistics on the frequency of informational manipulation. These are displayed in Table 4.1. This table presents each of the four previously discussed types of institutional resource abuse and displays whether each type was reported in an election by OSCE election monitors. This table shows that the most frequently observed type of informational manipulation was biased state media coverage, observed in 56 out of 88 elections, or 63.64%. This high rate is not entirely surprising, given the legacy of Communism as practiced in the Soviet Union among these ten states, where state media was regularly used as a propaganda arm of the party, rather than as an independent and objective source of information. The use of state employees at campaign events was observed in half of all elections included, while the other two types were reported in less than half of the cases. Still, the use of

Table 4.1. Observations of Informational Manipulation by Type

Type of Informational Manipulation	Zero Reports of Manipulation Type	One or more Reports of Manipulation Type	Percentage of Elections with Informational Manipulation Type
Use of State Employees at Official Campaign Events	44	44	50%
Use of state/government property or organizations for campaign activities	51	37	42.05%
Campaigning by officials during official state activities	58	30	34.09%
Biased coverage by state-owned media	32	56	63.64%

government property for campaign purposes and campaigning by state employees while performing official duties are both observed in at least over a third of the 88 elections covered. Based solely on this table, it is clear that informational manipulation has been observed at a far higher rate than the categories of instrumental manipulation presented in chapter 3.

I next examine the frequency of informational manipulation across the ten post-Soviet states covered in this book. Table 4.2 displays these rates for each state, listing the number of elections in which each type was present. This table reveals that four types were present in at least one election in every state[3]. This confirms that each manipulation type is general enough to not be a one-off or state-specific activity. Moreover, each type features a comparable range and median number of election observations. The usage of state employees at official campaign events has a median observation of occurring in 6 elections, while the median number of elections per state that government property was utilized for campaign activities was 4. Officials campaigning during official state duties has the lowest median number of election observations, 3, while biased state-run media coverage has the highest median score of 7 elections per state. Overall, these four median scores demonstrate that each type of manipulation is relatively balanced among the ten states.

Table 4.3 presents the instances where the four types of informational manipulation are combined with one another in a given election. This table reveals that just ten elections were completely free of informational manipulation altogether; this shows that in just under 90% of elections, at least one type of informational manipulation was observed. Moreover, these frequencies demonstrate that in more than two-thirds of elections, more than one type

Table 4.2. Number of Elections with type of Informational Manipulation, by State

	Use of State Employees at Official Campaign Events	Use of state/government property or organizations for campaign activities	Campaigning by officials during official state activities	Biased coverage by state-owned media
Armenia	8 out of 9	6 out of 9	3 out of 9	4 out of 9
Azerbaijan	7 out of 8	4 out of 8	3 out of 8	7 out of 8
Belarus	6 out of 8	4 out of 8	4 out of 8	8 out of 8
Georgia	5 out of 10	8 out of 10	3 out of 10	7 out of 10
Kazakhstan	7 out of 9	6 out of 9	8 out of 9	9 out of 9
Kyrgyzstan	5 out of 9	1 out of 9	1 out of 9	7 out of 9
Moldova	2 out of 8	3 out of 8	0 out of 8	4 out of 8
Russia	8 out of 10	8 out of 10	8 out of 10	10 out of 10
Tajikistan	6 out of 6	3 out of 6	2 out of 6	5 out of 6
Ukraine	5 out of 11	4 out of 11	4 out of 11	6 out of 11

Table 4.3. Observations of Informational Manipulation by Number of Combined Types

Combined Types of Informational Manipulation	Observations	Percentage of Observations per Election
Zero Types	10	11.36%
One type	12	13.64%
Two types	24	27.27%
Three types	19	21.59%
All Four Types	23	26.14%
Total	88	100%

of informational manipulation was deployed and present; it was in just twelve elections that one single type was reported. These rates suggest that it is far more common for two or more types to be observed, and that incumbent regimes may opt to combine types. As informational manipulation is expected to be used to enhance regime control over the institutions, this may be better achieved by selecting more than one type of manipulation.

I next present the rates of informational manipulation based on the conditions of the election: the degree of competitiveness, the level of incumbent dominance, and the type of election. Table 4.4 displays these results, and

Table 4.4. Descriptive Statistics of Informational Manipulation by Election Conditions

	Use of state employees at official campaign events	Use of state/ government property or organizations for campaign activities	Campaigning by officials during official state activities	Biased coverage by state-owned media
Type of Election				
Legislative	29	23	16	34
Executive	31	24	20	33
Degree of competiveness				
0 out of 3	16	11	11	21
1 out of 3	25	21	16	27
2 out of 3	18	13	8	16
3 out of 3	1	2	1	3
Incumbent Dominance				
0 out of 2	29	25	15	30
1 out of 2	18	14	13	24
2 out of 2	13	8	8	13

shows that these four types of institutional resource abuse indeed vary depending on the features of the election. First, the frequency of each of the four types of informational manipulation decreases as the competitiveness of the election increases. Second, informational manipulation is more frequent in elections with some amount of incumbent dominance than in elections where incumbent dominance is measured at a zero. Finally, the frequency of informational manipulation is higher in executive elections, with the exception of state media bias in favor of the incumbent. For this type, the distribution is almost equally split between legislative and executive elections.

I now turn to the empirical evidence. The results of the probit regression estimations are presented in Table 4.5. This table presents the results on the selection of informational manipulation. Each model presents the estimated coefficients for the individual types of informational manipulation. These individual models present some support for the theoretical relationships that are expected. First, the instances of public workers attending rallies in support of the incumbent have a positive, statistically significant relationship with executive elections. Second, the lack of distinction between the incumbent's official responsibilities and campaign behavior is negatively associated with the degree of previous competitiveness in the election; in other words, an increase in the inverted margin of victory is related to a decrease in the abuse of this state resource.[4]

I then estimate three additional models which combine the four types of informational manipulation; these results are presented in Table 4.6[5]. The first estimation uses a dichotomous variable which is coded as a one if two or more categories of informational manipulation were observed during the election; the second and third follow this example, being coded as a one if three or more of all four categories were observed, respectively. The most inclusive model, with two or more categories, finds a statistically significant relationship between incumbent dominance and informational manipulation; an increase in the level of incumbent dominance is positively associated with an increase in informational manipulation. This supports the proposition that dominant incumbents may be more likely to engage in informational manipulation so as to demonstrate power and enhance their political control of the state. Executive elections also have a statistically significant and positive association with informational manipulation, which follows my suspicion that such contests present especially effective venues for the demonstration of power. Finally, informational manipulation has a negative relationship with the rule of law observed in the state, presenting the intuitive finding that a more politicized or weak rule of law is associated with informational manipulation.

The remaining two models provide different support for the expected relationships. In both of these estimations, there is a moderate statistically significant negative relationship between the inverted margin of victory from the previous election of the same type and informational manipulation. This demonstrates that as the degree of previous competitiveness in an election is lower, incumbents are more likely to engage in more robust informational manipulation. The presence of three or four categories is also statistically related to executive elections; however, this is not the case for the model that only includes elections in which all four were present. Both models also demonstrate a positive association between GDP growth and informational manipulation, which suggests that these strategies correspond with more favorable economic circumstances. Finally, the abuse of all four categories is negatively related to the rule of law in these elections.

These results have demonstrated a different relationship than what was reported in chapter 3. More specifically, they show that a combined measure of informational manipulation has either no statistically significant relationship with the degree of competitiveness of the election, or a negative association. This is in stark contrast to the positive relationship between competitiveness and instrumental manipulation. These findings underscore the assertion that incumbents are likely to select particular types of manipulation tactics under certain circumstances, but not others. It also supports the argument that these manipulation strategies serve different electoral aims. I have argued that incumbent manipulation will vary depending on the optimal expected outcome associated with usage of the strategy. The optimal benefit of informational manipulation does not occur in the game level of the election, but rather with the meta-game level of the political institutions. Therefore, factors that may increase the attainability of the election, such a high degree of competition, would not be expected to increase the occurrence of such manipulation. The next section features two case studies that illustrate the positive relationship between incumbent dominance and informational manipulation, and a third case study with low incumbent dominance and low informational manipulation. These cases also suggest that informational manipulation can contribute to the long-term goal of greater control over the political institutions of the state.

CASE STUDY COMPARISONS

Azerbaijan's 2008 Presidential Election

Unlike the opposition victories and turnover in power witnessed in Georgia and Moldova, political power in Azerbaijan has been held by the Aliyev family since 1993. In 2003, after serving two terms, Heydar Aliyev put his support behind his son, Ilham, who was ultimately victorious. In that contest,

Table 4.5. Standard Errors in Parentheses, p-value *<0.10, **<0.05, ***<0.01, ****<0.001

	Use of state employees at official campaign events	Use of state/ government property or organizations for campaign activities	Campaigning by officials during official state activities	Biased coverage by state-owned media
Perceived Competitiveness	0.107 (0.278)	0.225 (0.263)	0.035 (0.348)	0.468 (0.334)
Previous Competitiveness	−0.007 (0.01)	−0.013 (0.009)	−0.021* (0.011)	−0.002 (0.014)
Incumbent Dominance	0.324 (0.5)	0.072 (0.546)	−0.472 (0.596)	13.304 (4997.04)
Executive Election	0.737* (0.387)	0.284 (0.362)	0.352 (0.384)	1.026 (0.63)
Proportional Representation	−0.74 (0.914)	0.182 (0.969)	0.906 (1.415)	−7.14 (16386.38)
Mixed Electoral System	−0.088 (0.94)	−0.129 (0.927)	0.016 (1.252)	−7.056 (16386.38)
GDP per capita, logged (lagged one year)	−3.468 (3.098)	−1.684 (2.6)	2.207 (3.069)	5.278* (3.04)
GDP% growth (lagged one year)	0.072* (0.04)	0.097** (0.039)	0.019 (0.04)	0.017 (0.062)
Experience with Elections	0.238 (0.166)	0.078 (0.156)	0.025 (0.183)	−0.499** (0.219)
Rule of Law (lagged one year)	−0.716 (0.778)	−0.836 (0.837)	−2.389** (1.174)	−4.325** (2.155)
Armenia	0.737 (0.881)	−0.098 (0.768)	0.287 (0.79)	0.279 (1.072)
Azerbaijan	0.742 (1.445)	−0.851 (1.427)	−0.668 (1.59)	−21.72 (7962.51)

Belarus	1.213	0.044	-0.53	-14.527
	(1.52)	(1.367)	(1.781)	(17831.68)
Georgia	-0.236	0.998	0.41	3.339*
	(0.827)	(0.882)	(0.878)	(1.986)
Kazakhstan	2.29	0.842	0.6	-6.548
	(1.742)	(1.529)	(1.806)	(6772)
Kyrgyzstan	-1.602	-3.034*	-2.439	1.036
	(1.697)	(1.74)	(1.103)	(1.811)
Moldova	-0.297	-0.549	-6.247	2.765
	(1.23)	(1.039)	(32534.05)	(1.799)
Russia	2.499	1.71	-0.479	5.674
	(1.763)	(1.474)	(1.655)	(4461.498)
Tajikistan	4.161	-1.472	0.045	Dropped
	(2681.67)	(1.596)	(1.856)	
Ukraine	—	—	—	—
Constant	9.776	4.719	-8.713	-12.439
	(10.137)	(8.518)	(10.516)	(16386.38)
N (countries)	10	10	10	10
N (total)	88	88	88	88
Wald Chi 2	20.61	19.58	17.52	12.33

Table 4.6. Standard Errors in Parentheses, p-value * <0.10, **<0.05, *<0.01, ****<0.001**

	Two or more types present	Three or Four types present	All Four Types present
Perceived Competitiveness	0.15	-0.097	-0.117
	(0.362)	(0.284)	(0.363)
Previous Competitiveness	-0.012	-0.023**	-0.021*
	(0.016)	(0.01)	(0.012)
Incumbent Dominance	5.493***	-0.524	0.195
	(2.144)	(0.554)	(0.59)
Executive Election	1.697***	0.957**	0.548
	(0.631)	(0.403)	(0.431)
Proportional Representation	-2.086	-0.309	0.403
	(2.25)	(1.24)	(1.084)
Mixed Electoral System	-2.553	-0.6	-0.127
	(2.288)	(1.217)	(1.018)
GDP per capita, logged (lagged one year)	0.823	-4.4	-1.237
	(4.789)	(3.106)	(3.352)
GDP% growth (lagged one year)	0.009	0.088**	0.091*
	(0.052)	(0.041)	(0.054)
Experience with Elections	-0.069	0.292	0.188
	(0.244)	(0.188)	(0.221)
Rule of Law (lagged one year)	-9.029***	-1.536	-2.182*
	(3.122)	(0.958)	(1.268)
Armenia	2.74**	-0.669	-0.836
	(1.297)	(0.802)	(0.964)
Azerbaijan	-10.675**	0.194	-2.328
	(4.254)	(1.512)	(1.788)
Belarus	-6.717*	0.447	0.031
	(3.827)	(1.606)	(1.802)

Georgia	8.43***	0.078	-0.829
	(3.24)	(0.869)	(1.052)
Kazakhstan	4.317	3.117*	0.064
	(6720.219)	(1.788)	(2.092)
Kyrgyzstan	-5.112	-5.245**	-3.271
	(3.121)	(2.215)	(2.37)
Moldova	3.743*	-1.465	-5.333
	(2.095)	(1.215)	(2855.038)
Russia	7.627	3.155*	0.77
	(6028)	(1.743)	(1.932)
Tajikistan	4.251	-2.742	-2.376
	(6854.568)	(1.83)	(1.994)
Ukraine	—	—	—
Constant	-7.5	13.538	1.802
	(15.772)	(10.146)	(10.551)
N (countries)	10	10	10
N (total)	88	88	88
Wald Chi 2	14.01	22.03	18.96

Ilham Aliyev won 75.3% of the vote, which continued the trend established by his father of winning over 70% of the vote in every election. The 2008 presidential election marked Aliyev's bid for reelection, in which the electoral system limited presidents to two terms at the time. During this time period, the political opposition held little power and maintained a decreasing number of seats in the legislature. Elections held in Azerbaijan have been monitored by the OSCE since 1995, and they have consistently reported irregularities, instances of manipulation and, in some cases, election day fraud. This case study examines the 2008 presidential election in particular and seeks to demonstrate a) how an executive election held with high incumbent dominance presents conditions conducive to informational incumbent manipulation and b) how the selection of this manipulation can serve the long-term goal of greater control over the political institutions.

As mentioned earlier, President Ilham Aliyev was first elected in 2003 in an election that marked his succession after his father's ten years in office. Aliyev's candidacy was presented as a continuation of the policies and regime of Heydar Aliyev, and he publicly supported and campaigned for his son during that election. After the elder Aliyev's exit from power (and subsequent death in late 2003), his support system of patronage networks and administrative staff shifted their focus to Ilham, which established the continuation of a dominant regime in Azerbaijan (Ergun 2009). This election further solidified the high degree of incumbent dominance present in Azerbaijan since Heydar Aliyev was first reelected with over 70% of the vote in 1998. This measure of reelection rates is the first of two indicators that comprise the incumbent dominance index used in this study. The second indicator concerns the percentage of the state's gross domestic product (GDP) that is produced from the export of energy natural resources. Natural resource exports can allow the regime to withstand domestic criticism and short-term crises, as well as provide the means for building support through patronage and suppressing opposition activity. As Azerbaijan is a major oil exporter, we should expect this number to be large. Indeed, in 2007, energy natural resource exports comprised 62.86% of Azerbaijan's GDP, according to the World Bank World Development Indicators. As this indicator surpasses the threshold of one third of overall GDP, it further contributes to incumbent dominance heading into Azerbaijan's 2008 presidential election. Overall, Azerbaijan measures a 2 out of 2 on the incumbent dominance index.

This executive election was also very uncompetitive. According to the index of competitiveness, this election measures a 0 out of 3. Prior to the 2008 election, held on October 15, the economy was doing well and was not in crisis. This was still in the early days of the global financial crisis of 2008–2009, and had had little effect on the election. Public opinion reveals that a majority of respondents considered the economy to be moving in the right direction between 2006 and 2010. Moreover, a plurality felt their own personal financial situations improved consistently during this same time period (Musabayov and Shulman 2010). Aliyev was also publicly confident of victory in this case, with his party and supporters mainly questioning by how much he would win. The previous margin of victory in the 2003 presidential election was also significant, with a 60-point difference between Aliyev, who won 76.4%, and the second place candidate Isa Gambar, who had won almost 14%. Additionally, the main opposition in Azerbaijan, composed of three political parties, announced two months prior to the vote, in August of 2008, that they would boycott the election and they publicly urged their supporters to do the same.[6] They argued that because they had no genuine chance of winning due to the unfair electoral circumstances, they did not want to legitimize Aliyev's inevitable reelection (Ergun 2009). This also contributed to an uncompetitive electoral contest. Nonetheless, five additional parties put forward candidates in this election, making Aliyev one of six contenders. These conditions establish an election where the attainability of the election was not in question; therefore, we should not expect incumbents to put their focus on benefits earned in the election level. Instead, incumbents are more likely to select manipulation strategies that present benefits in the long term, at the level of the political institutions.

Chapter 3 focused on instrumental resource abuse, which would not be expected in this election. Indeed, no instances of financial, regulatory, or enforcement resource abuse were reported by election observers. However, monitors from the OSCE did observe multiple examples of institutional state resource manipulation in this election. First, there were multiple reports of campaign rallies being held that were filled with public sector employees. OSCE observers were told of public rallies held in support of Aliyev's reelection where, on five separate occasions, public workers were encouraged or compelled to attend. Second, the OSCE notes that the New Azerbaijan Party (YAP) enjoyed clear institutional advantages due to its dominant position in the Aliyev government. In particular, multiple YAP offices were located in government buildings, contrary to recommended electoral practices that urge a clear separation between campaign behavior and government infrastructure. In addition, OSCE observers reported situations in which local public officials used their influence to secure locations and organize YAP rallies held in support of Aliyev's reelection.

Thirdly, while Aliyev's official campaign behavior was limited, he engaged in significant public outreach in the months prior to the election. He personally attended the openings of museums, parks, factories, schools, and even an airport. These frequent trips across the country presented Aliyev in an official capacity, "making it difficult to distinguish between the official activities of the President and his campaign" (OSCE 2008: 13).

Finally, state media coverage in this election was biased, according to the OSCE. First, it provided significant coverage of the touring activities of Aliyev throughout the country. This coverage was not neutral in its tone, but instead demonstrated support for Aliyev's reelection hopes. Moreover, state-run media outlets provided little coverage of the five other candidates running in this election. One exception to this dearth of coverage were the public forum roundtables organized to give voters information on the candidates and their policies. However, Aliyev himself never participated in these events, instead being represented by another regime official. This suggested a two-tier campaign to viewers where the incumbent president was above the act of campaigning. Even with these events, negative coverage and criticisms of Aliyev were virtually nonexistent in the state-run media. These instances represent an indirect, but very public form of electoral manipulation. Collectively, they send a message to voters, regime elites, and opposition actors that Aliyev's power is significant, unchallenged, and inevitable.

This case clearly presents an example of an election held in conditions of significant incumbent dominance and with extremely low competitiveness, as well as an election where all four types of informational manipulation were observed. This is clearly in support of the theory of this book. Aliyev was ultimately victorious in this election, winning with 87.34% of the vote. As a result of this, I would expect Aliyev to translate his victory and the usage of informational manipulation into greater control over Azerbaijan's political institutions. Changes to the political institutions indeed took place following this election. First, in 2009, the two-term limit for presidents was abolished through a public referendum and an amendment to the constitution of Azerbaijan (Ergun 2009). This has meant that since 2008, Aliyev has been able to run for, and secure, reelection in the 2013 and 2018 presidential elections. Second, both prior to, and following the 2008 election, changes have been made to the electoral code of Azerbaijan, with the mandatory campaign period being reduced to 22 days. The electoral code also eliminated the possibility for opposition candidates to receive public funding in subsequent elections, which further skews the political system in favor of Aliyev and the supportive YAP party that benefits significantly from its access to state resources. In 2016, another referendum was held to further alter the political institutions in ways that seem to benefit Aliyev. The referendum included amendments increasing the presidential term to seven years and those that diminish the power of the legislative branch by granting the president the ability to dissolve it. These measures were approved by voters with wide margins (84.2% in favor of the longer presidential terms, for example).[7] Moreover, Azerbaijan has become more inhospitable to external election monitors. In 2015, the OSCE stated that because they were not granted adequate time and resources, they were not able to monitor Azerbaijan's parliamentary elections.[8] However, the OSCE monitors were able to return for the 2018 early Presidential Election. Thus presidential power has been significantly concentrated among Aliyev and his regime and these moves have gone largely unchecked.

Additionally, the regime's intention to signal control and power through informational manipulation appears to have been effective. One way this can be observed is through the presence or absence of elite defections. In other post-Soviet states, such defections have created structural weaknesses within the incumbent regime and openings for opposition victory.[9] This was not the case in Azerbaijan. Following Aliyev's reelection in 2008, the main pillars of power that supported and were supported by the regime remained in place. In fact, Hale (2015) notes how the patronage networks around Aliyev have been remarkably stable, with the key top figures remaining in key positions throughout his presidency, and even dating back to the regime of Heydar Aliyev. Moreover, many of the main economic actors in Azerbaijan have highly visible connections to the regime and elites, which informs the public on just how dominant the regime is. Finally, the political party that supports Aliyev, the YAP, has also played a crucial role in maintaining stability and fending off defections through its ability to provide benefits (Hale 2015). The absence of defections indicates that attempts to consolidate power have been effective and that high incumbent dominance remains.

The public in Azerbaijan also remains highly supportive of Aliyev and his policies. In addition to the public economic windfalls associated with the exports of oil and natural resources, the popular support is also based on the enduring rivalry and territorial conflict with Armenia over Nagorno-Karabakh. While this remains a frozen conflict with little change since 1993, Aliyev has been a constant proponent of retaking the territory with no compromises. This conflict was even used to justify the 2009 constitutional change on term limits, specifying that presidents could serve more than two terms during times of war (Hale 2015). Given that the ongoing conflict remains the most important concern for Azerbaijanis, according to public opinion polls, this was effective.[10]

The opposition has also been further marginalized since the 2008 election. While they united behind a single candidate in the 2013 presidential election, they were unable to gain any traction due to the public consensus that Aliyev would win (Hale 2015). Opposition forces have been regularly weakened by regime pressure and tools of suppression, including being blocked from many government agencies and positions, extreme financial scrutiny, and the absence of media coverage (LaPorte 2015). Intimidation and pressure have been relentless, as seen by the recent imprisonment of many notable opposition actors, including Tofig Yagublu of the Musavat Party and Ilgar Mammadov.[11] Yagublu faced further charges just months after his release, which have also been seen as politically motivated.[12] The issue of political prisoners has become one of the most salient among opposition actors; it motivated a demonstration held in September of 2016, which according to estimates had hundreds in attendance.[13] Anti-regime forces remain active in Azerbaijan, but their numbers are clearly deteriorating amid the growing pressure and control by the Aliyev regime.

The political consolidation under Aliyev and the increased marginalization of the opposition both follow the expectations of this book. The usage of informational manipulation in an executive election with high incumbent dominance as well as low competitiveness does little to serve the short-term goal of winning the election, since that was never in question. Yet it has contributed to greater incumbent control and the projection of invincibility, which both bolsters their own legitimacy and also discourages support for the opposition.

Russia's 2008 Presidential Election

Like Azerbaijan, Russia also presents a case where the position of president has been closely held among regime elites since independence. In both cases, successors have been identified by the outgoing president with the implication of stability and the preservation of the status quo. After serving two terms, in 2007, President Vladimir Putin adhered to the constitutional consecutive two-term limit and announced his support for his first vice prime minister, Dmitri Medvedev, to be Russia's next president. Yet both Putin and Medvedev made clear that Putin would remain heavily involved in politics, as he would head the United Russia ticket in the parliamentary elections held in December of 2007, and would be appointed prime minister if victorious.

The 2008 Russian presidential election experienced extremely low competition. This election receives a zero out of three on the perceived competitiveness index. As discussed earlier, this index is based on incumbent confidence of victory, public perceptions of the economy, and public perceptions of an economic crisis. According to Hyde and Martinov (2011), Medvedev, as the officially endorsed candidate by the incumbent president, and as a member of the incumbent administration himself, was virtually assured of victory in this election. This confidence can be attributed to multiple factors. First, even before Putin's announcement, opinion polls conducted just days before showed Medvedev as the favorite among the potential successors that Putin could endorse. When considered with all the other potential Putin-backed and opposition candidates, 35% of respondents said they would vote for Medvedev. When the other potential Kremlin candidates were removed, 63% of respondents said they would support Medvedev.[14]

Second, Putin maintained notably high approval ratings heading into the election, which at the time of his official endorsement on December 10, 2007, hovered around 88%.[15] Third, United Russia, along with four other small political parties, officially endorsed Medvedev just days after their landslide parliamentary victory. Their victory would provide support for Medvedev's candidacy, and their endorsement meant that their considerable resources could be deployed on his behalf. Finally, just two days after Putin's announcement that Medvedev was his preferred candidate, Medvedev stated that he would appoint Putin as his prime minister once elected.[16] These factors all contributed to Medvedev's confidence in this election.

Public perceptions of the economy were also good prior to this election. In the year preceding the March 2nd election, survey data show a generally positive view of the economy. In April of 2007, 66% of respondents reported having positive perceptions of the current economic situation. Just seven months later, that figured climbed to almost 77% of respondents in December of 2007.[17] Thus, like Hyde and Martinov's (2011) classification, the economic situation in Russia prior to the presidential election was perceived to be good. This also removes the possibility that Russian respondents perceived the existence of an economic crisis. These factors both contribute to the very low degree of competitiveness present within this election.

Furthermore, the Putin regime maintained very high incumbent dominance heading into this election. In the previous presidential election of 2004, Putin was reelected with over 70% of the vote, which meets the criteria for classification as a hegemonic authoritarian state, one indicator on the index. Second, energy natural resource exports also support the classification of Russia as having high incumbent dominance. As discussed in the Azerbaijan case, scholars have argued that when energy exports exceed at least a third of total GDP, this can provide incumbents with necessary resource assets to secure dominance. Energy exports as a percentage of GDP exceed at least 30% from 2003 to 2006, and only in 2007 do they drop just below that threshold. This trend reveals that energy exports have exceeded 30% of Russian GDP for six of the eight years of Putin's presidency. Combined, these two measures put Russia at a 2 out of 2 on the incumbent dominance index. This means that informational manipulation is to be expected in this election.

Despite the low degree of competition and the high level of incumbent dominance in this election, electoral interference was observed and linked to Medevedev's campaign. According to the Russian election monitoring organization "GOLOS," the abuse of state or administrative resources was excessive in this election.[18] This book has categorized the abuse of state resources into four categories, each with particular subtypes: institutional, financial, regulatory, and enforcement resource abuse. Based on the election monitoring reports produced, the 2008 Russian presidential election witnessed all four subtypes of institutional resource abuse and one out of three subtypes of regulatory resource abuse. First, GOLOS noted the widespread usage of government properties for campaign operations. In particular, such campaign offices in favor of Medvedev were present in multiple administrative buildings throughout Russia. GOLOS noted that, of their entire deployment of observers around Russia in 38 different regions, about 20% noted seeing such campaign operations take place in state buildings.[19]

Second, state employees, who while not officially campaign workers, were observed working on campaign duties for Medvedev's team. GOLOS observed that within the administrative buildings that often housed such campaign offices, state workers actively contributed to campaign obligations during official business hours. Such activities were reported in 15% of the observed areas.[20] Bureaucrats and state workers were also observed participating in campaign gatherings. Moreover, GOLOS and media observers reported that regional governors felt compelled to use their staff to ensure significant voter turnout. Regional bureaucrats and governors reported feeling that they must generate voter turnout above 60% to demonstrate their loyalty to Medvedev, as the president maintained the authority to appoint regional governors.[21]

Next, GOLOS observed that in principle, there was no differentiation between Medvedev the candidate and Medvedev the deputy first prime minister. This lack of distinction was visible through the advertisements found throughout the country, which typically featured Medevedev pictured with President Putin, despite the fact that Putin himself was not a candidate in this election. It also was observed through the travels and visits made by Medvedev, who seemed to portray his actions as official duties in combination with campaigning.[22] Finally, GOLOS reported a persistent imbalance in the coverage of the election on state TV channels. They stressed the sharp distinctions in coverage for the four candidates. Medvedev received four times as much airtime as the next candidate, Zhirinovsky, on the three main state TV channels. These disparities were even more pronounced regarding Zyuganov and Bogdanov. GOLOS reports that the media displayed a fundamental bias in favor of the incumbent-supported candidate.[23]

GOLOS also considered the decision by the Central Election Committee regarding Mikhail Kasyanov's candidacy to be political. It cited that the signatures rejected as invalid contained minor technical errors and that there was no process through which signatories could prove or correct these errors.

Within the segment of flagged signatures. GOLOS reported that less than one percent was deemed fraudulent, with the vast majority merely having technical problems. This level of scrutiny was not applied to the same degree to the two million signatures provided for Andrei Bogdanov's candidacy. Thus GOLOS deemed the rejection of Kasyanov's signatures as political, due to his vocal opposition of Putin and the Kremlin. This provides evidence of one type of regulatory state resource abuse in favor of the incumbent.

This case follows the theory as well as the quantitative evidence presented on informational manipulation. As an executive election with low competitiveness and high incumbent dominance, consolidation over the political institutions becomes more important than the election itself. Medvedev was indeed victorious in this contest, winning 71% of the vote. Informational manipulation can establish the circumstances for the further consolidation of power through changes to the political institutions. In examining the aftermath of the 2008 presidential election in Russia, such changes indeed occurred. First, the constitutional rules on the terms of the president and members of the parliament were officially altered in December of 2008. The president's term was extended from four to six years, while the term for members of both houses of the parliament were increased from four to five years (Clark 2012). While Medvedev argued that such a change enhanced the stability of the political system, it also clearly increases the amount of time between elections and gives those in power greater latitude without being accountable to voters. More recently, new laws have been passed to put additional scrutiny on the funding sources of domestic NGOs and to add restrictions and regulations to internet behavior.[24] Such laws augment regime control and demonstrate how a highly dominant regime can manipulate political institutions to consolidate its position.

In addition to the constitutional changes, the political system in Russia remained highly centralized. Even with the change in the position of president, the ruling elite remained coherent, with no notable cases of elite defection. The political regime of Medvedev primarily represented the continuation of the status quo in Russia. His rule alongside Putin was characterized as a "tandem," and it maintained the ongoing political elite surrounding Medvedev and Putin. Hale (2015: 280) remarks that although this tandem arrangement could be seen as one with two distinct sources of power, it was still a "single pyramid system because the two were so clearly in the same network and never ruptured these ties." This arrangement may actually have prevented elite defections, since it provided frustrated elites contained within the different hierarchical networks of influence with an alternative authority figure to influence and raise issues (Hale 2015). Although Medvedev also criticized the political and economic structures within Russia, voicing concern over an economy so dependent on natural resources, no significant actions were taken on these fronts (Mommsen 2010). Since Putin has returned to power in 2012, talk of such reforms have evaporated, even as Medvedev has remained, at least publicly, within the inner circle of the political elite.

Moreover, the popularity of the Medvedev-Putin regime remained strong. Putin in particular worked to cultivate a public persona in ways similar to the informational manipulation witnessed during the election. State-run media often featured footage and photos of Putin engaging in physical activities, signaling hyper-masculinity and simply demonstrating Russian power through military and economic might (Mommsen 2010). State media coverage of Putin tagging a Siberian Tiger, retrieving an ancient artifact from a diving trip in the Black Sea, and posing shirtless on horseback are just some examples of attempts to build legitimacy through highly visible acts of strength. These behaviors have been associated with the high degree of regime approval from the public even while Putin was prime minister. For many years, Putin has been known to use informal, and in some cases vulgar or suggestive language, which also endears him to the populace and distinguishes him from previous, more formal Russian leaders (Sperling 2014) Approval ratings reached their lowest levels in 2013, after Putin returned to the position of president, but have since peaked again at close to 90% approval; this most recent surge in support has been widely attributed to Russia's annexation of Crimea and its intervention in the conflict in Eastern Ukraine. As recent political science research has demonstrated, such high public approval ratings for Putin are for the most part genuine and not the result of confirmation bias or self-censorship by survey respondents (Frye, Gehlbach, Marquardt, and Reuter 2017).

The Russia case further illustrates the informational manipulation of elections. This 2008 executive contest featured a high degree of incumbent dominance and a low degree of competitiveness, and as expected, informational manipulation was widespread. This despite the fact that, as in the case of Azerbaijan, such manipulation was not necessary for Medvedev's victory. This case also led to long-term benefits for the regime, including constitutional changes to term lengths and the further minimization of opposition forces.

Negative Case: Kyrgyzstan's 2015 Parliamentary Election

The previous two case studies illustrated the ideal conditions under which informational manipulation is to be expected. With low competition and high incumbent dominance, the manipulation in these elections promoted the long-term consolidation of control over the political institutions and contributed to the stabilization of authoritarianism. Informational manipulation has been theorized to be less impactful, and therefore less utilized, when it cannot serve this long-term strategy. The theory of this book hinges on the expectation that regimes vary their manipulation strategies, and act based on the conditions of the election. Therefore, this final case study departs from the previous two by presenting an example with opposing conditions that were not conducive to such incumbent interference. Kyrgyzstan's 2015 parliamentary election meets these criteria and, as expected, generally does not offer any observations of informational election manipulation.

As referenced earlier in this book, Kyrgyzstan was home to 2005's Tulip Revolution. This event came in response to its parliamentary elections of the same year, where demonstrators took to the streets to protest the officially reported results of the election, which saw many pro-presidential candidates and regime insiders elected despite numerous claims of fraud and manipulation. That election came after multiple constitutional and election reforms had been implemented, many of which further concentrated power around the president at the time, Askar Akayev. After two weeks of protests and significant violent unrest, the prime minister as well as Akayev stepped down and resigned (Abazov 2007). This led to early presidential elections being held, the election of opposition candidate and acting President Kurmanbek Bakiyev, and some glimmers of hope that the political system would become more open and competitive (Bunce and Wolchik 2011). However, in the years following, Kyrgyzstan's political system remained unstable and witnessed the rise and fall of another manipulation-prone, authoritarian government led by Bakiyev. The previous parliamentary elections were held in 2010, just months after another period of chaos and serious instability, including the deaths of an estimated 86 protestors, that led to Bakiyev's ouster and the installation of a transitional government (Husky and Hill 2011). Those 2010 elections saw the most seats go to two competing parties, Ata-Jurt and the Social Democrats (SDPK). These elections were also the first since a constitutional referendum was held in 2010. This established a semi-parliamentary system and an upper limit of 65 seats from any one party in the Jogorku Kenesh, Kyrgyzstan's parliament, so as to mandate compromise and prevent any dominant parties from taking control. Since 2011, Kyrgyzstan had been led by President Almazbek Atambayev of the SDPK, who was elected in one of the cleanest elections in both Kyrgyz history as well as in the Central Asian region (Fumagelli 2012). The outgoing parliament in 2015 featured a coalition between three parties, Ata-Jurt, the SDPK, and Respublika.

These events illustrate the dramatic and often shifting political landscape in Kyrgyzstan since its 2005 Color Revolution. The 2015 parliamentary elections highlighted the continued fractious nature between the parties but also featured renewed hopes that the democratic prospects in Kyrgyzstan were within grasp. Incumbent president Atambayev made clear his support for his former party, the SDPK, as the campaign began, and many saw this party as the frontrunner in the election. Nonetheless, both the perceived and previous competitiveness in this election were high. The 2010 election saw a very small margin of victory between the top two parties, Ata-Jurt and the SDPK, which won 15.3% and 14.1% of the vote, respectively, and a 1.2-point margin of difference. The index of perceived competitiveness reveals a score of 2 out of 3 heading into this election. First, there was no public confidence of victory from any of the three coalition parties heading into the election. The SDPK had become more prominent over the course of the last five years, but the election atmosphere was one of genuine uncertainty as to which party would come out victorious.[25]

Second, economic problems were quite pronounced as the election approached. Kyrgyzstan has long been home to economic instability and suffered heavily after the 2008–2009 Global Financial Crisis (Huskey and Hill 2011). Due to severe fluctuations, the Kyrgyz economy posted both notable growth (10.9% in 2013) as well as numerous contractions (-0.47 and -0.08 in 2008 and 2010, respectively. In the year before the 2015 election, its economy grew at just above 4%, while its GDP per capita was recorded as $1279 in 2014.[26] This puts Kyrgyzstan as one of the poorest states among the ten post-Soviet states covered in this book; only Tajikistan reports lower figures. Public opinion further illustrates the economic problems mounting. A July 2015 survey found 59% of respondents listing unemployment as the most pressing issue facing Kyrgyzstan, and 34% reported financial problems and a low standard of living as the most important problem facing their households; these were the top answers from both questions, respectively.[27] However, the economy did not reach crisis levels prior to this election, so this leaves the remaining indicator of competitiveness unobserved.

Additionally, incumbent dominance was low prior to the 2015 parliamentary election. First, presidents have been limited to just one six-year term since the 2010 constitution (Fumagalli 2012), although the ousted president Bakiyev was reelected in 2009 with 76% of the vote, which briefly gave Kyrgyzstan one indicator of incumbent dominance. This was not the case prior to the 2015 election. Second, unlike its neighbor Kazakhstan, Kyrgyzstan is not a significant exporter of oil, which means that a reliance on energy exports is absent from the indicators of incumbent dominance. In 2014, natural energy resource exports comprised 7.8% of its total GDP, which falls short of the 30% threshold meant to capture its ability to bolster authoritarian regimes.

This backdrop establishes a competitive election with a genuinely unknown result faced by a government with a low degree of dominance in the state. Such conditions are argued to be unfavorable to informational manipulation for two reasons. First, informational manipulation only indirectly influences the election, so it is less able to serve the short-term goal of tipping the scales in favor of incumbents. Instead, it prioritizes long-term control over the political institutions. Second, informational manipulation is highly visible, which carries both short-term and long-term costs. In the short term, it detracts from the legitimacy of the election, which can spur post-election protests and discord. In the long-term, it may diminish the prospects for democracy from both internal and external supporters of democracy. These costs carry more weight in a competitive election, and are therefore expected to make informational manipulation less likely.

The OSCE's election observation mission of the 2015 election reports that, as expected, informational manipulation was generally not witnessed during this contest. As was done for the previous two case studies, I scrutinized the OSCE's final report for any of the four types of institutional resource abuse use to measure informational manipulation. First, the OSCE did not note any reports of state workers serving in campaign-related roles, nor did they observe any instances of state workers being pressured to attend campaign events and meetings. Second, the OSCE observers did not report any improper usage of state resources for campaign activities. Instead, they noted that all major parties secured private office space and that numerous posters and advertisements for their candidates were visible on either paid billboards or on the vehicles of private citizens. Third, the OSCE report lacks any observations of any of the three ruling coalition parties from blurring the distinction between their official duties and their campaign activities. The SDPK did promote its accomplishments and those of the president during the campaign, but this did not reach the level of campaigning while performing official functions. Finally, biased or slanted campaign coverage was generally not observed in the state media by the OSCE. However, the OSCE report did lament the fact that many news channels provided little in-depth analysis or examinations of the parties' platforms and policy positions.[28] This type of occurrence reflects the still nascent political system in Kyrgyzstan, but it does not reveal any attempts at informational manipulation. However, the OSCE did note some more concerning developments in state media in the final week before the election. Specifically, they observed that one of the state-owned television networks, KTRK, presented more slanted editorial coverage that painted the SDPK in a more positive light while putting more negative attention on Respublika-Ata Jurt and Ata Meken. This approaches a positive occurrence of informational manipulation. Even with this caveat, informational manipulation overall was mostly absent from the 2015 parliamentary election.

While informational manipulation was mainly lacking from this contest, given the competitive nature of the election, instrumental manipulation would be expected and was indeed observed. The contrast between the lack of informational manipulation and the presence of more directly influential instrumental manipulation comes across from the OSCE's report itself, "[i]n a positive development, misuse of state administrative resources did not appear to be a major concern in these elections. However, allegations of vote-buying were widespread, and some criminal investigations were launched" (OSCE 2016a: 2). Additionally, one of the big controversies of the campaign was the deregistration of a candidate from Respublika-Ata Jurt, Kamchybek Tashiev, with just a week remaining before the election. These examples point to clear abuses of financial and regulatory sate resources, respectively.

Summary of Case Studies

These three cases reveal starkly contrasting patterns in selection and employment of manipulation strategies. Table 4.7 displays these differences. The 2008 presidential elections in Russia and Azerbaijan both were considered to have low competitiveness and high incumbent dominance. Moreover, both of these elections were the sites of significant informational manipulation, observed through the abuse of each of the 4 types of institutional resources. This is a notable contrast with Kyrgyzstan's 2015 election, where instrumental manipulation was present but informational manipulation generally

Table 4.7. Summary of Three Informational Manipulation Case Study Findings

Indicators	Azerbaijan, 2008	Russia, 2008	Kyrgyzstan, 2015
Type of Election	Presidential	Presidential	Parliamentary
Competitiveness	0 out of 3	0 out of 3	2 out of 3
Incumbent Dominance	2 out of 2	2 out of 2	0 out of 2
Informational Manipulation Types			
Use of State Employees at Official Campaign Events	Yes	Yes	No
Use of State/Government Property or Organizations for Campaign Activities	Yes	Yes	No
Campaigning by Officials during Official State Activities	Yes	Yes	No
Biased Coverage by State-Owned Media	Yes	Yes	Partial
Total	4 out of 4	4 out of 4	0-1 out of 4

was not. The results of the Kyrgyz election were also different. Once again, no party won a majority, and the margin of victory between the first and second place finishers was small. The SDPK won the most seats, 38, while the Respublika-Ata Jurt alliance won 28. Six parties, representing different policies and political orientations, now hold representation in the Jogorku Kenesh. These case study contrasts echo the findings from chapter 3. The authoritarian regimes of Aliyev and Medvedev/Putin both have enjoyed significant incumbent dominance in their respective states. This means that any and all types of manipulation could in all likelihood be deployed with great ease. And yet, these case studies paint the opposite picture of restraint when it comes to instrumental manipulation, while displaying perceptible eagerness toward informational manipulation. This bolsters the second intention behind these case studies: to illustrate how informational manipulation in the short term can further authoritarian consolidation in the long term.

CONCLUSION

This chapter has examined the role that informational manipulation plays in elections. In particular, it has demonstrated the conditions that make the selection of informational manipulation more likely, and what's more, that these conditions differ from those presented in chapter 3. While instrumental manipulation shared a positive association with highly competitive elections, the same was not true for informational manipulation. Instead, incumbents are more likely to select informational manipulation in executive elections, as well as when incumbent dominance is high, or when the degree of competitiveness is low. This distinction suggests that these manipulation strategies are not interchangeable and that they may serve different goals depending upon the circumstances of the election. These findings also demonstrate that informational manipulation is a common feature of post-Soviet elections no matter how uncompetitive the election or dominant the incumbent regime is. Even in regimes with established incumbent dominance, manipulation continues to be observed. The case studies of Russia and Azerbaijan illustrate how such manipulation can occur despite the ample dominance of the regime and low degree of competitiveness.

As theorized in this book, the optimal benefits of informational manipulation lie in the level of the political institutions. Informational manipulation can further the goal of consolidating an authoritarian regime through enhanced control over the political institutions in place. This implies that elections that experience significant informational abuse in service of nondemocratic incumbents are more likely to experience long-term effects that strengthen the authoritarian regime. The two positive case studies of Azerbaijan's 2008 presidential election and Russia's 2008 presidential election both bear this relationship out. In both cases, clear steps were taken to consolidate regime control through changes to the political institutions of the state. In the case of Azerbaijan, term limits for the president were removed and steps were taken to further marginalize the political opposition. In Russia, term lengths for both the president and parliament were increased. Moreover, in both cases, the opposition experienced further electoral losses or saw fewer and fewer opportunities for victory and political change. The dominant political regimes remained so, and even when faced with worsening economic or geopolitical circumstances. As of this writing, no force nor set of actors seem positioned to effectively challenge these consolidating political regimes.

The frequency of such events should come as no surprise to practitioners of election monitoring. Organizations like the OSCE that author election reports regularly detail such activities, even as they note that the will of the people may still have been met in the unfair contest. As Simpser (2013) argues, blatant manipulation that only indirectly affects the election is still problematic, and should be treated as such. Election observers should continue to publicize the occurrence of these events in their reports, and they should continue to highlight how they violate the norms of democracy. However, reports could go further in outlining the potential for the long-term consolidation of non-democratic regimes and the further marginalization of opposition forces. It is true that these types of manipulation may only have an indirect effect on the election, but as demonstrated in this chapter, the effects are more notable in the long term.

Additionally, OSCE monitors could attempt to gather more longitudinal data on some of these manipulation tactics to track whether they are increasing, decreasing, or remaining stagnant over time. This suggestion definitely requires more resources and greater in-country access, which may not be attainable in every case. Nonetheless, more precise observations on, for example, the number of campaign offices located in government buildings observed, could offer additional data on whether regimes have demonstrated limited improvements, or conversely if they have expanded this manipulation practice. The GOLOS observation reports used for the 2008 Russian Presidential Election presented similar statistics and it can add an extra layer by conveying the visibility of the manipulation. The OSCE already reports such detailed statistics in its media coverage and monitoring, so this would not be entirely out of their purview. The overarching implication of this chapter is that informational manipulation matters and deserves attention regardless of its effects in the short term. As discussed in the case studies, it is clearly the long-term effects that are far more impactful and far more crucial in the consolidation of authoritarianism.

NOTES

1. Maxim Shemetov. "With Russia's Presidential Elections Looming, Ksenia Sobchak Has Already Moved On." *The Moscow Times*. March 16, 2018.

2. The 2018 Russian Presidential Election is not included in the 88 elections analyzed as the economic indicators and rule of law scores from 2017 were not available at the time of writing.

3. There is one exception: there are no reported instances of officials campaigning while conducting official state business in Moldova.

4. As discussed in the previous chapter, I have inverted the margins of victory so that this indicator can be interpreted in the same direction as the competitiveness index.

5. Each model was also estimated by omitting incumbent dominance, previous competitiveness, and perceived competitiveness to address multicollinearity. These models did not produce differences in statistical significance.

6. The three parties that boycotted the 2008 election were the Musavat Party, the Popular Front Party, and the Liberal Party.

7. "Azerbaijani Voters Said to Approve Greater Powers for Aliyev," *Radio Free Europe/Radio Liberty*, September 27, 2016.

8. Charles Recknagel, "'Never Been Worse': Opposition, Election Monitors Boycott Vote in Azerbaijan," *Radio Free Europe/Radio Liberty*, October 31, 2015.

9. Georgia and Ukraine in the early 2000s present especially clear examples of this.

10. Rasim Musabayov and Rakhmil Shulman. 2008. *Azerbaijan in 2007: Sociological Monitoring* (Baku: Friedrich Ebert Stiftung and Pulls).

11. "Freed Opposition Leader Says Azerbaijan's President Orchestrates Imprisonments" *Radio Free Europe/Radio Liberty*, March 31, 2016.

12. Liz Fuller. "Jailed Former Azerbaijani Minister Hit With New Criminal Charges," *Radio Free Europe/Radio Liberty*, October 17, 2016.

13. "Hundreds of Azerbaijani Opposition Supporters Rally in Baku," *Radio Free Europe/Radio Liberty,* September 18, 2016.

14. Levada Opinion Poll. December 13, 2007. "Presidential Election." *Levada Center Press Release*. http://www.levada.ru/13-12-2007/vybory-prezidenta.

15. New Russian Barometer. December 2007: 88% approve of Putin, 10% disapprove, 1% unsure. Sample size: 1601 observations.

16. Rodin, Ivan, Natalia Kostenko, and Vladimir Razuvaev Jr. 2007. "Reciprocal Post." (Ответный пост). *Nezavisimaya Gazeta*. December 12, 2007. http://www.ng.ru/politics/2007-12-12/1_post.html.

17. New Russian Barometer. Views of Economic Situation. April and December 2007. Sample sizes: 1470 and 1404 respondents, respectively.

18. The OSCE decided not to send international monitors to this election, citing restrictions put on the quantity and duration of visas offered to its observers (Clark 2009). Therefore, I have relied on three reports issued during and after the campaign by GOLOS, a domestic election monitoring organization, for evidence of electoral

interference. GOLOS is also widely respected by Western election monitoring organizations.

19. GOLOS. 2008. *Statement No. 2 from Organization GOLOS concerning the results of the long-term observation of the voter campaign for President of the Russian Federation on March 2, 2008. (*Заявление № 2 Ассоциации «ГОЛОС» по результатам долгосрочного наблюдения хода избирательной кампании Президента РФ 2 марта 2008 года.*)* February 28, 2008. http://archive.golos.org/asset/75.

20. Ibid.

21. Ibid. Francesca Mereu. 2008. "Voters Pressured to Choose Medvedev." *The Moscow Times*. February 22, 2008. http://www.themoscowtimes.com/news/article/voters-pressured-to-choose-medvedev/361374.html.

22. Ibid.

23. Ibid.

24. Steven Wilson, "The Logic of Russian Internet Censorship" Monkey Cage blog, *Washington Post*, March 16, 2014.

25. "Election Campaign Kicks Off in Kyrgyzstan." *Radio Free Europe/Radio Liberty*. September 4, 2015; "Elections in the Kyrgyz Republic: 2015 Parliamentary Elections." *International Foundation for Electoral Systems*. Washington, DC: September 28, 2015.

26. All figures come from the World Bank World Development Indicators.

27. Poll conducted by the International Republican Institute between July 22nd and 31st, http://www.iri.org/sites/default/files/wysiwyg/2015-09-25_survey_of_kyrgyz_public_opinion_july_22-31_2015.pdf.

28. "Kyrgyz Republic Parliamentary Elections 4 October 2015." *OSCE/ODIHR Election Observation Mission Final Report*. Warsaw: 28 January 2016.

Chapter Five

The Conditions for Opposition Pre-Electoral Coalitions

The previous two chapters have dealt with incumbent strategies of electoral manipulation. These chapters have demonstrated how the conditions of an election alter the likelihood of some strategies being selected, and how the different strategies can in turn contribute to varied effects on the incumbent authoritarian regime. In the next two chapters, I shift my attention to opposition political actors, examining how they too can and do pursue different strategies depending on the conditions of the election. As in the previous chapters, these two chapters will also use case studies to illustrate how the conditions of the elections encourage these strategies to be used. Additionally, these case studies will highlight how the different strategies can have varied long-time effects on the degree of organization and the influence of opposition actors in electoral authoritarian states.

This chapter focuses exclusively on opposition pre-electoral blocs or coalitions. I have argued that this electoral strategy can help opposition actors reach victory in a contest that otherwise puts incumbents and regime candidates at a distinct advantage; this yields a clear short-term benefit. While opposition pre-election coalitions can yield benefits in the long term, these can be potentially subdued by the possible long-term costs of which outcome is produced. Given this, I assert that the optimal expected outcome for a pre-election bloc lies within the level of the electoral contest. As such, I expect conditions that alter the attainability of the election to be especially important in the decision to form a pre-election coalition. In particular, I expect such coalitions to be more likely in elections where the degree of competitiveness is low, where incumbent dominance is low, and in legislative elections. This chapter proceeds as follows. First, it discusses the logic and practice of opposition pre-electoral coalitions, and how the usage of this strategy is distinctive within electoral authoritarian regimes. Second, it introduces the descriptive statistics on when this strategy has been used within the states of the former Soviet Union, as well as its effectiveness as a strategy. It then presents the quantitative statistical analysis between a pre-election coalition and the conditions of the election. Then this chapter introduces three case studies of particular elections—Georgia's 2012 parliamentary election, Armenia's 2012 parliamentary election, and Russia's 2011 parliamentary election. The first two case studies demonstrate a similarity in conditions and the selection of a strategy, echoing the quantitative evidence; yet they also present two different potential outcomes after the selection of this strategy. Given this, the chapter examines the long-term trajectory of opposition actors following the deployment of a pre-election coalition and how their role and organizational power has shifted in response. The third election presents a negative case where the main difference is a higher degree of incumbent dominance; it demonstrates that in an otherwise similarly situated parliamentary election with similar competitiveness, a coalition was not present. Combined, the three case studies illustrate the conditions in which opposition actors operate and make decisions within the more limited setting of an electoral authoritarian regime.

OPPOSITION PRE-ELECTION
COALITIONS ACROSS POST-SOVIET STATES

As discussed in chapter 1, an opposition pre-election coalition represents a political decision among at least two parties or candidates to combine campaign efforts and unify into a presumably larger political entity. The shapes and dimensions of coalitions will vary depending on many different factors, including the type of the election. In a legislative contest, parties or candidates can unite to create a bloc of candidates and/or parties that compete as a team in seeking to win seats in the legislature. In an executive contest, the members of a coalition must agree which candidate will be at the top of the ticket and assume the position, if victorious.

Opposition pre-election coalitions have become an increasingly visible occurrence across the former Soviet Union (FSU). Globally, pre-electoral coalitions have been the most frequent in the FSU, in comparison with electoral authoritarian regimes in other regions. About 30% of all pre-election coalitions have been observed in these states (Gandhi and Reuter 2013). These entities have also grown in frequency over the last fifty years as the number of electoral authoritarian regimes has increased as well.

A pre-election coalition works in particular to achieve the short-term goal of winning the election for the included set of opposition actors. It is in a position to further this goal for multiple reasons. First, it can alter the electoral math in a way that makes the opposition more viable against the authoritarian incumbent regime. Many studies have documented how authoritarian incumbents seek to maintain a divided opposition so that none is in a position to mount an effective challenge against a dominant regime or party. This can be done through cooptation efforts by a dominant party, where politicians and legislators are compelled or incentivized to leave the opposition and join the regime for greater rewards, access, and influence (Reuter and Remington 2009). Conversely, when at least part of the opposition is unified, the regime is in less of a position to woo away potential defectors and water down their influence. Moreover, a divided opposition can lead to split votes among two or more alternatives to the regime. This can make victory virtually impossible when faced with a dominant incumbent party or regime that already commands a sizable majority of seats or votes.

Second, voters may be more willing to cast a vote for a unified opposition rather than for one of many in a divided landscape. Voters typically have a strong preference against wasting their vote by supporting a party or candidate that has little likelihood of winning. This impulse can be especially strong when the opposition has been repeatedly marginalized and has seen their vote share decline after multiple election cycles of incumbent dominance. Yet when two or more opposition actors unite into a pre-election coalition, this can provide a signal of viability to voters. As Bunce and Wolchik (2011: 252) state, "collaboration sends out a clear signal that the opposition is serious about contesting power, and that it has the commitment and the political skills to form an effective government." Therefore, voters that may have abstained from voting altogether or who would have voted for the incumbent regime simply due to its presumed victory may instead be willing to cast their ballot for a combined opposition grouping.

Finally, the decision to form a pre-election coalition can help resolve the inherent resource imbalance that defines electoral authoritarian regimes. Incumbent actors always operate in advantageous positions when facing reelection, but as discussed in chapters 3 and 4, this can be exploited and exaggerated in nondemocratic elections. Such behavior is exemplified by the abuse of state resources and electoral manipulation, regardless of whether it falls within the instrumental or informational variety. This reality can put opposition actors at an extreme organizational and resource disadvantage, infringing upon their ability to mount effective campaigns. This situation can be at least somewhat improved when two or more opposition actors unite in a pre-election coalition. Existing parties can maximize their already limited resources by combining voter outreach efforts and coordinating campaign events. Coalitions can benefit from the integration of staff by addressing any inadequacies or holes in expertise, as well as reinforcing any strengths that might be shared across the previously separate organizations. As Bunce and Wolchik (2011) have demonstrated, innovative campaign strategies have been linked to electoral victory in post-Soviet electoral authoritarian states. Such new approaches may emerge in some cases due to personnel strengths.

Yet while a unified opposition coalition presents many advantages in the already unfair electoral environment, this is not an easy strategy to pursue. It carries with it serious short-term costs in the level of the electoral contest, which may help us understand the fact that under 30% of elections in post-Soviet states have contained at least one opposition pre-election coalition. First, opposition parties and organizations can become even more rigid and ideological after years of electoral deterioration and defeat (Greene 2007). This can make pre-existing differences in policy and approach even more pronounced, thus complicating any possibility of compromise and coopera-tion. Second, the opposition in post-Soviet states is especially vast, in some cases featuring an enormous landscape of different opposition entities (Bunce and Wolchik 2011). Such a disparate setting can make unification logistically difficult and improbable. Finally, as mentioned in chapter 2, groups may be hesitant to cooperate due to the likelihood of future disagreements about governing (Dawisha and Deets 2006). Coalition governments in Eastern Europe and post-Soviet states have mixed, but mostly negative track records of maintaining unity after electoral victory. Following both Georgia's Rose Revolution and Ukraine's Orange Revolution, the pre-electoral coalitions experienced significant internal dilemmas over policy direction as well as the relative influence of the different personalities. In both of these cases, the coalitions ultimately fragmented and returned to their previous positions of separate, opposing entities.

QUANTITATIVE EVIDENCE ON PRE-ELECTION COALITIONS

Having discussed the role that pre-election coalitions can and have played across the former Soviet Union, I now turn to the quantitative data available on the relationship between such coalitions and other electoral factors. Table 5.1 displays the descriptive statistics on the universe of cases included in this study. First, this reveals that opposition pre-electoral coalitions are more frequent in legislative elections than in contests for the executive. Second, coalitions occur more often in elections with a higher degree of competitive-ness and in elections with a lower degree of incumbent dominance. Finally, opposition pre-election coalitions have been formed in at least one election in every post-Soviet state with the exceptions of Kazakhstan and Tajikistan. Georgia has been the site of the most coalitions, with six having participated

Table 5.1.

	Low Incumbent Dominance	Medium Incumbent Dominance	High Incumbent Dominance
Low Competitiveness	Armenia's 2012 Parliamentary Election Georgia's 1999 Parliamentary Election Georgia's 2004 Parliamentary Election Georgia's 2013 Presidential Election	Belarus's 2001 Presidential Election Belarus's 2004 Parliamentary Election Belarus's 2006 Presidential Election Belarus's 2008 Parliamentary Election	Azerbaijan's 2005 Parliamentary Election Azerbaijan's 2010 Parliamentary Election Azerbaijan's 2013 Presidential Election
High Competitiveness	Armenia's 2003 Parliamentary Election Georgia's 2008 Presidential Election Georgia's 2008 Parliamentary Election Georgia's 2012 Parliamentary Election Kyrgyzstan's 2007 Parliamentary Election Kyrgyzstan's 2015 Parliamentary Election Moldova's 2010 Parliamentary Election Russia's 1999 Parliamentary Election Ukraine's 2002 Parliamentary Election Ukraine's 2004 Presidential Election Ukraine's 2012 Parliamentary Election Ukraine's 2014 Parliamentary Election		Azerbaijan's 2003 Presidential Election

in elections dating back to 1999. Moreover, despite the ongoing focus on opposition pre-electoral coalitions academically and by political actors themselves, a total of only 24 total coalitions have been observed out of 88 total elections between 1995 and 2016. This underwhelming statistic suggests that opposition actors may demonstrate restraint in selecting this electoral strategy, that they may face notable hurdles in forming coalitions in the first place, or that calculus behind such coalitions depends on both the short- and long-term circumstances.

Next, I present the multivariate statistical estimations on the formation of opposition pre-election coalitions. For this analysis, I use a dichotomous variable coded as a 1 if a coalition of at least two opposition actors formed, competed, and campaigned together in the election. I performed a probit regression estimation to assess the presence of any statistically significant relationships between the independent variables and the presence of an opposition pre-election coalition. Table 5.2 displays these results.[1] First, in congruence with the theoretical expectations, incumbent dominance has a significant and negative relationship with coalitions. As incumbent dominance decreases in the state, a coalition is more likely to form, all else being equal. Second, executive elections are also significantly associated with coalitions in a negative direction. This confirms the hypothesis that coalitions would be more likely in legislative elections rather than in executive contests. However, based on the two measures meant to capture the degree of competition in the election, there is no statistically significant relationship between either indicator and pre-election coalitions. The only other primary variable that reaches statistical significance is GDP growth lagged by one year. As the previous year's GDP growth increases, an opposition pre-election coalition is more likely to be formed.

These empirical results have demonstrated some support for expected relationships, namely that incumbent dominance and executive relationships have negative correlations with opposition pre-election coalitions. Yet this only provides us with a big-picture finding, with limited details about how coalitions form and how these factors may play into the decision by opposition actors to unify. In other words, the causal mechanisms are still unclear from the statistical results. The following section aims to explore two positive cases where opposition pre-election coalitions did form and use these cases to understand how the level of incumbent dominance and the type of election figures in to this calculus. It then includes a negative case where an opposition pre-election coalition did not form in a contest with a higher degree of incumbent dominance.

Table 5.2.   Standard Errors in Parentheses, p-value * <0.10, **<0.05, *<0.01, ****<0.001**

Variables	Opposition Pre-Election Coalition
Perceived Competitiveness	0.29
	(0.309)
Previous Competitiveness	−0.008
	(0.01)
Incumbent Dominance	−1.519*
	(0.921)
Executive Election	−0.745*
	(0.416)
Proportional Representation	−1.191
	(1.083)
Mixed Electoral System	0.092
	(0.994)
GDP per capita, logged (lagged one year)	1.072
	(2.787)
GDP % growth (lagged one year)	0.071**
	(0.036)
Experience with Elections	−0.004
	(0.162)
Rule of Law (lagged one year)	−0.181
	(0.872)
Armenia	−1.567*
	(0.847)
Azerbaijan	2.122
	(1.814)
Belarus	0.656
	(1.514)
Georgia	−0.166
	(0.845)
Kazakhstan	−4.754
	(2740.357)
Kyrgyzstan	0.103
	(1.705)
Moldova	0.411
	(1.325)
Russia	−1.374
	(1.657)
Tajikistan	−6.39
	(4143.954)
Ukraine	Omitted
Constant	−3.118
	(9.246)
N (countries)	10
N (total)	88
Wald Chi 2	14.8

PARLIAMENTARY ELECTION CASE STUDIES

Georgia's 2012 Election

Georgia's 2012 election previously received attention in chapter 3, but with a clear focus on the actions of the incumbent regime actors. It presented an example of an election with high perceived competitiveness and low incumbent dominance that in turn witnessed a high degree of instrumental incumbent manipulation. These same conditions are also theorized to influence the decision to form an opposition pre-electoral coalition; given this, I return to this case to examine how the opposition behaved during this election, and what long-term effects have been observed since then.

As discussed in chapter 3, the degree of perceived competitiveness was low heading into the 2012 contest. While Saakashvili and his UNM party had been reelected in 2008, their regime suffered from poor economic conditions and increasing public discontent with the political situation. This election scores a 2 out of 3 on the perceived competitiveness index due to perceptions of ongoing economic troubles and the lack of confidence in victory held by the UNM Party. Moreover, the margin of victory in the 2008 parliamentary election represented a decline in the share of seats and a smaller margin of victory for the UNM. Also, a significant scandal emerged following the release of video recorded incidents of prisoner abuse (discussed in greater detail in chapter 3) in the months before the 2012 election. These developments added greater uncertainty to the 2012 election and definitely represented a major problem for Saakashvili and the UNM Party.

Additionally, incumbent dominance was low in Georgia prior to the 2012 election. This has been observed and measured using the incumbent dominance index: Saakashvili had not been reelected with at least 70% of the vote, nor is Georgia's GDP reliant on oil and natural resource exports. Since his reelection, Saakashvili was in the position of a lame duck president, given Georgia's two-term limit for presidents. However, in 2010 he assisted the parliament in restructuring the Georgian political system to shift power away from the executive and to the parliament and prime minister. These constitutional changes would maintain a presidential system but would weaken the president's ability to remove the prime minister without the necessary actions by the parliament. It was widely perceived that Saakashvili would, within the context of these institutional shifts, decide to put himself forward as a candidate for the position of prime minister (Hale 2015). These changes would definitely alter the power structure and regime dynamics in Georgia, but also set the stage for Saakashvili to retain his power and influence in the newly enhanced position of prime minister, a role with no term limits.

Yet even with the potential for increased incumbent dominance looming, Saakashvili's regime also suffered from additional setbacks after the 2008 elections. Multiple prominent regime elites defected from Saakashvili's administration. First, in late 2008, UNM member and speaker of the parliament Nino Burjanadze, UN ambassador Irakli Alasania and former prime minister Zurab Noghaideli all defected with the explicit intentions to form rival political organizations in opposition to the regime. Then, in 2011, Bidzina Ivanishvili, a mega-rich oligarch and patron of Saakashvili (and someone once identified as a potential successor to Saakashvili as president)[2] publicly distanced himself from Saakashvili, and began forming an opposition political movement of his own. These highly public defections demonstrated a growing and sustained frustration with Saakashvili and also made clear that his regime lacked significant dominance within Georgia.

To recap, with conditions of high competition and low incumbent dominance, opposition political actors are likely to recognize that the election is more attainable under these circumstances. Therefore, strategies that can work to improve their own odds of winning the election are especially appealing; one such strategy is forming an opposition pre-electoral bloc. As theorized, such a coalition was indeed formed to compete in the 2012 parliamentary election in Georgia. The formation of such a bloc also faces costs in the short term, namely the need to compromise on policy and campaign positions as well as the need to cooperate among different, often rival, politicians. As the example in Georgia will demonstrate, the perceived benefits of uniting clearly outweighed the potential costs, leading to not just the formation of an opposition pre-electoral coalition, but the attainment of the game through electoral victory.

As stated earlier, after Ivanishvili's defection in 2011, he set forth to build an opposition political movement with the intention to run as a candidate himself, and to use his significant net worth to finance this operation. Shortly after Ivanishvili made these intentions public, President Saakashvili and his regime began to create problems for Ivanishvili related to his multiple citizenships. As of October 2011, Ivanishvili maintained French and Russian citizenships in addition to his Georgian citizenship. While he was born in the Georgian Soviet Socialist Republic, he resided in Moscow at the time of the fall of the Soviet Union, leaving Ivanishvili with Russian citizenship. His Georgian citizenship was personally approved by President Saakashvili in 2004 when Ivanishvili was still supportive of his regime. Later, in 2010, he was granted French citizenship after his marriage to a French citizen. He made clear that he intended to renounce both the French and Russian citizenships by the end of the year in a statement made on October 7, 2011. Yet three days later, President Saakashvili personally revoked the Georgian citizenships of both Ivanishvili and his wife in an executive decree. Ivanishvili did indeed renounce his Russian citizenship in December but said he would maintain his French citizenship until his Georgian citizenship was restored.[3] He then applied for Georgian citizenship through naturalization, but his application was refused in April of 2012.[4] Members of pro-regime political parties sought to create a way to allow Ivanishvili to run for parliament through a new constitutional amendment even without Georgian citizenship. However, Ivanishvili himself criticized the law for being a cynical way to prevent him from regaining Georgian citizenship.[5]

Despite these events, Ivanishvili went forward with the creation of an opposition political organization that sought to challenge Saakashvili's pro-regime UNM Party. First, Ivanishvili formed a new public movement, the Georgian Dream-Democratic Georgia (GDDG), largely seen as the first step toward establishing a political party. He announced this new movement in December of 2011, amid ongoing challenges due to his dual citizenship with France and the loss of his Georgian citizenship. Despite these questions about Ivanishvili's citizenship, his ability to run for office, and his right to fund a political party, two other opposition parties demonstrated their public support early on. Both the Our Georgia-Free Democrats Party, of which Saakashvili defector Alasania is a member, and the Republican Party were present at Ivanishvili's announcement.[6] Furthermore, the Conservative Party and the Party of People joined the movement at its inception. Ivanishvili maintained early on that the presence of these party leaders signified an electoral and political union, but not a formal political merger; the different entities would remain separate.[7] The newly formed GDDG organization quickly worked to create alliances and formal connections. The National Forum Party officially announced its intention to join in February of 2012, citing the prospect of electoral victory as a key motivating factor in their decision.[8] Finally, the party Industry Will Save Georgia also joined the movement. This meant that the Georgian Dream movement now included six opposition parties that had campaigned individually in previous elections.

One of the possible short-term costs for opposition pre-election coalitions is their potential to create new logistical, political, or organizational struggles through the merger of previously separate political entities. Different wings of the coalition may disagree on policy directives or campaign strategies. This scenario could be especially likely when the most visible member, and presumed leader, is a newcomer to politics, as is the case with Bidzina Ivanishvili. Despite these circumstances, such discord was mostly absent in the 2012 parliamentary campaign. The leading party in the new coalition was the newly created Georgian Dream Party, introduced to the public on April 21, 2012. This event culminated the activities by the coalition over the previous few months with the opening of unified campaign offices throughout the country. The submission of candidates for the single mandate districts were announced throughout June and July, including candidates from the National Forum, the Republican Party, the Conservative Party, as well as the Georgian Dream-Democratic Georgia.[9]

From this, the overall program of the unified bloc focuses largely on three key issues: Georgia's foreign policy orientation, the improvement of social welfare, and the development of Georgia's political system toward democracy. Georgia's relationship with Russia was the largest component of the GDDG's foreign policy positions. In particular, the 2008 war with Russia continued to linger in Georgian politics. It had consequences for Saakashvili, as it has been linked to at least some of the previously mentioned defections from his regime in late 2008. Ivanishvili in particular emphasized his own disapproval of how the conflict was handled, stating in his first appearance with the press that Georgia started the war and behaved recklessly.[10] Ivanishvili later distanced himself from this position, but remained critical of how Saakashvili behaved during the war, and its effects on Georgia.[11] The six-day-long war also produced severe long-term economic effects by eliminating one of Georgia's biggest trading partners and cutting off diplomatic contacts with Russia. Thus Ivanishvili and the GD coalition emphasized renewing economic relations with Russia, while still maintaining a more pro-European political and security orientation.[12] The GD also promised voters that it would increase pensions and adjust the tax code.[13] At campaign events, Ivanishvili typically spoke very generally about social improvements to education and healthcare, as well as reducing unemployment in Georgia.[14] Yet, as is the case in many post-Soviet states, many of the GD's campaign events were focused less on policy positions than on distinguishing the party from the incumbent regime. In its founding statement, the GD asserted that Georgia was at a political crossroads between democracy and dictatorship, and that they were the only actors able to guarantee the advancement of democracy. Five of the twelve points established in the founding statement emphasized their commitment to democracy and their goal of advancing and protecting it once in office.[15] Ivanishvili continued to emphasize the pro-democracy positions of the coalition throughout the campaign, and he also warned of authoritarian behavior on the parts of the incumbent President Saakashvili and the United National Movement Party that supports him.[16] These attacks on Saakashvili only grew as the videos showing prisoner abuse were released less than two weeks before election day.[17]

As already discussed in chapter 3, the release of videos from a Tbilisi prison depicting the violent physical and sexual assault of prisoners in the final ten days before the election hurt the UNM. Protests emerged over the issue, demanding that it be addressed by Saakashvili and his administration. As a result, multiple prison officials were fired, and senior figures resigned in response to this scandal. Saakashvili also acknowledged the scandal in his speech to the United Nations General Assembly, taking responsibility for it and defending how his government had handled it.[18] Yet in a campaign speech just days earlier, he alleged that "Russian money" had been linked to the release of the video, and that it was a conspiracy to hurt his party's chances at the polls.[19] These allegations could be interpreted as implicit connections to the Georgian Dream coalition, due to Ivanishvili's past in Russia where he had earned much of his wealth.

Ultimately, the Georgian Dream coalition were successful in their bid for a parliamentary majority. They won 54% of the vote in the proportional electoral system, while the UNM won 40.7%. Moreover, the GD won 41 out of the 73 single, member districts in the country. Combined, this gave them a clear majority in the new parliament. As a result, Ivanishvili ultimately was elected prime minister by the parliament, a move that was only possible due to a constitutional amendment allowing non-Georgian citizens to be elected to public office if they had lived in the country for at least five years.

The formation of this opposition pre-election coalition illustrates many of the ways in which such groupings can counter an incumbent regime. First, this decision indeed created more mathematical opportunities for victory. Ivanishvili noted at one point the percentage of votes he hoped the GD to receive both from the proportional representation seats as well as from the single mandates. He pointed to their unified position as the sole genuine opposition to the UNM, and how this would be noticed at the polls. Also, opposition figure Nino Burjanadze, the leader of a party that did not join the GD, decided not to challenge the GD so as not to force voters to pick one opposition party over another.[20] Second, Ivanishvili's Georgian Dream coalition received considerable support early on from public opinion polls. Georgian political analysts argued that this suggested that the coalition was attracting some apathetic or disengaged voters, as well as some who normally would have supported the government but saw the GD as a more viable alternative.[21]

These steps at unification clearly benefitted the smaller parties by improving the chances that they would win representation in parliament. According to a late 2011 poll, less than 5% of respondents reported that they would vote for either the Our Georgia-Free Democrats Party as well as the Republican Party.[22] Since Georgia's parliament is elected through a mixed system of single-member districts and party-list proportional representation with a 5% threshold, this suggests that had these parties not joined Ivanishvili's movement, they would have been shut out of the parliament. Instead, they joined forces with Ivanishvili early on so as to improve their own political position in Georgia.

This pre-election coalition also illustrates the long-term benefits from electoral victory through this strategy. In the following year, the Georgian Dream candidate Giorgi Margvelashvili won the presidential election, which ensured that they were firmly in control of the government. In addition to gaining power and creating a loss for the incumbent regime, coalitions can also produce long-term benefits through restructuring the political institutions. The case of Georgia following the 2012 election provides us with many examples of this. First, the new administration made changes to the Election Code regarding the thresholds for victory in single-member districts, and redrew some district boundaries to address disparities in district magnitude.[23] Also, the new administration agreed to an Association Agreement with the European Union, which went into effect in 2016. More recently, the Georgian Parliament has been debating several constitutional changes to the electoral system, including parliaments elected entirely using proportional representation, the abolition of direct elections for the president, and, most surprisingly, the banning of opposition pre-election coalitions.[24] The last of these would significantly alter the calculus of opposition parties in Georgia were they unable to unite and form the very type of organization that was crucial to the success of the Georgian Dream in 2012.

Armenia's 2012 Election

Similar to the 2012 election in Georgia, Armenia's 2012 election was also a legislative contest in a state with low incumbent dominance. However, the degree of competition was lower in this election than was observed in Georgia. There are a few other notable differences between the political dynamics in Armenia and Georgia. First, unlike Georgia, Armenia had not experienced a color revolution as of 2012. This term has generally come to mean an event where public demonstrations and protests erupted in response to an unfair election and ultimately succeeded in calling for a new election, in which an opposition party or candidate was victorious. Instead, up until this point, Armenia had had only one instance of a turnover in power between opposing political actors[25]; this occurred following the February 1998 coup and resignation of former president Levon Ter-Petrossian. The 1998 political crisis stemmed from the conflict with Azerbaijan over the territory of Nagorno-Karabakh, an issue that has remained unresolved since the collapse of the Soviet Union. Still, it represents a powerful issue and source of nationalist sentiment in Armenian politics. Since the events of 1998, a rival political network connected to subsequent presidents Robert Kocharian and Sergz Sargsyan remained in power until 2018. While both of these presidents have been officially politically independent, they have governed with the support of the Republican Party, and, at various times, the Law-Based State Party and the party Prosperous Armenia. The presence of this long-term political elite in Armenian politics has distinguished it from its neighbor Georgia. Yet a key difference between these two states is the degree of incumbent dominance, in which Armenia has far more in common with Georgia.

Despite the lack of change in Armenia, incumbent dominance has remained low since its independence. First, no president in Armenia has been reelected with over 70% of the vote. The 2012 parliamentary election was preceded by the 2008 presidential contest, which saw the succession in power from Kocharian to Sargsyan. In contrast to events in Azerbaijan, discussed in chapter 4, Kocharian made no effort to amend the constitution to allow him to run for a third term. Instead, he made clear that he planned to leave office at the end of the second term and designate a successor. In the 2008 election, Sargsyan ran against Ter-Petrossian, who sought to return to the position of president after his ouster; this despite the low levels of popularity and dwindling support for Ter-Petrossian among Armenians. Yet he intended to capitalize on his numerous connections throughout the state from his days as president by building a new political party that attracted some elite defections and by working to subvert the regime's own political machine. Ultimately, Ter-Petrossian lost the election to Sargsyan, who himself engaged in electoral manipulation. Sargsyan won 52.82% of the vote in the first round, enough to prevent the need for a run-off election, but still far below the 70% mark, while Ter-Petrossian secured 21.5%. Going even further back to the 2003 presidential election, Kocharian was reelected with 67% of the vote in the second round, after failing to cross the 50% threshold in the first round. According to this metric, incumbent dominance has been absent based on the incumbent's share of the vote in executive elections.

Second, and in contrast to Azerbaijan, Armenia does not rely on the export of oil or other natural resources. It is true that the export of natural resources as a percentage of its overall GDP has increased since Armenia's independence in 1991, from a low of 0.18% in 1998 to 5.22% in 2012. Nonetheless, these levels are far below the threshold of 30%, above which states are seen as reliant on natural resources and thus able to defy external pressure and reward elites through rent-sharing. Thus, like Georgia, Armenia's national economy is not dependent on the export of oil or other natural resources.

In this election, the degree of competitiveness was lower than in Georgia's 2012 election. According to the competitiveness index, Armenia's 2012 parliamentary election scored a one out of three. This score was due to general perceptions that the economic conditions in Armenia were poor in the year preceding the election. According to one survey conducted in October and November of 2011, Armenian respondents cited unemployment and poverty as the top two most frequently cited problems in the country.[26] However, there were no widespread perceptions that the economy was in crisis. The economy had begun to rebound after suffering a 14.5% decline in 2009, marking steady growth in 2010 and 2011.[27] Even so, Armenia's GDP per capita had not yet returned to its pre-2008 levels by 2012, suggesting that for the general population, the economic conditions were not optimal.[28] Finally, the incumbent Republican Party was publicly confident of victory in the May 6th contest, stating that they actually expected to increase the number of seats they held in parliament.[29] Indeed, during the election one of the main issues was not whether or not the Republican Party would win the most votes, but instead whether it would win an outright majority or simply a plurality.

The backdrop for the 2012 election was the protests and accusations of fraud following the 2008 presidential election. Former president turned opposition candidate Levon Ter-Petrossian immediately complained following the election that the contest was rigged and that widespread election fraud had prevented him from winning. He urged his supporters to take to the streets in protest and to demand that new elections be held. The day after the election, about 20,000 people gathered in a central square in the capital of Yerevan to denounce the election. Police responded with force and violence on March 1, 2008, seeking to break up the protests. Clashes between demonstrators and the police broke out, which ultimately left ten people dead and more than 100 injured. The OSCE and other international election monitors noted irregularities during the election, including many instances of pre-election incumbent manipulation. Nonetheless, they ultimately concluded that the contest did reflect the will of the people, and that there was not substantial evidence to support claims of massive election fraud and a stolen election. The events of 2008 marked an especially contentious period in Armenian politics, and have furthered suspicions among the opposition that the political process is rigged against them.

In this case, both incumbent dominance and the degree of competitiveness were low. Under conditions of low incumbent dominance, I expect opposition parties and actors to be more likely to form pre-election coalitions so as to improve their chances of winning the election. As the empirical results demonstrated, the degree of competitiveness does not hold a statistically significant relationship with opposition pre-electoral coalitions. Given that this is one main distinction between the Georgian and Armenian cases, we should see incumbent dominance and the type of the election being more important than the degree of competitiveness. This relationship is observed when examining Armenia's 2012 parliamentary election. While the degree of competition was lower, opposition actors nonetheless worked together to form a pre-election coalition. However, in contrast to Georgia's 2012 election, this coalition was not successful in Armenia; in other words, they did not achieve their goal of winning a majority of seats in Armenia's National Assembly.

The 2008 presidential election also revealed some further weaknesses in the incumbent regime in Armenia. Some previous members of the elite defected either prior to or following the 2008 election, a further indicator that incumbent dominance was low. The previous speaker of the parliament, Artur Baghdasarian, renounced his party, the Law-Based State Partys, for it's support for the regime in 2007, and ran for president in 2008. However, Baghdasarian ultimately returned to the regime elite after the election, accepting a cabinet position in Sargsyan's cabinet.[30] In a more permanent shift, Khachatur Sukiasian, an oligarch and former ally of Kocharian, publicly shifted his support to Ter-Petrossian during the 2008 electoral campaign. Finally, in 2009, the party Armenian Revolutionary Federation-Dashnaktsutyun, formerly an ally of the regime and a member of the governing coalition, cut its ties with the regime and went into the political opposition.

It was under these circumstances that the 2012 parliamentary elections occurred. Ter-Petrossian once again sought to challenge the regime and the political parties that supported it. To do this, he announced his intentions of competing alongside the opposition coalition, the Arnmenian National Congress (ANC), that he first established for his presidential run in 2008. The ANC was comprised of as many as 20 small opposition parties, none of which had representation in the current National Assembly. Ter-Petrossian first signaled his intention to take part in the election by organizing multiple demonstrations in early 2011 along with the ANC. These protests demanded that the regime hold snap elections, and that the elections be absent of fraud and manipulation, unlike their perceptions of the 2008 contest. Ter-Petrossian also advised the regime to take these issues seriously or risk provoking an Arab Spring–like backlash, due to the deteriorating economic conditions.[31] Of particular note were demonstrations held on March 1, 2011, three years after law enforcement violently broke up the post-election protests in 2008, utilizing the symbolism behind the date in disseminating their message.[32] These demonstrations emerged in the days and weeks following the public announcement by the three parties currently in power, the Republican Party of Armenia, Prosperous Armenia, and the Law-Based State Party, that they all agreed not to campaign against one another in the 2012 elections.[33] Ter-Petrossian and the ANC complained that such an alliance stifled competition and further reduced the legitimacy of the upcoming elections.

The ANC continued to press the regime on the need for new elections as well as other prominent concerns. One was the continued detention of political prisoners, individuals with connections to the ANC who had been arrested in the days and months following the 2008 presidential election. Ultimately, Sargsyan and his regime agreed to release these individuals, sending a public signal that they were making concessions to the ANC and Ter-Petrossian.[34]

Second, Ter-Petrossian and other ANC leaders pushed for permission to hold demonstrations in the main square, Liberty Square, in the capital, Yerevan. These concessions culminated in an up to that point unprecedented political dialogue between the ANC and the government. The two sides began meeting in July of 2011 in order to further address the areas of disagreement and bring calm to the political environment.[35] These talks proceeded for about a month and a half, producing six separate meetings, but ultimately collapsed in late August after new ANC protesters were arrested and not immediately released.[36]

As the election drew nearer, the incumbent regime's hold on power witnessed a public setback. The political party Prosperous Armenia (PA), which had previously agreed not to challenge or campaign against other pro-government parties and candidates, pulled out of this February 2011 agreement.[37] This was notable, as PA was the second largest party in the National Assembly at the time, and had been a loyal ally to both presidents Kocharian and Sargsyan since its formation in 2006. Instead, it announced that it had formed an agreement with another opposition party for the May 2012 election.[38] PA, led by businessman Gagik Tsaruukian, was increasingly seen as a tool for former president Kocharian to retain influence in Armenian politics, and this shift in allegiance signaled that Kocharian no longer supported Sargsyan or his regime.[39] Ter-Petrossian stated in the preceding months that his ANC coalition in principle was open to the idea of PA joining their pre-election coalition, and other members had made public overtures to PA, despite previous criticisms of the party's support for Sargsyan.[40] The political maneuvering by PA further suggests that Sargsyan's incumbent dominance was low and that this reality helped establish the conditions for the formation of opposition pre-election coalitions.

After almost a year of staging anti-regime protests, Ter-Petrossian officially announced the ANC's intention to compete in the May 2012 elections in January of the same year. At this point, the coalition was comprised of 18 parties, who would work together to produce a party list for the proportional representation seats, and would decide whether to run any candidates for the single-member district seats.[41] This opposition coalition, the Armenian National Congress, demonstrated very little ideological or policy commitments. The different parties and actors were mainly unified in their hostility toward Sargsyan and his regime, rather than along any clear shared ideology or policy programs. Yet this resembles the same characterization of the Georgian Dream in Georgia, where actors were generally committed to democracy and regime change, but avoided more specific policy proposals. They were also genuinely mixed in terms of their foreign policy orientation. On the one hand, they argued that they hoped for more pro-Western policies, but on the other hand, they sometimes criticized the West for not standing up to Armenia's regime and Sargsyan on human rights abuses. Ter-Petrosian remained one of the main voices and public representations for the ANC coalition, and continued to reiterate not just his displeasure with Sargsyan and his government, but also his perception that things were collapsing beneath him. In particular, he claimed Sargsyan was a "sinking ship" amid developments that the party Prosperous Armenia had pulled out of the pro-government coalition (RFE/RE 2012a).

Another example of Ter-Petrosian's influence on this campaign was the creation of a multi-party agreement on strategies to prevent voter fraud and manipulation. The ANC, along with the Armenian Revolutionary Federation-Dashnaktsutyun, the Zharangutiun Party, and even the newly critical PA, all signed a pledge committing themselves to a free and fair election. They established demands on the regime, including the publication of voter rolls. Doing so was believed to reduce the ability for the government to engage in electoral fraud. This opposition pre-election agreement was unprecedented in Armenian politics, and definitely relates to the previous experiences with electoral manipulation in Armenia. However, this grouping still experienced disagreements. Most notably, the leader of the Zharangutiun Party, Raffi Hovannisian, urged the other party leaders to explicitly ban practices of vote-buying and the provision of goods to communities during election campaigns. Yet the PA opposed this provision, which led Hovannisian to pull his party's support from the agreement.[42]

Additionally, during the election, the Armenian National Congress demonstrated many of the short-term challenges expected with the opposition pre-election coalition. In the months before the election, four parties displayed frustration with the list of candidates submitted. More specifically, the number of candidates selected from the different parties struck some party leaders as imbalanced and too connected to the preferences of Ter-Petrosian. As a result, these four parties pulled out of the coalition in March, two months before the vote.[43] In combination with the challenges experienced in the pre-election agreement on the integrity of the election, these incidents illustrate the short-term organizational and logistical difficulties that can accompany opposition pre-election coalitions.

Ultimately, Ter-Petrossian and the Armenian National Congress (ANC) were unsuccessful in their ambitions to win power. In the official results, the ANC won 7.1% of the vote in the proportional representation races, just exceeding the 5% minimum threshold for winning seats. Moreover, the newly defiant Prosperous Armenia Party (PA) also failed to win a majority of seats in the National Assembly; they came in second under the proportional representation system with 30% of the votes. They ultimately ended up with 36 out of 131 seats, far behind the clear winner, the Republican Party of Armenia (RPA), which secured 69 seats. While this did produce an increase in total seats for both of these parties, it also gave the RPA a complete majority in the National Assembly. This indicates the resilience of the regime even in the face of low dominance.

While the Armenian National Congress was ultimately unsuccessful in challenging the incumbent regime parties, the 2012 election did ultimately produce a new political reality. One illustration of this was the defection of the party Prosperous Armenia away from the pro-government coalition. A few weeks after the election, oligarch and head of the party Gagik Tsarukian announced officially that it would not continue its alliance with the Republican Party of Armenia and the Law-Based State Party. The Armenian National Congress even took some credit for this turn of events, saying in a statement, "Political developments in the country show that ANC's strategy that was adopted in October 2011 and aimed at eroding the political monopoly of Serzg Sargsyan's Republican Party...was an accurately calculated step that is contributing to the regime's political isolation" (RFE/RE 2012b)

The concessions granted by Sargsyan and his regime in response to the ANC's protests were also notable. One of the motivations behind opposition pre-election coalitions is to seek access to the political institutions so as to re-shape them; often this is under the assumption that pro-democracy opposition actors would institute democratic reforms. While these sets of circumstances did not come to pass in Armenia, Sargsyan still made some minor (some would say cosmetic) changes due to pressure from Ter-Petrossian and the ANC; these included the freeing of political prisoners and greater legal rights for holding demonstrations. Moreover, it may have been the incumbent regime's relative weakness that prompted Sargsyan to make these concessions. As early as May of 2011, there were public indications that the Prosperous Armenia Party, PA, might be less reliable as supporters, due to former president Kocharian's renewed interest in Armenian politics and his ties to the party.[44] The future trajectory of the ANC, PA, and RPA will all be discussed in far greater detail in chapter 6, which includes a case study of Armenia's 2013 presidential election.

Negative Case: Russia's 2011 Parliamentary Election

While the previous two case studies have examined elections that featured opposition pre-election coalitions, the majority of elections across the FSU are void of such groupings. This book argues and seeks to demonstrate that certain electoral conditions may make the opposition more likely to opt for this strategy. By examining an election without such a bloc, we can see further evidence for the importance of certain electoral factors. In particular, the common factor across the 2012 parliamentary elections in Georgia and Armenia was the low degree of incumbent dominance. To further illustrate the importance of this factor, this chapter introduces a third and final case study on Russia's 2011 parliamentary election. This election features greater incumbent dominance, but also similar competitiveness to that of Armenia's 2012 contest. Despite this, the Russian case did not witness the formation of an opposition pre-election coalition.

The 2011 parliamentary election in Russia took place while still under the presidency of Dmitri Medvedev, as discussed in chapter 4. As president, he oversaw multiple constitutional changes to both the term lengths of members of parliament as well as to the president. The 2011 contest was slated to be the first election to take place under these new rules, and thus would be electing MPs to five-year terms instead of the previous four-year terms. Like previous Russian parliamentary elections, it was scheduled to take place just months before the presidential election, which in the past has given the parliamentary contest the status of political bellwether on the president's support in the state. These elections also took place in the wake of the announcement by then prime minister Vladimir Putin that he and Medvedev had agreed to essentially switch places in terms of their political roles. Putin announced that he intended to run for a non-consecutive third term in 2012, that Medvedev supported him in this decision, that Medvedev had his support to become prime minister, and, crucially, that this had been their plan all along (Clark 2013).

While both Putin and Medvedev enjoyed high approval ratings prior to the 2011 election, the same was not entirely true for the pro-presidential party United Russia. Its approval rating fell to about 40% with just over two months before the December 2011 election.[45] Medvedev himself was tasked with campaigning for United Russia, and for helping to reenergize voters to support the party.[46] As discussed in chapter 4, United Russia currently enjoyed a supermajority in the State Duma, the lower house of Russia's parliament, with 315 out of 450 seats. As one of four parties serving, it did not even need to count on votes from the other three to pass legislation, and typically faced muted opposition from those parties. The other three parties, the Communist Party of the Russian Federation (CPRF), the Liberal Democratic Party (LDPR), and A Just Russia (JR), have all been considered part of the "systemic" opposition due to their ability to win seats in the increasingly dominant political system. Therefore, even though United Russia had seen its favorability fall, most agreed that it would still win an outright majority in the Duma, even if it lost some of its seats.[47]

The degree of competition for this election was considered moderate. Based on the previous competitiveness, the prediction would be for this election to be more of the same and feature an enormous margin of victory between United Russia and the second-place finisher. In 2007, the difference in the voter results saw United Russia win 64.3 % of the vote, while the CPRF came in second with 11.6%; this 52.7-point difference is quite massive and suggested a very uncompetitive election. However, the index of perceived competitiveness provides a more blurred image. When Medvedev accepted his nomination as the head of the party's list of candidates at the United Russia National Congress held in September of 2011, he said that he was confident the party would win the election. This is an indicator that the incumbent is confident of victory, which usually points to a lower degree of perceived competitiveness. And yet, there was still a growing sense of concern over the party's fate in the December elections. While election watchers and political observers felt confident that United Russia would continue to hold the most seats in the Duma, there was a widespread sense that it was bound to lose control of at least some of them.[48] A Russian newspaper article published the week before the election even made clear the methods available to United Russia for manipulating the election in their favor, but noted that they could probably only add about 5% to the party's overall vote total. This emphasized that the party was prepared to even falsify the results, but could only do so to a certain degree.[49] This sense of impending losses was also visible in Putin's decision to run for president as a United Russia candidate. At the party's second National Congress held on November 27, 2011, just a week before the parliamentary vote, United Russia formally nominated Putin to be its candidate for the 2012 presidential elections; Putin appeared at the Congress and accepted their nomination. This marked the first, and currently only, time that Putin would run for the presidency as a party nominee rather than as an independent. This move further indicated that the party, and Putin, knew it was facing reduced support for its upcoming parliamentary elections.[50] The official nomination of a leading presidential candidate (and former president) may not seem significant in a democratic state with a stable and developed political party system, but in Russia, parties have always been subordinate to the president. That Putin and the party felt this move was necessary suggests that they were preemptively engaging in damage control for the upcoming elections. The party's leader may have been confident in winning the most seats, but the party, and most observers, also sensed that it would lose seats and end up with a simple majority, rather than a supermajority.

Additionally, Russia's economy had suffered under the 2008–2009 Global Financial Crisis, and these issues were far from resolved as the 2011 election approached. Russia's economy contracted by over 7% in 2009, but posted 4.5% growth in 2010. Similarly, its GDP per capita had fallen, and had not yet returned to its pre-2009 levels; it stood at $10,674 in 2010, which was still the highest of the ten FSU states included in this book.[51] Public opinion provides support for this reality. When asked what the biggest problems were facing Russians just three months before the 2011 election, economic concerns, specifically rising prices, unemployment, and the ongoing economic crisis were identified as the top three. Moreover, 66% were dissatisfied with the economic and political course of the country.[52] This clearly meets the criteria for perceptions of the economy being negative within the index of perceived competitiveness. However, the economy was no longer considered to be in full crisis, as things had turned around since 2009. Given these indicators, officially this election receives a 1 out of 3 on perceived competitiveness, with the asterisk that the incumbent party made clear they expected vote losses in the upcoming election. This leaves the election with a moderate degree of competitiveness.

Incumbent dominance in this election was also moderate. Medvedev was elected in 2008 with 71.25% of the vote, and as the incumbent-picked successor to Putin, this provides us with one of the two indicators of dominance. This was the second election in Russia to report such a pronounced victory, and it signals that the already powerful president had the ability to widely shape the political institutions of the state. However, natural resource reliance had continued to decrease in Russia since 2007, as noted in chapter 4. In 2010, energy exports comprised just 21.09% of Russia's overall GDP, which falls below the one-third minimum threshold used in this index. Nonetheless, this leaves the 2011 election with a higher degree of incumbent dominance than what was observed in Georgia and Armenia's 2012 parliamentary contests.

Under these conditions, incumbent dominance may overpower any added elements of uncertainty present with the moderate degree of competition. Once a dominant regime is in place, it can stifle opposition, development and reduce the space for organizing in the state. This means that the formation of an opposition coalition would face additional hurdles either in its inception or practice, and that these hurdles are the result of increased incumbent dominance. Such a strategy would be unlikely due to changes made in political institutions that can limit such opportunities, through the lack of prominent elite defectors, through further marginalization of the opposition and through inter-opposition disagreements about policies or strategies. All four of these realities were present in the lead-up to Russia's 2011 parliamentary election, which ultimately did not feature an opposition pre-election coalition.

First, the regime made clear that it was fully in control of the political institutions. One example were the changes to the electoral system for the 2007 and 2011 parliamentary elections. Until 2003, the Russian State Duma was elected using a mixed system that combined single-member districts with a closed list proportional representation system and 5% minimum threshold.

Under these rules, opposition parties were able to win at least some seats, usually in particular districts. The parliament elected in 2003 saw only four parties surpass the 5% PR threshold, but four additional parties won SMD seats, as well as 67 independent candidates (Clark 2005). However, since 2005 the Duma converted all of its 450 seats into the PR system, with a raised electoral threshold of 7%. This new system was first implemented in the 2007 parliamentary election, which resulted in just four political parties winning seats (White 2009). The elimination of the single-member districts clearly reduced the ability for opposition parties to win seats.

The regime exerted additional influence through the registration process for the election. In the months leading up to the 2011 election, multiple opposition parties were prevented from registering any candidates. One of these was the Party of People's Freedom (PARNAS), founded in 2010 by opposition figures, including former regime insiders Mikhail Kasyanov and Boris Nemstov.[53] Kasyanov in particular was previously denied registration for Russia's 2008 election, and so has been essentially blocked from electoral competition since his dismissal from the position of prime minister in 2004. This was part of a larger trend, as explained by the OSCE, which wrote that, "[s]ince the 2007 parliamentary elections several parties have been denied registration by the Ministry of Justice" due to various reasons including, "mistakes and inaccuracies in the documentation submitted, ineligible party members, or insufficient membership or regional representation" (OSCE 2012: 4)

Second, Russia has not seen the prominent elite defections or turnover in power that Georgia or Armenia witnessed. Those that have previously been in power can hold greater credibility amongst the electorate. Moreover, elite defections can signal to voters that the regime is untenable and harmed by internal dissent. Elite defectors can also prove successful organizers of opposition movements and coalitions due to their perceived legitimacy of having been in government and of leaving voluntarily. It is true that some of Russia's most prominent opposition figures have come from the regime, but through entirely different circumstances. Instead of elite defections, Russia has witnessed prominent elite dismissals, which seems to have had negative effects on opposition strength and organization. The aforementioned Kasyanov provides a key example of this, as he was dismissed as prime minister in the weeks before Putin sought reelection in 2004 (Shevtsova 2005). Another example came in the months leading up to the December 2011 election. Former Kremlin political strategist Gleb Pavlovsky was dismissed after serving in the Putin and Medvedev administrations for over ten years.[54] In both of these cases, Kasyanov and Pavlovsky have become outspoken critics of Putin, Medvedev, and their administrations, but this hasn't given them widespread public support or legitimacy. One of the few exceptions to the dearth of defections did occur in the lead-up to the 2011 election. The former finance minister Alexei Kudrin announced his resignation, reportedly due to disagreements between himself and then president Medvedev. However, Kudrin did not completely leave the inner circle, as he remained on the National Banking Council and the Council on Financial Markets, and continued to be seen as a strong ally of Putin.[55] Elite cohesion therefore serves as a further by-product of incumbent dominance in the state, which hinders opposition strength or cooperation.

Third, the opposition in Russia had been successfully marginalized since Putin was first elected to the presidency in 2000. As has been observed in other non-democratic regimes, the opposition in Russia has been split between those that do not threaten or seek to change the broader political system, the systemic opposition, and those that fight against the system itself, the non-systemic opposition (Linz 1973; Gel'man 2015). The systemic opposition are often considered semi-complicit, or token opposition parties, in the electoral authoritarian regimes due to the presumed concessions or limitations faced by those that are allowed to participate. This has driven a schism through Russia's opposition, and fosters inter-party hostility, which makes coalitions unlikely. The systemic opposition typically includes all parties with seats in the Duma, including the Communist Party of the Russian Federation, the Liberal Democratic Party, and A Just Russia. The first two present such radically different policy prescriptions and have been led by two long-time party insiders, Gennady Zyuganov and Vladimir Zhirinovsky, respectively, that cooperation between the two has been unthinkable. A Just Russia was created prior to the 2007 elections largely as a pro-Kremlin, left-leaning party that could actually attract voters away from the Communists (March 2009). This reduced the likelihood of any cooperation between the CPRF and A Just Russia.

Yabloko is one party that arguably straddles this systemic/non-systemic dichotomy. A liberal, pro-Western party, Yabloko is typically allowed to compete in elections but has fallen short of the 7% threshold in the proportional representation system. Yet it also vocally criticizes the regime. The leader of Yabloko, Grigory Yavlinksy, has challenged the characterization that the party is systemic, but he did not deny the state of the disunity among Russia's opposition. Prior to the 2011 elections, he made it clear that he and Yabloko followed a different strategy than the other opposition actors, systemic or not, and that he saw no chance of that changing.[56] This seemed to preclude the potential for a coalition with other similarlymsuited parties such as the Party of People's Freedom in the 2011 election.

Even setting aside the systemic/non-systemic distinction, Russia's opposition has been described as hopelessly divided on the issue of working together and following a coherent strategy. Both systemic and non-systemic parties have been burdened by strong leading personalities that have tended to clash with one another, and have made cooperation too difficult. This can be seen in earlier failed efforts at uniting forces into a coalition. For example, Boris Nemtsov, as the leader of the former liberal party Union of Right Forces, reportedly sought out a coalition with Yabloko for the 2003 parliamentary elections. He attributed this failure to Yavlinsky's preference for independence, while Sakwa (2005) argued that the two parties also differed on several key policy issues. In another attempt, prior to the 2008 presidential campaign, Mikhail Kasyanov briefly allied with the opposition movement Other Russia, but then publicly left after they failed to agree on submitting a single candidate.[57] These previous attempts have left Russia's opposition severely fragmented and showing little interest in a political alliance for the 2011 election.

Taken together, these three factors help explain why incumbent dominance in Russia worked against the strategy of an opposition pre-election coalition. However, the biggest takeaway from the 2011 elections was not the lack of a coalition, but the massive post-election protests that emerged due to widespread perceptions of fraud and falsification at the ballot box and in the tabulation process. These protests ultimately marked the largest such demonstrations since Russia's independence from the Soviet Union in 1991. What's more, these protests were seen to represent a broad swath of Russia's political spectrum, including both systemic and non-systemic opposition groups including the pro-Western liberals, the more pro-regime nationalists and the Communists (Greene 2014). The general demand of the protests was for new elections to be held. While they ultimately failed on this, the protests did lead to changes to the electoral system, including the reintroduction of a mixed electoral system where half the seats are filled using proportional representation while the other half come from single-member districts. Additionally, the minimal threshold for seats was reduced from 7% to 5%. Yet despite this, the first election with these new rules in place, the 2016 parliamentary election, did not yield any substantial inroads for any of the regime's biggest opponents and critics. Ultimately, much of the legacy of these protests eventually evaporated. Gel'man (2015: 181) notes that "[i]t would not be too much of an exaggeration to state that the Russian opposition in the period of the 2011–2012 mass protests became a victim of its own success. It was poorly prepared to solve its new tasks, both organizationally and strategically." A large part of this was due to its inability to coalesce around the same long-term vision for greater success.

"[S]ome opposition leaders attempted to bargain with the Kremlin . . . but these attempts were premature: the scope and duration of mass protest mobilization in late 2011 were insufficient, and the Kremlin felt strong enough to reject any proposals for roundtable talks a la 1989 in Poland. Not only had elite defection from the regime's side been avoided, but even system opposition refused to cooperate with protesters." (Gel'man 2015: 181)

The aftermath of the 2011 election, in which United Russia could only claim to have won 49% of the vote, provided an opportunity for opposition cohesion, but many of the forces discussed earlier worked against those efforts.

What's more, the events in Ukraine in 2014 have in many ways further marginalized the political opposition in Russia. The only systemic political party that was at least nominally critical of the Putin regime on some occasions was the Communist Party of the Russian Federation. They were more willing to vote against the pro-regime parties in parliament and have always received the second most votes in presidential elections; indeed, they were the only bloc that opposed and voted against the constitutional changes on term limits made in December of 2008 (Clark 2012). Yet after the annexation of Crimea and the ongoing Russian support for the separatists in Donetsk and Luhansk, the Communists have followed the regime and voiced their support for such actions. Their votes in parliament have also shifted, revealing a decidedly more pro-regime orientation.

The most notable exception to the further deterioration of any opposition to the regime with representation or public support is Alexei Navalny. A former anti-corruption blogger and leading force behind the December 2011 protests, he has since transitioned into politics and maintained a very public anti-regime position. Navalny challenged the incumbent mayor of Moscow in the 2013 election as a candidate submitted by Kasyanov and Nemtsov's Party of People's Freedom. While he did not receive enough votes to win, he still impressed political observers by winning over 25%. Since then, Navalny has remained active despite repeated attempts to hurt his credibility through lawsuits and criminal charges. His main message has focused on anti-corruption, and apart from this, he has remained decidedly non-ideological, and has since severed any connections to existing political parties.[58] This approach may actually make him more appealing to a public that holds negative ratings of all parties. This type of approach also holds a greater potential in challenging Putin, who himself has positioned himself as "above" politics (Lassila 2016). Most recently, Navalny announced that he sought to run for president in 2018; however, his candidacy was rejected by the Central Election Commission for what many perceive to be biased criminal convictions. Navalny currently heads the non-governmental organization Anti-Corruption Foundation (ACF) and in March of 2017, his organization released a well-produced forty-nine minute video on YouTube chronicling the suspected corruption of now Prime Minister Medvedev, calling for his resignation.[59] The video went viral, with millions of views and led to a new wave of anti-corruption protests across Russia. His ACF continued to release videos on other high-level regime elites throughout 2017. Yet as a national political figure, Navalny is far less well-known than other long-standing political figures. A poll taken in late March and early April of 2017 put his approval ratings at close to 10%.[60] However, a larger number, 38%, reported supporting the demonstrations inspired by Navalny and his anti-corruption message.[61] Nonetheless, the political establishment in Russia is still very consolidated around Putin, and Putin was unsurprisingly reelected in March of 2018 with 76.7% of the vote.

Summary of Case Studies

These three case studies have presented three elections with similar degrees of competitiveness, but differences on the degree of incumbent dominance. Table 5.3 displays these factors and results. While competition can seem encouraging to an opposition pre-election coalition, this was not borne out in either the quantitative evidence nor in the case studies. In electoral authoritarian regimes, incumbent dominance serves as the bigger influence on the state of the opposition, and thus shapes the conditions in which this strategy may be considered. While Russia's 2011 election matched Armenia's 2012 election in terms of perceived competitiveness, it did not observe the formation of a coalition. That case illustrates the ability for hegemonic regimes to use their dominance to curtail opposition organizational and political space.

DISCUSSION

This chapter has considered the strategic decision making among opposition actors to form a pre-election coalition. The empirical estimation demonstrated that such formations are indeed tied to the conditions of elections in electoral authoritarian states. Specifically, the formation of coalitions is positively related with low levels of incumbent dominance and with legislative elections; however, this means that the degree of competition has no statistically significant relationship with the formation of a pre-electoral bloc. Furthermore, the empirical evidence revealed that the type of electoral system was not associated with an opposition pre-election coalition, contrary to what is typically seen in democratic elections. Instead, coalitions are likely to form in both competitive and uncompetitive elections, so long as incumbent dominance is low, or the election is for the legislature. This echoes the findings of Gandhi and Reuter (2013), who found that coalitions were negatively related to the number of seats held by the ruling party as well as to the age of a dominant

Table 5.3. Summary of Opposition Coalition Case Study Comparisons

Indicators	Georgia's 2012 Election	Armenia's 2012 Election	Russia's 2011 Election
Type	Parliamentary	Parliamentary	Parliamentary
Perceived Competitiveness	2 out of 3	1 out of 3	1 out of 3
Incumbent Dominance	0 out of 2	0 out of 2	1 out of 2
Opposition Coalition?	Yes	Yes	No

political party. The three case study illustrations further demonstrated this, with two examples of opposition coalitions in elections with low incumbent dominance (Georgia 2012 and Armenia 2012), but with no coalition in a similarly situated election with greater incumbent dominance (Russia 2011).

Second, this chapter reveals the trade-off between short-term and long-term benefits and costs for opposition actors. While both the level of the electoral contest and the level of the political institutions yield benefits for opposition actors upon victory, the costs are far more significant in the long term. Opposition actors can clearly benefit by achieving electoral victory through the decision to unify, and they can also benefit through changes and reforms made to the political institutions once in power. However, forming a pre-election coalition can produce costs, no matter the outcome of the election. If victorious, then the newly established union can lead to more profound disagreements over policy and political decision making. But if unsuccessful, then electoral defeat can be especially demoralizing; if the opposition could not unseat the incumbent regime through unification, then it highlights just how enduring the incumbent regime is. Georgia's 2012 election demonstrates the best-case scenario for opposition pre-election coalitions: the newly connected grouping won the most votes and then also proceeded to reshape the political institutions. They also have rarely suffered, at least publicly, from in-fighting and disagreements among the actors. Yet Armenia's 2012 election instead illustrates all the potential costs to opposition actors. The Armenian National Congress endured internal frustrations and challenges during the campaign, with some parties leaving the movement before any voting took place. Moreover, the coalition led by Levon Ter-Petrosian has suffered further marginalization after this defeat, including his eventual exit from Armenian politics altogether.

Yet this chapter further suggests that opposition pre-election coalitions can yield results even if unsuccessful. In Armenia, Ter-Petrosian and the ANC managed to produce concessions from the incumbent regime well before the election took place. The success of their protests in 2011 and the mere threat of their participation in the election ultimately seemed to convince President Sargsyan that they deserved to be taken seriously. This has profound implications for opposition actors in electoral authoritarian states as well as for democracy promoters and civil society activists. The possibility of concessions from the incumbent regime may in and of itself represent a new motivation for the formation of pre-election opposition coalitions. Of course this chapter has highlighted legislative elections that also experienced low incumbent dominance, so either or both of these factors may be especially powerful for this outcome. This was not a relationship that was explicitly examined in this chapter, but the experience in Armenia may be suggestive of a broader pattern.

The overall takeaway from this analysis is that opposition pre-election coalitions are not panacea for politics in electoral authoritarian regimes. Opposition actors consider numerous factors in determining their electoral strategies, and therefore exercise caution before embarking on the formation of a coalition. Moreover, coalitions are not without their own complications and require a mutual commitment from all actors to unite and cooperate effectively. Opposition actors may be better positioned to overlook these challenges when the electoral conditions are right, but they still remain ongoing hurdles. These complications are more likely to grow and multiply as incumbent dominance swells, which can have adverse effects on opposition unity into the long term. Ultimately, opposition actors behave strategically even in the face of unfair elections, and consider the full gravity of forming coalitions for both the short and long term.

NOTES

1. Additional models that omitted incumbent dominance, perceived competitiveness, and previous competitiveness did not produce substantially different results.

2. Ia Antadze, "Next in Line? Saakashvili's Possible Successors as Georgian President," *RFE/RL*, September 12, 2008.

3. "Ivanishvili Revokes His Russian Citizenship," *Civil Georgia*, December 26, 2011.

4. "Ivanishvili Refused in Citizenship through Naturalization," *Civil Georgia*, April 4, 2012.

5. "Ivanishvili Hopes Constitutional Amendment, Related to Him, Will Be Dropped," *Civil Georgia*, April 11, 2012.

6. "Ivanishvili Launches Public Movement," *Civil Georgia*, December 11, 2011.

7. "Ivanishvili Speaks of His Planned Political Party," *Civil Georgia*, November 7, 2011.

8. "National Forum Joins Ivanishvili's Coalition," *Civil Georgia*, February 6, 2012.

9. "Ivanishvili Starts Naming Majoritarian MP Candidates," *Civil Georgia*, June 10, 2012; "Ivanishvili Names Majoritarian MP Candidates in Kvemo Kartli," *Civil Georgia*, July 9, 2012; "Ivanishvili Names 17 More Majoritarian MP Candidates," *Civil Georgia*, July 12, 2012.

10. "Ivanishvili's First-Ever Press Conference," *Civil Georgia*, November 1, 2011.

11. "Ivanishvili's Campaign Rally in Gori," *Civil Georgia*, July 15, 2012.

12. "Ivanishvili on NATO, Russia," *Civil Georgia*, February 7, 2012.

13. "Ivanishvili-Led Coalition Vows to Increase Pensions," *Civil Georgia*, May 23, 2012.

14. "Ivanishvili Launches Campaign with Large Rally," *Civil Georgia*, May 27, 2012.

15. "Founding Declaration of the Political Coalition Georgian Dream," *Civil Georgia*, February 21, 2012.

16. "Ivanishvili Warns Supporters Over Majoritarian Contest," *Civil Georgia*, August 26, 2012.

17. "Ivanishvili Holds Huge campaign Rally," *Civil Georgia*, September 29, 2012.

18. "Elections, Russia and Prison Scandal in Saakashvili's UN Speech," *Civil Georgia*; September 26, 2012.

19. "Saakashvili: Those Who Want to Bring in 'Putinist Rules' Will Be Disappointed," *Civil Georgia*, September 23, 2012.

20. "Ivanishvili Meets Burjanadze," *Civil Georgia*, August 19, 2012; "Ivanishvili Speaks of Worst, Best and Average Case Scenarios for His Coalition," *Civil Georgia*, August 3, 2012.

21. "Poll Shows Two-Way Parliamentary Race," *Civil Georgia*, December 8, 2011.

22. "Poll Shows Two-Way Parliamentary Race," *Civil Georgia*, December 8, 2011.

23. "Georgia Parliamentary Elections, 8 and 30 October 2016" *OSCE/ODHIR Election Observation Mission Final Report*. Warsaw 3 February 2017.

24. Liz Fuller, "President, Speaker Trade Barbs Over Georgia's Draft Constitutional Changes," *Radio Free Europe/Radio Liberty*; June 15, 2017.

25. The more recent events in Armenia since April of 2018 will be discussed in the section on long term effects in Chapter 6.

26. Respondents were asked to state what they saw as the greatest problem facing Armenia. Of the response, 44% stated unemployment, making this the most frequent response. The second more frequent response was poverty, listed by 22% of the respondents. (Caucasus Barometer 2011, Armenia.)

27. According to the World Bank World Development Indicators, GDP % growth in Armenia was 2.2% and 4.7% in 2010 and 2011, respectively.

28. According the World Bank World Development Indicators, Armenia's GDP per capita in 2011 was $3266; in 2008, it was recorded at $3547.

29. Emil Danielyan. "Armenian Government and Parties Gear Up for Parliamentary Race," *Eurasia Daily Monitor*: Volume 8, Issue 216.

30. Since 2014, Baghdasarian has again abandoned the incumbent regime and joined forces with another small opposition party.

31. "Ter-Petrossian Insists on Snap Polls, Warns of Anti-Government Unrest," *Radio Free Europe/Radio Liberty*. February 19, 2011.

32. "Armenia Stuck Between Stagnation and 'Mubarakization'," *Radio Free Europe/Radio Liberty*. March, 2, 2011.

33. Ibid

34. Anush Martirosian, Karine Simonyan, and Satenik Vantsian. "Prominent Armenian Opposition Figures Are Released Under Amnest," *Radio Free Europe/Radio Liberty*, May 27, 2011.

35. "Armenian Government, Opposition Preparing for Landmark Talks," *Radio Free Europe/Radio Liberty*, July 12, 2011.

36. "Armenian Opposition Suspends Dialogue with Leadership," *Radio Free Europe/Radio Liberty*, August 26, 2011.

37. "Armenian Political Parties Wary of Parliamentary Election Alliances," *Radio Free Europe/Radio Liberty*, January 31, 2012.

38. "Armenian Election Alignments Take Shape," *Radio Free Europe/Radio Liberty*, March 7, 2012.

39. Emil Danielyan, "Battle Lines Drawn in Armenian Parliamentary Race," *Eurasian Daily Monitor* 9 (54).

40. "Armenian Coalition Party Mum on Offer to Join Opposition," *Radio Free Europe/Radio Liberty,* November 29, 2011.

41. "Armenian Opposition Bloc Parties Unite For Parliamentary Elections," *Radio Free Europe/Radio Liberty*, January 27, 2012.

42. "Armenian Authorities, Opposition At Odds Over How to Prevent Vote-Rigging," *Radio Free Europe/Radio Liberty*, April 29, 2012.

43. "Armenian Election Alignments Take Shape," *Radio Free Europe/Radio Liberty*, March 7, 2012.

44. Emil Danielyan, "Armenian Government, Opposition Opt for Far-Reaching Dialogue," *Eurasia Daily Monitor* 8 (93).

45. Matthew Rojansky. "Putin's Return" *The Global Think Tank: Carnegie Endowment for International Peace.* Moscow: September 26, 2011.

46. Nikolay Petrov. "Dumping Dead Weight and Adding Medvedev." *The Moscow Times.* October 25, 2011.

47. Matthew Rojansky. "Putin's Return."

48. Nikolay Petrov. "Russian Elections: The Abandoned Script." *Open Democracy.* 19 October 2011; Matthew Rojansky. "Putin's Return"; Timothy Heritage "Putin's Party Set to Lose Ground in Russia." *Reuters.* December 1, 2011.

49. Анастасия Корня и Максим Гликин. "Как избирательная система помогает «Единой России» побеждать на выборах." Ведомости. 30 Ноября 2011.

50. Gleb Bryanski and Thomas Grove. "Putin launches Kremlin bid with swipe at opponents." *Reuters.* November 27, 2011.

51. Data from the World Bank World Development Indicators.

52. "Кто виноват, что нам плохо." Публикации в Прессе: Левада-Центр. 21.09.2011.

53. "Russian Opposition Party Denied Registration." *Radio Free Europe/Radio Liberty.* June 22, 2011.

54. Юлия Таратута. "Глебу Павловскому закрыли вход в Кремль." Ведомости 27 Апреля 2011.

55. "What's Ahead for Russia's Economy Now that Kudrin is Gone?" *Radio Free Europe/Radio Liberty.* October 5, 2011.

56. Brian Whitemore. "Grigory Yavlinksky: 'Change Is Only Possible if There Is an Alternative.'" *Radio Free Europe/Radio Liberty.* October 12, 2011.

57. "Russian opposition coalition divided." *New York Times*: July 3, 2007.

58. Andrey Pertsev. "Splits Force Russia's Opposition to Rethink." *Carnegie Moscow Center.* 13.05.2016.

59. "Он вам не Димон." March 2, 2017. https://www.youtube.com/watch?v=qrwlk7_GF9g.

60. "Рейтинг Навального вырос вдвое за месяц." *Republic.* April 6, 2017. https://republic.ru/posts/81580.

61. "Мартовские протестные акции одобряет 38% россиян." *Politsoviet Information Agency.* April 6, 2017.

Chapter Six

The Strategy Behind Electoral Boycotts

This chapter continues to devote its attention to opposition political actors. While chapter 5 examined a strategy that has been associated with electoral victories in non-democratic regimes, this chapter instead turns to a strategy in which defeat is not just unlikely, but predetermined. This chapter focuses on the decision of opposition actors to not participate in the election at all by boycotting the contest entirely. A boycott can be an understandable, if self-defeating, strategy in electoral authoritarian regimes. Not only is the political environment marked by the uneven and often unfair electoral field of competition dominated by incumbents, but the very nature of elections in such regimes can actually serve the function of maintaining and consolidating authoritarian rule, rather than offering an opportunity for turnover in power. Opposition actors therefore face the unappealing dilemma of participating in an unfair contest in which they may have little realistic chance of winning, or by sitting out the election altogether. Both strategies carry costs. By participating, the very involvement of opposition actors may be inadvertently providing legitimacy to the flawed election. And by boycotting, they are resigned to remain on the sidelines for the foreseeable future. Therefore, opposition actors within electoral authoritarian regimes face the dilemma of whether and under what circumstances they should participate at all, or whether they should abandon the electoral process altogether.

This chapter explores whether or in what ways the conditions of the election may influence which elections are boycotted, using the logic of nested games established in chapter 2. Since a boycott represents a strategy in which electoral victory is not an option, logically we must assume that opposition actors make this decision in hopes of more long-term benefits at the level of the political institutions. Given this, a boycott may be more likely when the election is already not attainable. Therefore, this chapter explores whether boycotts are associated with a low degree of competition, high incumbent dominance, or with executive elections. This is done with statistical estimations of boycotts that have taken place in post-Soviet electoral authoritarian regimes. Furthermore, this chapter also includes two illustrative case studies of elections where at least some opposition actors have boycotted the election, and examines what these cases tell us about this strategy. I present Armenia's 2013 presidential election, a continuation of the political events contained within chapter 5, and Belarus's 2012 parliamentary election as two cases of elections that were in some degree boycotted by certain opposition actors. This chapter also presents Belarus's 2010 presidential election as a negative case where a boycott did not occur.

ELECTION BOYCOTTS AS AN OPPOSITION STRATEGY

As previously noted in chapter 1, boycotts represent the most puzzling and counter-intuitive election strategy included in this book. Why would any political actors, who by definition are motivated by their desire to obtain and maintain political power, instead decide not to participate in the election at all? No matter which type of election is being considered, the lack of participation by at least some political actors ensures that the incumbent regime will remain in power. Moreover, a boycotting candidate or party typically goes one step further than merely refraining from participation: they usually also publicly discourage voters from turning out at the polls at all. So what motivates opposition actors to signal such an explicit and public rejection of the electoral process? The primary assumption is that boycotting opposition actors are so frustrated and dissatisfied with the political situation in the state that they have decided to focus more on long-term goals beyond the election rather than the short-term goal of winning political representation.

In the short term, victory in the election is not in question. This means that not only can electoral victory represent a potential benefit for the opposition, but it actually serves as the primary cost of this strategy. Instead, a boycott presents two potential short-term goals. First, opposition actors can seek to delegitimize an election that the incumbent is all but assured to win. By reducing the number of participants, it can signal to voters, to election monitors, and to the international community in general that the election could not possibly represent the genuine will of the people. The reduced number of viable alternatives may demotivate voters from participating as well. An election with low voter turnout, even if it produces a victory for the incumbent regime, may actually convince elites and outside actors that the incumbent regime has lost its perceived legitimacy. This does not directly benefit opposition actors themselves; instead it potentially harms the incumbent regime in the short term, which could be regarded as an indirect benefit for boycotting actors. The main incentive here is to emphasize through the missing opposition that the political system is inherently flawed and problematic. Ideally, this reality leaves a strong impression on voters and may serve as a catalyst for future action. Similarly, the ideal reaction to an enormously lop-sided win may produce strong denouncements from international election monitors or observers. If such actors view boycotted elections with skepticism or mistrust, it could potentially affect international relationships in the future. Yet even with these two scenarios, the emphasis is on potential long-term effects.

One additional alternative benefit that may be enjoyed by boycotting actors in the short term is the conservation of resources. The electoral playing field is already skewed during elections in electoral authoritarian states, leaving opposition, non-regime candidates and parties with an especially uphill path to representation and victory. Electoral manipulation can further exacerbate this situation, and may convince some opposition actors that the regime only wins due to fraud or malpractice (Beaulieu 2014). Opposition parties therefore need to spend more money or engage in more creative campaign efforts, often with the support of international civil society organizations, to be viable and competitive (Bunce and Wolchik 2011). By deciding to not participate in the election, opposition parties and actors can conserve limited resources. In this case, an election boycott can become a strategic decision to evaluate the circumstances of an election and decide if participation or protest makes better political sense.

Finally, an election boycott may serve as a preservationist strategy for opposition parties and candidates. By failing to participate openly in the contest, they may actually be sparing themselves some of the wrath of the regime by evading direct electoral competition. Ash (2015) notes that opposition candidates and actors in Belarus were often subject to the most extreme and concentrated regime repression *after* the election had taken place. He argues that victory is futile in most cases anyway, that opposition actors are not office-seeking actors in the first place, and that the subsequent post-election repression contributes to the further deterioration of any genuine or viable alternative to the regime. Extending this logic, a boycott may actually present the opposition with the opportunity to avoid such harsh treatment and potentially preserve their existing organization and resources. However, a boycott could also produce a short-term cost, as Ash (2015) reports that the primary motivation for participation is the receipt of outside funding and support. By staying out of the contest altogether, they would be forgoing such resources.

In the long term, boycotting opposition actors typically hope that this act of protest will alter the political environment in some way. This could happen in a few ways. First, some countries may realize that they depend on economic trade or support from developed, democratic states. This can give the West leverage over the state, encouraging them to fall in line with international norms and practices; democratic elections are increasingly viewed as one such norm. If an election is boycotted and produces an outsized victory for the incumbent regime, this could threaten further economic or political connections, since Western powers may punish the state for its deteriorating democratic institutions. Such circumstances may therefore make the incumbent regime less legitimate and more vulnerable, which may hasten their political exit. Eventually, this could create a new opening for the previous boycotters to participate and have a real shot of winning an election (Levitsky and Way 2010; Smith 2014).

Second, boycotted elections may depress voter turnout. Prospective voters may decide that there is no real need to show up at the polls since the incumbent candidate or party is guaranteed victory; this reaction applies to both voters that support the regime as well as those who are more sympathetic to opposition actors. Apathetic or uninterested voters would be especially unlikely to vote in elections where at least one candidate boycotts the election. Therefore, voter turnout is expected to be threatened by a boycott. In electoral authoritarian regimes, voter turnout is often an especially powerful priority for incumbent leaders. Elections often provide them with one of clearest tools for evaluating genuine voter support as well as determining policy preferences among the electorate (Little et al. 2015; Miler 2015). Regimes have been observed to alter policies or redirect certain priorities in response to changes in voter support. Yet if elections witness low voter turnout, incumbent regimes lose this opportunity for gathering information from voters. This means that, over time, the regime may fail to pick up on areas of discontent from the electorate and may not make adjustments to address weaknesses or threats to continued public support. In the long term, this could make the regime more vulnerable to opposition electoral challenges.

The previous two scenarios describe theoretical and ideal circumstances in response to a boycotted election, and likely suggest to opposition actors that a boycott can bring long-term benefits in the form of greater political access and viability. Unfortunately, research on these hypotheticals has provided mixed conclusions on the effectiveness of boycotts as democratic stimuli. In general, subsequent elections are not associated with greater democratic ratings or openness (Schedler 2009b). This could be because the effects of a boycott occur slowly and need more than one election cycle to be constructive. At the same time, boycotted elections probably have the greatest impact immediately following an election, as voters may be unlikely to remember an unfair contest more than a few years out from the event. This may especially be the case if opposition actors return to the political arena in the next election; they could even potentially undo the effects of the boycott by reengaging too quickly and convincing voters that the political situation is more open than previously thought.

Indeed, Smith (2014) has found that boycotted elections are associated with regime turnover and the collapse of an incumbent regime, both in the short term but especially in states that have witnessed multiple boycotts. This provides some support for the notion that a boycott may be most effective if the actors keep such a strategy in the electoral playbook, rather than returning to the status quo of participation that existed prior to a boycott. Clearly a long-term perspective is crucial in achieving political change from an opposition boycott. It is unclear whether such changes are due to reduced voter turnout or to international pressure from boycotted elections. In the case of the latter factor, Western political leverage is far less powerful in regions where China or Russia maintains significant influence (Levitsky and Way 2006). This has particular resonance within the former Soviet Union, where Russia often continues to exert its power within its perceived sphere of influence.

QUANTITATIVE EVIDENCE OF OPPOSITION BOYCOTTS

While opposition boycotts may have the potential to produce turnover in power in some regions, this particular strategy may be less effective within the former Soviet Union. This section examines the frequency of boycotts among post-Soviet electoral authoritarian regimes and whether their occurrence is related to electoral factors. Table 6.1 displays how many opposition boycotts have occurred and the circumstances of these elections. For this book, I include both minor and major opposition boycotts, but I do not include elections where the opposition simply threatened to boycott. Among the ten states of the FSU included in this study, 15 opposition boycotts have occurred between 1995 and 2016. Of these 15 observations, a slightly larger number have occurred during executive elections, although this figure is split between the two types of elections. Opposition boycotts are clearly more frequent in states with higher incumbent dominance; only one boycott occurred in a state with low dominance (Armenia's 2013 presidential election, which will be discussed in greater detail in this chapter). Finally, the frequency of boycotts declines as the degree of competitiveness increases in an election. Both of these latter frequencies suggest that the decision to boycott may be associated with either incumbent dominance or with competition in the election.

Table 6.1. Elections in which one or more opposition actor staged a boycott

	Low Incumbent Dominance	Medium Incumbent Dominance	High Incumbent Dominance
Low Competitiveness	2013 Presidential Election in Armenia	2004 Parliamentary Election in Belarus 2004 Presidential Election in Russia 2006 Presidential Election in Tajikistan 2008 Parliamentary Election in Belarus 2012 Parliamentary Election in Belarus 2013 Presidential Election in Tajikistan	1998 Presidential Election in Azerbaijan 1999 Presidential Election in Kazakhstan 2000 Parliamentary Election in Azerbaijan 2006 Parliamentary Election in Azerbaijan 2008 Presidential Election in Azerbaijan 2011 Presidential Election in Belarus 2011 Presidential Election in Kazakhstan
High Competitiveness		1995 Parliamentary Election in Azerbaijan	

Next, I turn to the statistical examinations of opposition boycotts. Table 6.2 presents the results of a cross-sectional time-series probit regression on elections that have included a major or minor opposition boycott.[1] In this estimation, both measures of competitiveness are negatively associated with the presence of an opposition boycott. As the index of perceived competiveness decreases, the odds of a boycott occurring appears to increase. Similarly, the larger the scale of previous competitiveness, the more likely at least one opposition actor is to boycott the election.[2] Boycotts are also negatively associated with the level of economic development in the state, as measured by GDP per capita. This suggests that as economic conditions deteriorate, the odds that one or more opposition actors will boycott an election increase.

Since Beaulieu (2014) argues that opposition boycotts may be influenced by previous cases of electoral manipulation, I include an additional model to test this relationship. This model includes two lagged variables of the types of instrumental and informational manipulation observed in the previous election; however, it loses ten observations due to the lack of previous manipulation figures for the first election in each state. This model finds that the index of perceived competitiveness continues to have a significant and negative relationship with opposition boycotts, which reinforces this finding. These results also find a significant and positive association between informational manipulation and opposition boycotts. As the types of informational manipulation increase in the previous election, so too do the odds that one or more members of the opposition will decide to boycott the following election. This follows Beaulieu's (2014) argument that boycotts may be in response to electoral manipulation. Since instrumental manipulation is not significant in this model while informational manipulation is, this also emphasizes the distinction between these different varieties of manipulation. Informational manipulation covers highly public actions that indirectly shape the election; its use is to consolidate regime power, rather than affect the election in the short term. This relationship suggests that the opposition is more likely stay out of elections that occur amid growing authoritarian consolidation, rather than short-term manipulation. This actually aligns with the argument that boycotts are a strategy focused on long-term goals rather than any short-term benefits that may come from participating in an unfair contest. In contrast, instrumental manipulation may signal that the elections are still in play but that authoritarian elements are also at work. Opposition actors thus may not regard this manipulation as a clear indicator for their future strategies. Finally, in this model with a reduced number of observations, boycotts are positively related to executive elections.

These models generally follow the theory proposed in this book. In particular, the estimates suggest that opposition actors are likely to be strategic

Table 6.2. Probit Regression of Electoral Factors and Opposition Boycotts

	Model 1	Model 2
Perceived Competitiveness	−3.495***	−3.178**
	(1.24)	(1.599)
Previous Competitiveness	−0.071**	−0.024
	(0.028)	(0.029)
Incumbent Dominance	−0.509	14.809
	(1.688)	(1084.021)
Executive Election	0.555	3.33*
	(0.691)	(1.967)
Previous Informational Manipulation	—	1.603*
		(0.942)
Previous Instrumental Manipulation	—	1.72
		(1.132)
Proportional Representation	−2.495	−7.714
	(2.178)	(6.649)
Mixed Electoral System	1.962	1.569
	(1.622)	(2.419)
GDP per capita, logged (lagged one year)	−15.061*	−8.513
	(9.128)	(6.686)
GDP % growth (lagged one year)	-0.025	−0.052
	(0.066)	(0.145)
Experience with Elections	0.597	0.059
	(0.514)	(0.351)
Rule of Law (lagged one year)	3.415	21.794
	(2.827)	(14.3)
Armenia	6.808	9.245
	(8380.005)	(1084.013)
Azerbaijan	10.714	−9.804
	(8380.006)	(1084.016)
Belarus	9.99	−2.125
	(8380.005	(4.014)
Georgia	−2.262	−15.06
	(12969)	(1460.682)
Kazakhstan	13.861	−10.964
	(8380.006)	(1084.017)
Kyrgyzstan	−9.255	14.68
	(12419.98)	(1073.168)
Moldova	−6.826	9.561
	(12115.79)	(1523.787)
Russia	14.451	(Dropped)
	(8380.006)	
Tajikistan	−0.838	(Dropped)
	(8380.006)	
Ukraine	omitted	omitted
Constant	48.547	27.291
	(8380.062)	(1084.353)
N (countries)	10	10
N (total)	88	78
Wald Chi 2	10.77	7.68

Standard Errors in Parentheses, p-value * <0.10, **<0.05, ***<0.01, ****<0.001

in their decision to boycott, and assess the competitiveness of the election in making this decision. The absence of a statistically significant relationship between incumbent dominance and opposition boycotts is surprising, given that the observed boycotts have almost all taken place in elections with medium or high incumbent dominance. This could point to the crucial, or almost necessary, role that incumbent dominance may play on boycotts, even if it is not a sufficient explanation. Overall, the data and estimations suggest that some elections are far more likely to be boycotted than others, and that opposition actors likely consider the trade-off between the perceived costs and benefits before opting out of the election entirely. Next I will examine two elections where boycotts occurred, examining how these cases follow the quantitative results, and what they suggest about the short-term and long-term benefits and costs of opposition boycotts.

OPPOSITION BOYCOTT CASE STUDY COMPARISONS

Armenia's 2013 Presidential Election

Armenia's 2013 presidential election occurred in the political aftermath of the 2012 parliamentary election, which was discussed in detail in chapter 5. The opposition coalition led by former president Levon Ter-Petrosian did not succeed in removing the loyal pro-regime parties from power; however, they did receive enough votes to win the minimum number of seats in the National Assembly. That election instead left the incumbent regime in a stronger position than before the 2013 election, as the pro-regime Republican Party of Armenia increased its vote share and the number of seats it held. Other than the entrance of the opposition coalition, the Armenian National Congress, the make-up of the parliament did not change significantly; it now contained six political parties and coalitions instead of five. After the 2012 election, the political party Prosperous Armenia further distanced itself from President Sargsyan and his regime, and refused to join the governing coalition. As explained in chapter 5, Prosperous Armenia was led by oligarch Gagik Tsarukian and was affiliated with former president and former ally of Sargsyan, Robert Kocharian. So while the regime maintained a majority in the National Assembly, the pro-presidential faction within parliament had diminished as a result of the defection of Prosperous Armenia.

Since parliamentary elections have historically been held one year before presidential elections, they have typically served as bellwethers for the president's position. The 2012 election suggested that President Sargsyan was in a favorable position for the 2013 presidential election, given that the most prominent pro-regime party increased its vote share. Yet despite this, incumbent dominance remained low in Armenia. Sargsyan was first elected in 2008, and while he was the regime-supported successor to Robert Kocharian, Sargsyan's electoral victory did not cross the 70% threshold. This marker of executive reelections has been used as one of the primary indicators of incumbent dominance and hegemonic authoritarian regimes, but it was absent from Armenia heading into the 2013 contest. Second, as stated in chapter 5, Armenia does not rely on the export of oil or natural resources. Such exports comprise a very minimal percentage of Armenia's total GDP, just under 4% in 2012 according to the World Bank. According to these indicators, incumbent dominance was low prior to the 2013 election. The theory proposed in this book argues that opposition actors would be more likely to boycott an election in which incumbent dominance was high. Indeed, this appeared to be the pattern according to the descriptive statistics presented in the previous section: only one boycotted election, Armenia's 2013 contest, took place under conditions of low incumbent dominance. The statistical estimations did not find a statistically significant relationship between a boycott and incumbent dominance, so this chapter includes this sole case for closer examination.

In this case, the degree of competitiveness was also fairly low. The previous margin of victory between the Republican Party and Prosperous Armenia, the two parties who came in first and second, respectively, in the 2012 parliamentary elections, was 24.5%. This figure demonstrates that the Republican Party won the plurality of votes quite decisively. The 2008 presidential election, the previous election of the same type, provides an even more substantial difference: 31.3% between Sargsyan and Ter-Petrosian, who came in second. Turning to the index of perceived competitiveness, the 2013 presidential election scores a 1 out of 3 on this scale. The incumbent, Sargsyan, was indeed confident that he would be reelected and said so during the campaign. While the economy was not in economic crisis, public perceptions of the general economic situation were negative. Armenia's GDP per capita had continued to rise in the years since its independence in 1991; in 2012, it was recorded at $7401, according to the World Bank. This put it behind its neighbors in the Caucasus, Georgia, and Azerbaijan. This figure also left Armenia ahead of just three other post-Soviet states: Moldova, Kyrgyzstan, and Tajikistan; every other state's GDP per capita exceeded Armenia's in 2012.[3] This is reflected in public opinion polls taken in Armenia in the year before the 2013 election. When asked to state the most important issue facing the country, 38.3% of the participants responded with unemployment. In the same survey, when asked to describe their family's current economic situation, only 10% considered their situation to be good or very good; the rest answered fair, poor, or very poor.[4] Ongoing economic strife in Armenia adds one dimension of uncertainty to the electoral environment. This leaves the degree of competitiveness to be medium-low, according to the index utilized in this book.

Armenia's 2012 election also featured electoral manipulation, setting the stage for the 2013 presidential contest. The quantitative results presented earlier found that informational manipulation, but not instrumental manipulation, was linked to an opposition boycott. Considering Armenia's 2012 election, two out of four types of informational manipulation were observed by international election monitors from the OSCE. First, they received many reports of state employees being encouraged to attend pro-regime rallies and being discouraged from attending any campaign rallies held by opposition candidates. Furthermore, public sector employees were reportedly urging their coworkers to vote for pro-regime candidates on government property and during business hours. Second, observers also noted the usage of state property for campaign purposes. They noted that public ambulances, local government transportation, and public schools all displayed pro-regime campaign posters and advertisements. These observers also noted one type of instrumental manipulation, the provision of financial goods to voters. Monitors were very concerned about widespread reports of vote-buying that was taking place in direct connections with the Republican Party of Armenia.[5]

To summarize so far, Armenia's 2013 presidential election took place under conditions of a low degree of competitiveness. This could provide a strategic opportunity for opposition actors to decide not to participate in the election at all and instead focus on more long-term goals. Indeed, the election did feature either a formal boycott or the decision not to participate by multiple opposition actors. First, former president Levon Ter-Petrosian, head of the opposition pre-electoral coalition that competed and won seven seats in 2012, announced that his Armenian National Congress (ANC) would not submit a candidate in 2013. This decision then transformed into a more explicit boycott, evidenced by his organization's public statements that told voters not to go to the polls at all. Second, the party Prosperous Armenia that had recently defected from the governing coalition, also decided not to field a candidate for the election, even though they had just come in at second place in the 2012 parliamentary elections. Two other opposition parties, the Armenian Revolutionary Federation-Dashnaktsutyun and the Free Democrats, both also declined to submit candidates; the former of these maintained representation in the National Assembly. The absence of candidates from these four political organizations left a weak slate of candidates to run against incumbent president Sargsyan; only one candidate, Raffi Hovannisian of the Heritage Party, came from an established political party that had representation in parliament.

Ter-Petrosian and his ANC coalition were in a mixed, but ultimately disadvantageous position in Armenian politics after the 2012 election. Amid this, Ter-Petrosian announced his decision not to run in December of 2012, less than two months before the February 18th election. Initially, he asserted that his decision was based primarily on his age; he was 68 at the time. Yet even with this non-political reasoning, he was already accusing the elections of being illegitimate, comparing Sargsyan's anticipated victory with those of Saddam Hussein.[6]

The opposition Armenian Revolutionary Federation held the same number of seats as the Armenian National Congress prior to the 2013 election. They initially voiced their support for a unified opposition candidate to compete against the incumbent president if the opposition had any hope of victory. Instead, they decided not to participate in the election, even earlier than Ter-Petrossian announced his decision. The Armenian Revolutionary Federation worried about the unfairness of upcoming election, citing the increasing voter fraud and vote buying that took place in Armenia's elections as reasons for their decision not to participate.[7]

At the time, Gagik Tsarukian was seen as the second most popular politician in Armenia after Sargsyan, and was also perceived to be the best positioned challenger to the incumbent president. After officially declining to re-enter the governing coalition after the 2012 election, Tsarukian and his Prosperous Armenia (PA) Party remained coy about their position in Armenia politics; they typically referred to themselves as "a constructive alternative" to Sargsyan, rather than an explicit opposition party (RFE/RE 2013). This veneer of uncertainty compounded in early December of 2012 when Tsarukian abruptly announced that he had no plans to run in the 2013 election, and further that the PA would not support any candidates. This announcement came after a private meeting between Tsarukian and Sargsyan, leading to speculation about whether the president had pressured Tsarukian to leave the race.[8] Tsarukian and the PA failed to provide an explicit reason for this decision; the party spokesperson stated that the party had different priorities other than contesting the post of president.[9] In January, a different PA figure, Ruben Ayvazyan, briefly announced plans to run for president and represent the party, but quickly abandoned these plans. After this, Tsarukian and the PA remained silent and did not endorse any candidates. While they did not explicitly tell their supporters to boycott the election, a December 2012 public opinion poll suggested that only about 10% of PA voters were confident that they would turn out for the 2013 election.[10]

The election proceeded with a very limited campaign environment. While the election officially contained eight candidates, it was in many ways characterized by protest and frustration with the election environment. In fact, of the eight registered candidates, two also openly criticized the process and urged their supporters to boycott the process altogether. One of these candidates, Andrias Ghukasyan, embarked upon a hunger strike during the campaign to protest what he saw as unfair electoral conditions. He had petitioned the Central Election Commission to deregister incumbent president Sargsyan due to the misuse of administrative resources; when this request was denied, Ghukasyan then announced his intention to stage a hunger strike for the duration of the campaign and promoted a general boycott. Ghukasyan also publicly voiced his desire that all other candidates drop out of the race so as to make blatantly clear that the incumbent president was the only one able to win the election.[11] Another registered candidate, Aram Harutyunyan, formally withdrew less than two weeks before the election, urging the other candidates to follow his lead and produce an explicitly illegitimate election. Additionally, every candidate, with the exception of Sargsyan, discussed at one point or another that the election was unfair and that the government was abusing its power during its campaign activities.[12] On January 31, candidate Paruyr Hayrikian was shot leaving his campaign office. He survived the shooting and subsequently did not ask that the election be postponed. This event heightened the tensions in the election even as the motive was officially unclear.[13] The visible lack of candidates from the major opposition and non-government parties was observed to be glaring; the subdued election atmosphere was reportedly highly affected by the actions of these parties. In particular, it may have reduced voter interest and emphasized the one-sided nature of the contest.[14]

Raffi Hovannisyan was the most active candidate during the election, aside from the incumbent Sargsyan. He regularly held meetings with supporters, and he visibly toured the country in the weeks leading up to the February 18th contest. His campaign style was observed to be a departure in Armenian politics, focusing mostly on grassroots-style personal meetings and one-on-one interactions with Armenians out on the street. As the election drew near, he stated confidently he would win while also emphasizing that the election was significantly marred by irregularities and incumbent manipulation. He did not urge voters to boycott, instead calling on Armenians to turn out in large numbers.[15] Electoral manipulation and fairness seemed to be the defining issues of the 2013 campaign; Hovannisyan regularly focused on instances of fraud and manipulation and considered these behaviors to be among the most significant facing Armenia. He alleged that "there are 100 types of Watergates here, and we must jointly expose those Watergates," making clear his distrust in the government actors and the incumbent president Sargsyan (Harutyunyan 2013). He also asserted that the election was a contest between good and evil, further illustrating the reliance on criticizing the status quo, rather than engaging with the issues.[16]

For his part, president Sargsyan conducted a relatively low-key campaign. He regularly held large rallies and emphasized how his reelection would continue his agenda of economic development and political stability.[17] He also demonstrated his continued confidence in his victory in especially blatant terms; while being interviewed by a journalist he noted that "the real question is whether he will hit 90, 80, 70 or 60 out of 100" in Shirak Marz, a region of Armenia (Stepanian 2013). This comment suggested that he had the ability to manipulate his own vote share, and was being especially egregious in describing it.[18] In adherence with his generally confident campaign behavior, Sargsyan mostly refused to criticize opponents, and in some instances actually offered praise for their ideas and actions; this especially illustrated the lack of real competition in the election. However, one exception to this was seen in his angered response to Hovannisyan's claim that the election was divided between forces of good and evil. He condemned such divisive language and argued that his conduct and policy proposals were more responsible.[19]

One foregone conclusion of opposition boycotts is that the incumbent is expected to win in a landslide due to the reduced field of competition. Yet this is not exactly what occurred in Armenia's 2013 presidential election. The official election results gave Sargsyan 59% of the vote, while Hovannisyan came in second with 37%. This figure for Hovannisyan is actually larger that the percentage of votes won by Ter-Petrosian in the polarized 2008 contest. Moreover, public opinion polls actually suggested that a majority of Armenians may have preferred Hovannisyan to Sargsyan (Nedolyan 2013). Allegations of voter fraud and ballot box stuffing emerged after the election, and Hovannisyan maintained that he was the actual victor. So why didn't we see a landslide victory for the incumbent when faced with multiple abstentions, including the second most popular politician, Gagik Tsarukian? It appears that in this case, many voters were frustrated with the incumbent regime and pooled this discontent into support for Hovannisyan, despite his relatively minor role in Armenian politics up until that point. This may be related to the low degree of incumbent dominance in Armenia as well; the incumbent regime is in power, but lacks a supermajority of support. Moreover, the protests and demonstrations against Sargsyan since his 2008 election signal that his power has definitely not been fully consolidated.

Elections that feature boycotts are typically expected to feature lower voter turnout than those without such abstentions. Indeed, this was the case in 2013: the official turnout was recorded at 60.62%, while turnout for the 2008 presidential contest was instead at 72.14%.[20] Given the perceived public apathy toward the election, combined with pre-election polls showing an increase in protests votes in support of Hovannisyan, voter fraud and vote buying were witnessed in the final days before the election. Hovannisyan's own party, the

Heritage Party, noted many particular precincts where Sargsyan's support was disproportionate when compared with the bulk of the surrounding areas (Sargsyan 2013). Thus one implication of these accusations is that voter turnout was in fact even lower than the recorded figures. International observers conversely gave general support for the election, but did note some irregularities in the vote count.[21] Protests emerged in the days after the election in response to what opponents of Sargsyan saw as blatant fraud. Hovannisyan filed official complaints with the Central Election Commission and also appealed to the constitutional court that the allegations be investigated, charged, and that the election be held again; he lost in each of these instances.[22] He did not give up his protest, and engaged in a 21-day hunger strike to signal his lack of acceptance with the election results.[23]

This case illustrates that in the short term the election was indeed a guaranteed defeat for the protesting parties and coalitions. It also demonstrates that the regime worried about voter participation in this context, allegedly engaging in ballot box fraud, and thus potentially harming the regime's legitimacy as Sargsyan entered his second term. The protests immediately following the election definitely signaled short-term frustration, but a boycott is most effective if it damages the legitimacy of the regime in the long term. So has there been evidence that this electoral protest strategy has had any effect on Armenian politics in the long term? In short, both no and yes. If one pays attention to election results in the wake of the 2013 presidential election, then it is clear that the pro-government parties initially continued to be successful and victorious. The 2013 mayoral election in the capital, Yerevan, as well as parliamentary by-elections later that year both saw vote gains and victories for pro-government candidates and parties. After the 2013 boycott, all of the parties that did not submit candidates suffered losses in the 2017 parliamentary election. Prosperous Armenia, led by Gagik Tsarukian, lost two seats, while Levon Ter-Petrosian's Armenian National Congress lost representation entirely. The newly formed ORO alliance, which included 2013 presidential candidate Raffi Hovannisyan, also won no seats in the new National Assembly. Therefore, opposition parties and coalitions fared poorly in 2017, regardless of their decisions in the previous presidential election.

However, other political developments have revealed a remarkable turn of events in Armenia's government. A 2015 referendum on constitutional amendments proposed by Sargsyan transformed Armenia into a parliamentary republic with an indirectly elected president. This meant that, barring any further institutional changes, the 2013 presidential election was Armenia's last, and that the prime minister would become a more significant figure in Armenia's political system. Sargsyan and those in the pro-government coalition supported this switch, while critics saw it as a way for the regime to remain in power. Yet the 2017 general election for the newly established parliamentary system produced vote losses for the pro-government Republican Party; they received 58 seats in the 131-seat National Assembly, a drop of 11 seats from the previous session. Despite this, the party formed a pro-government coalition with another party and thus maintained a majority. Amid the changing political system, Sargsyan had previously stated publicly that he had no intention of serving as Armenia's prime minister when his term as president ended. However, this changed in April of 2018 when the coalition government voted to install him in that position. This spurred massive spontaneous protests in Yerevan as well as in other cities across Armenia, and within the span of a week, Sargsyan resigned from his position.[24] Opposition figure Nikol Pashinyan became the perceived leader of the protest movement, and within weeks after Sargsyan's exit, Pashinyan was elected prime minister by the parliament.[25] These surprising turns of events seemingly changed the balance of power in Armenia within the span of a month. Pashinyan's political career dates back to Levon Ter-Petrossian's 2008 presidential campaign, when Pashinyan himself was arrested and served three years in prison for post-election protests. In the aftermath of the 2013 election, Pashinyan formed a political party, Civil Contract, which participated in an opposition coalition for the 2017 elections and successfully won seats.

These events have all occurred in the aftermath of the 2013 presidential election. While the boycott itself did not seem to play an active role in the events of 2018, it may have set the stage for growing frustration with the status quo in Armenian politics. These events are still ongoing, and their implications for democracy remain unclear. The contrast between Armenia and Belarus, the setting for the next two case studies, will be even starker, given the political upheaval that Armenia has recently experienced.

Belarus's 2012 Parliamentary Election

The second election under examination in this chapter is the 2012 parliamentary contest held in Belarus. This election came after more than a decade and a half of rule by president Aleksander Lukashenka, who has dominated the political landscape in Belarus since coming to power. Unlike most other executives in the post-Soviet region, Lukashenka rules without the dominant backing of an organized political party or pro-government coalition (Wilson 2011). Instead, he relies on support from non-affiliated, independent members of parliament who support his rule and draft legislation in line with his policy agenda. The share of independent members of parliament has risen dramatically in Belarus since Lukashenka took office in 1994. After the first parliamentary elections held after independence in 1995, independents held about 37% of the seats; however, this number has surged to about 94% after the 2008 parliamentary elections. Moreover, since Lukashenka took power, genuine opposition parties, those that explicitly oppose Lukashenka and criticize his authoritarian behavior, have been almost unable to win any representation in the parliament. One exception to this occurred in the 2000 parliamentary election, when the Social Democratic Party of Popular Accord won one seat. Additionally, eleven independent members once formed an anti-regime coalition named the Respublika faction, but that grouping failed to last beyond the 2004 election cycle. The Communist Party of Belarus, the Agrarian Party, and the Liberal Democratic Party have been the most successful pro-government parties in Belarus, and the first two of these three were the only two parties to hold seats in the outgoing House of Representatives heading into the 2012 election (Frear 2014).

Lukashenka has consolidated power through multiple institutional changes. In 1995, just one year after his first election, he held a referendum that, among other things, reduced the powers of the parliament in relation to the president. Next, he held another referendum in 1996 that approved a new constitution drafted by Lukashenka. The new constitution changed the parliament into a bicameral institution in which the lower house was elected while the upper house was appointed; this new parliament also lost any ability to directly challenge Lukashenka, and its power of legislation was rendered weaker than the president's authority to grant decrees. Moreover, the judiciary was severely weakened through this new constitution (Wilson 2011). Finally, a third referendum held in 2004 removed the term limits for Lukashenka, ensuring that he could continue to seek reelection without any institutional barriers (Hale 2015). In addition to changing the institutions so as to consolidate presidential power, many prominent opposition figures disappeared in 1999 and 2000. During this time period in the run-up to a potentially contentious 2001 presidential election, four (or possibly five) opposition figures disappeared under mysterious circumstances (Wilson 2011).[26] This meant that Lukashenko occupied a dominant position in a state with few genuine opponents.

Anti-Lukashenka opposition parties and actors have sought to challenge the regime and gain representation through various strategies. In 2006, following the models of the Color Revolutions, multiple parties joined together to form an opposition pre-election coalition and support one candidate, Alyaksandr Milinkevich, to challenge Lukashenka in the presidential election (Bunce and Wolchik 2011). Additionally, Alyaksandr Kazulin also ran with the support of the newly unified Social Democratic Party, which also opposed Lukashenka. Both were ultimately unsuccessful in their bids for the presidency, with the official results putting their vote shares at 6.1% and 2.2%, respectively, while Lukashenka received 83% of the vote. However, these figures were highly questioned and perceived to be highly manipulated, both increasing the votes for Lukashenka and depressing support for anti-regime candidates (Marples 2006). The OSCE reported that the vote count was performed without transparency and that many of their observers were denied access to crucial activities for monitoring the vote tabulation process. This led them to issue a strong negative assessment of the election and process.[27] Both candidates organized rallies and protests in response to the election results, and also officially challenged the results with the Central Election Commission, but the election's outcome was upheld. The protests held on election night were some of the largest in Belarus's history, with tens of thousands of individuals turning out. Law enforcement responded forcefully, arresting hundreds of individuals (Korosteleva 2009). One candidate, Kazulin, was imprisoned for two years after this, and was only released in 2008 after EU pressure and engagement with Lukashenka (Padhol and Marples 2011).

In 2010, Lukashenka was reelected to a fourth term in another highly imbalanced election.[28] The official results of the December 19, 2010, election gave Lukashenka 79% of the vote, while the main opposition candidate received just 2.56%. As in 2006, anti-regime forces protested the election results, with over 20,000 people turning out at a demonstration in Minsk, including every presidential candidate except Lukashenka. The response to these protests was incredibly harsh, with riot police and security officials arresting and beating hundreds of protesters. Two of the candidates themselves suffered serious injuries, and seven of the candidates were arrested and held in police custody overnight. In the days after the election, more members of anti-regime parties were arrested and offices of organizations seen to be sympathetic to or affiliated with the opposition were also attacked and shut down.

The violent and repressive circumstances of the 2010 election provided the backdrop for the 2012 parliamentary election. In this election, as was the case in Armenia's 2013 contest, the degree of competitiveness was low. First, Lukashenka was explicitly confident that pro-regime candidates would prevail in the majoritarian electoral system. Relatedly, Lidziya Yarmoshyna, the chair of Belarus's Central Election Commission, criticized the ability of the opposition to ever be genuinely competitive prior to the 2012 election. She suggested that their ages and lack of experience would hinder their efforts to succeed.[29] While Yarmoshyna's position would expect impartiality, she is seen as an ally of Lukashenka, and this statement directly suggested the government felt no threat from regime foes. Second, the economy had improved since 2010, with negative perceptions being alleviated. According to public opinion polls from late 2011 and early 2012, the number of Belarusians who felt that the economic situation was improving continued to grow in the run-up to the September 23, 2012, vote.[30] GDP per capita in Belarus had continued to improve since the 2008–2009 Global Financial Crisis, and by 2011, it had reached an all-time high of $6,519 in USD. Still, the economy grew at a slower rate than in 2010, but nonetheless reported a 5.54% growth in 2011.[31]

Incumbent dominance was higher in Belarus than it was prior to Armenia's 2013 presidential election. As already described, Lukashenka has completely dominated politics in Belarus since he took office in 1994. He has guided institutional changes that have seriously weakened the powers of the legislative and judicial branches, and firmly consolidated power in the hands of the president. He has also enjoyed immense electoral victories, one of the two indicators used to capture incumbent dominance in this book. His first election in 1994 was the only one in which Lukashenko did not win at least 50% of the vote, sending the contest into a second round. In every subsequent election since then, Lukashenka has won over 70% of the vote in the first round; the highest of these official results was the 84.4% he received in 2006. These massive victories demonstrate that the regime is indeed hegemonic. Despite these official results, public opinion surveys have consistently revealed support for Lukashenka to be at or below 50%. This supports the claims of opposition activists that manipulation and fraud are significant aspects of these victories. However, as in Armenia, Belarus is not economically dependent on the export of natural resources or fossil fuels. In 2011, such exports represented about 1.8% of Belarus's total GDP. The highest point this figure has ever reached was 3.3% in 1996.[32] Thus the export of natural resources does not add to incumbent dominance in this case.

Given this, the 2012 legislative election occurred under conditions of extremely low competitiveness and moderate incumbent dominance. The theoretical expectations assert that such a case would be especially ripe for an opposition boycott; moreover, the empirical analysis singled out the degree of competitiveness as an essential indicator in this relationship. As expected, an opposition boycott did occur in this election.[33] Multiple anti-regime parties and organizations similarly decided not to participate in the 2012 parliamentary elections. Three organizations, the European Belarus movement, the Young Front, and the Belarusian Christian Democratic Party, announced their intent not to participate just after elections were called in June. Their reasoning was precisely to protest a process that grants legitimacy to Lukashenka and his regime. They also cited the continued imprisonment of political opponents of Lukashenka, and the failure to level the playing field in elections.[34] More boycotts emerged as the election drew nearer. Two additional parties, the United Civic Union and the Belarusian National Front, that had initially registered candidates, withdrew them in protest of the political situation. They urged voters to "go fishing or visit your parents" or go "to the forest to pick mushrooms" rather than turning out to the polls to legitimize the electoral process (RFE/RE 2012c; Marples 2012).

Six different groups held a press conference a week before the election and explicitly called for voters to stay home in the election. Opposition actors made clear that they hoped the boycott strategy would highlight the illegitimacy of the Lukashenka regime. One leader, Anatol Lyabedzka, stated that " it is better to cancel the imitation [of democracy] we have witnessed," while another, Vital Rymasheuski, asserted that "the isolation of the main opponents of the regime . . . is alone enough to consider this election illegal and undemocratic" (RFE/RE 2012d). These actors tried to become especially visible in the week before the election. One organization, the Tell the Truth movement, sought to hold a demonstration urging voters to boycott the election. However, four activists from the movement were arrested before they had the chance, and were held in jail until after the election.[35] The opposition boycott was publicly criticized by the Central Election Commission. Mikalay Lozovik, the Commission Secretary, asserted that the boycott revealed, "disrespect for voters" and a "travesty of law" (RFE/RE 2012e).

Not all opposition parties officially pulled out the election, even if they also voiced agreement with the decision to boycott. The aforementioned Tell the Truth movement supported the boycott, but 13 of its members still stood as candidates in the election (Frear 2014). Overall, out of the 110 total seats available in this election through the single-member district system, only 70 candidates ran that represented a genuine opposition to the Lukashenka regime, representing about 24% of the total candidates registered. Moreover, candidates in 16 districts ran in uncontested races.[36] Thus, even without a complete boycott, the opposition anti-regime presence in the election was minimal.

The electoral campaign itself was quite underwhelming. The OSCE noted that even two weeks out from the election day, parties and candidates had engaged in virtually no explicit acts of campaigning or voter engagement; parties asserted that they preferred to save such activities until just one week before the voting took place.[37] The OSCE observed only a modest increase in overall campaign activities in the final weeks, but noted that pro-government candidates appeared to hold more rallies and to have greater access to farmers and other government-affiliated workplaces.[38]

The results of the 2012 parliamentary election provided another significant victory for pro-government candidates and parties. Of the opposition candidates that still chose to participate, none were successful in winning a seat in the House of Representatives. Of the 109 total seats, 104 were won by independent candidates, with three pro-government parties winning the remaining five seats (Frear 2014). An opposition boycott seeks to reduce the legitimacy of the incumbent regime. Yet in Belarus, elections have already been complete landslides for the pro-government candidates, so there was little room for the electoral results to demonstrate fictitious or overzealous victories for the regime. Reduced voter turnout, however, could reveal public dissatisfaction and frustration with the incumbent regime. Despite calls for voters to boycott the election entirely, the official turnout was listed at 75%, according to the Central Election Commission. While opposition activists publicly disputed this figure, independent observers reported that it may have been about 10 percentage points lower (Frear 2014). This suggests that while a boycott is typically associated with a decrease in voter turnout, regime manipulation makes it difficult to effectively observe this in Belarus.

Another way to consider the effectiveness of the boycott in the short term would be to consider how the public reacted to the strategy. Prior to the election, only a small portion of Belarusian survey respondents reported that they agreed with the opposition boycott. Yet, less than half (36.8%) answered that they thought the election would be free and fair, while a larger share (39%) instead thought that the elections would not be democratic.[39] While the population was not universally supportive of the boycott, it is clear that many already viewed the elections as severely flawed. Following the election, a survey found that only 10% of respondents stated that they had heeded the call to boycott the vote, and that about a quarter judged the elections to have been unfair (Frear 2014).

In the years following the 2012 election, circumstances have not improved much for the anti-regime opposition in Belarus. Lukashenka was reelected a fifth time in 2015, with an official vote share of 83.5%, while the top opposition candidate, Tatiana Korotkevich, received 4.4%. While this election undoubtedly also contained manipulation and election day fraud, there was far greater genuine support for Lukashenka leading up to this election than had been the case in the previous presidential contests (Crabtree, Fariss, and Schuler 2016). Interestingly, the following year's 2016 parliamentary elections witnessed victory for two opposition candidates. One candidate, Elena Anisim, ran as an independent in a district in the capital of Minsk, and won the seat, while Anna Konopatskaya, a member of the united opposition coalition, "The Right to Choose," also won a seat.[40] These remarkable victories are quite small in the grand scheme of things, but offer some evidence that anti-regime forces have made progress. As the first legislative election held after the boycotted 2012 contest, this could be considered a long-term benefit from such a strategy.

Given the very small gains made by anti-regime parties and candidates, it is unsurprising that indicators of democracy have not changed much in Belarus. The Polity IV measure of political regimes has consistently given Belarus the score of-7 since 1996 (Marshall, Jaggers, and Gurr 2017). This actually gives Belarus the lowest score among all ten post-Soviet cases included in this book, and firmly plants it in the authoritarian category. Similarly, Freedom House has classified Belarus as "Not Free" since it began to offer such assessments in 1998. Its overall freedom rating has not changed from a 6.5 over the last five years, either.[41] As previous scholarship has observed, the existence of a boycott in Belarus has, at least so far, not been associated with any democratic breakthroughs.

Negative Case: Belarus's 2010 Presidential Election

While the two previous cases contained opposition boycotts, the majority of elections in the former Soviet Union have not. This also means that generally opposition actors prefer to participate even when the odds are stacked against them. This leaves many potential elections to serve as a counterpoint to the two positive case studies on Armenia and Belarus. One particularly attractive case also comes from Belarus in the years prior to the already discussed election. While the 2012 Belarusian election did feature a boycott, the same strategy was also considered but ultimately rejected in its 2010 presidential contest. Given this, the 2010 presidential election in Belarus serves as a negative case to contrast with the previous two elections discussed in this chapter.

This election follows the authoritarian consolidation already discussed earlier, with Aleksander Lukashenka seeking a fourth term as president. The Belarusian anti-regime opposition had suffered under the repressive conditions of the regime, and in particular after their pre-election coalition in the 2006 election. As it was their most thorough and explicit attempt at unseating Lukashenka, the political space closed even further in response. This presidential election was scheduled for late December of 2010, four months before Lukashenka's term would officially end.

Incumbent dominance, as was also the case in the 2012 election, was moderate prior to the 2010 contest. Lukashenka's massive official victory in 2006, with a reported 83% of the votes, firmly placed Belarus in the hegemonic authoritarian category. Also similar to the 2012 case, Belarus's economy remained not dependent on the export of energy natural resources, which comprised just 2.13% of the overall GDP in 2009. This leaves Belarus with a 1 out of 2 on the index and a moderate degree of incumbent dominance.

However, it is on the amount of competitiveness that this election differs from the 2012 case. That election featured an extremely low amount of perceived competitiveness, which was argued to contribute to the opposition boycott. However, the 2010 election contained a higher degree of competition. This came largely through the notably negative economic conditions that had overwhelmed Belarus. Described as facing, "profound, even unprecedented, economic problems," both the national economy and the people of Belarus were adversely affected by the 2008–2009 Global Financial Crisis, although in different ways than other post-Soviet states (Padhol and Marples 2011: 6). Its economy just barely posted positive growth, with a meager 0.2% increase reported in 2009. Additionally, its GDP per capita fell for the first time since 2001.[42] As Rovdo (2011) notes, Belarus maintains a huge public sector and the state serves as the primary economic driver even two decades after the end of communism. An estimated 55–60% of the population works for the state, and relies on subsidies or other social services for their economic well-being. To prevent massive outcries, the Belarusian state engaged in massive borrowing to maintain its spending, which destabilized its economic position. Ultimately, these worries contributed to the 2010 election being held a few months early, before the situation could potentially get much worse (Rovdo 2011). Public opinion also revealed the deteriorating economic conditions, with more than 80% responding that there was an economic crisis in Belarus at the start of 2010. Moreover, close to a third of Belarusians reported that their economic situation worsened over the last year (Yefimova 2011). All of these points illustrate how perceptions of the economic situation were negative heading into the 2010 election, and that this increased the perception of competitiveness.

Despite these conditions, Lukashenka was publicly confident of his reelection in the summer of 2010 at least six months before the election. With just one week to go, he stated, "There will definitely be political changes . . . but no change of power in Belarus" (Stern 2010). While public opinion had consistently revealed marginal support for Lukashenka, with usually between 40 and 50% of survey respondents reporting that they intended to vote for him, the previous elections have demonstrated that there is little correlation between the support revealed in surveys and the official voter results (Nikolyuk 2011). Lukashenka himself stated in June of 2010 that "I have enough political intuition, enough methods to see it. The election can only confirm that" (Rovdo 2011: 54). This statement appears to show that Lukashenka viewed the election as a way to give himself the results he wanted, rather than as an exercise in public scrutiny and voter preferences.

With this added amount of competitiveness, a boycott may conflict with the goal of remaining active in the political realm and showing consistent opposition to the regime. In the lead-up to this election, an opposition boycott was actually suggested by two different opposition figures, Zyanon Pazniak and Alyaksandr Milinkevich. Both publicly worried that participating carried the long-term cost of legitimizing an authoritarian regime (Padhol and Marples 2011). Pazniak did speak publicly about a boycott after Syarhey

Haidukevich, who had run in 2006, decided not to run in 2010.[43] Milinkevich had also run for president in 2006 as the united opposition's candidate, but he ultimately decided not to participate in the 2010 election either. Yet he did not support a boycott. Instead, he voiced his support for other opposition candidates with similar views.[44] As noted, this election highlighted the growing economic problems in the state, as well as more tense relations with Belarus's imposing neighbor, Russia. This led to the perception that perhaps Lukashenka's regime was vulnerable and that opposition participation was more valuable than the protest sentiment of a boycott (Padhol and Marples 2011). Therefore, despite Pazniak's urging, opposition actors did not heed his recommendation to boycott.

Nine other candidates competed against Lukashenka in this election. The two front runners among this crowd were Uladzimir Nyaklayeu and Andrei Sannikau, which one poll showed receiving 16% and 10% of support from voters, respectively (Padhol and Marples 2010). The opposition appeared to have multiple goals for participating in this election separate from (or instead of) focusing solely on winning. One was to prevent Lukashenka from securing a majority in the first round, which would force the contest into a second round run-off. This would signal a close election with genuine competition and would accordingly harm Lukashenka's image and legitimacy (Padhol and Marples 2010). Another was to maintain the position of the opposition parties on the political landscape and to prevent the loss of support. As Chausov (2011: 15) explains, "[o]pposition political parties' engagement in the presidential election was determined by the need to retain their political identity." Third, many opposition candidates hoped that because Belarusian–Russian relations were deteriorating, Russia might not recognize the results of the election. Thus multiple candidates presented themselves as pro-Russian so as to curry favor with Russia and draw attention to Lukashenka's lackluster relationship with then-president Dmitri Medvedev (Rovdo 2011).

Unfortunately for the opposition, this election once again featured regime repression, obstacles to the fulfillment of their goals, and an ultimately manipulated result. Three months before the election, Aleh Byabenin, an opposition activist and supporter of the anti-regime candidate Sannikau, was found hanged. Byabenin had worked for years to bring attention to the deaths of other opposition activists in the 1990s. His death was ultimately ruled a suicide, a conclusion shared by the OSCE, but his friends and families rejected this narrative and alleged government involvement (Padhol and Marples 2010). Second, just ten days before the election, Lukashenka signed a partnership with Medvedev in Russia, which seemed to remove any likelihood that Moscow would reject the results of the Belarusian election (Rovno 2011).[45] Finally, once the voting had taken place, OSCE observers noted that the tabulation process was handled poorly and that the officially announced figures seemed untrustworthy.[46]

On election day, Uladzimir Nyaklayeu and Andrei Sannikau had agreed to meet as the polls closed and to protest if the results seemed incorrect. As they marched with an estimated one thousand-plus supporters, police and security forces met them and responded with violence. Nyaklayeu and Sannakau were both badly beaten and by the next morning, seven of the presidential candidates had been arrested and were being held in jail. Moreover, leaders of parties and those affiliated with any of the opposition activities were also either arrested or saw their offices searched (Padhol and Marples 2011). This election ended with the opposition in complete disarray and facing further repression from the Lukashenka regime.

DISCUSSION

In summation, these three cases present different scenarios on opposition engagement with the electoral process. Actors generally chose to participate in the unfair elections, so when a boycott is performed, it is a salient event. Table 6.3 presents the indicators and outcomes from the three case studies featured in this chapter. The first two case studies of Armenia, 2013, and Belarus, 2012, reveal examples where the degree of competitiveness was quite low, and where a group of opposition actors opted to boycott the process entirely. In the case of the 2010 Belarusian presidential election, a boycott was considered, but this strategy was rejected due to perceptions that the poor economic conditions could offer the opposition a genuine opportunity to fulfill certain goals. Yet in the 2012 election, when the Belarusian economy had shown more improvements, opposition actors decided to follow through on this strategy. The violence and arrests inflicted on opposition actors in Belarus in both 2006 and 2010 emphasized the importance of weighing the costs and benefits of participation. When the election offers little productive opportunities due to extremely low competition, a boycott can make the most

Table 6.3. **Summary of Opposition Boycott Case Study Comparisons**

Indicators	Armenia's 2013 Election	Belarus's 2012 Election	Belarus's 2010 Election
Type	Presidential	Parliamentary	Presidential
Perceived Competitiveness	1 out of 3	0 out of 3	1 out of 3
Incumbent Dominance	0 out of 2	1 out of 2	1 out of 2
Opposition Boycott?	Yes	Yes	No

rational sense. This suggests that perceptions of competition are connected to the decision to select the protest strategy of boycotting the election.

IMPLICATIONS AND CONCLUSION

This chapter examined the conditions under which one or more opposition party opts to protest the regime by boycotting the election entirely. The empirical results as well as the illustrative case studies yield several implications on this electoral strategy. First, the statistical estimations report that the degree of competitiveness in the election is related to this strategy, but that incumbent dominance and the type of the election are not. It makes intuitive sense that opposition actors would take their own chances in the election under consideration when choosing to boycott. If opposition actors felt they had a chance in the electoral contest, then they likely would not forego that possibility. Moreover, as Table 6.1 showed, incumbent dominance is almost a perfect predictor of boycotts. In every case observed in the region, except for Armenia's 2013 election, the boycott took place amid conditions of either medium or high incumbent dominance. Even though the quantitative results revealed no relationship with incumbent dominance, the universe of cases may suggest a necessary but not sufficient condition for opposition boycotts.

One particular boycott mentioned earlier in this book was staged by opposition anti-corruption activist Alexei Navalny in Russia's 2018 presidential election. I address this boycott as it received great international attention, even though the 2018 election was not included in the data of this book. As discussed in chapters 1 and 5, Navalny intended to run for president in the election, and behaved very much like a candidate through the year of 2017. Yet there was the looming issue of his ability to register, given his previous convictions for embezzlement (which many considered to be politically motivated charges).[47] Navalny attempted to register multiple times and appealed the rejections to the fullest extent possible.[48] Yet ultimately, when he had no other options available, he instead urged voters to boycott the elections and stay home. On the surface, this path to a boycott follows a different trajectory than what has been described in the book. And yet, it also adheres to the theoretical conditions more generally. The 2018 election featured Putin's campaign for a fourth term (and a second non-consecutive one), in the years following Putin's historically high domestic approval ratings. This election therefore featured low competitiveness, and would make a boycott appealing. Even other candidates in the election remarked that they knew Putin would be reelected, and that they were more interested in drawing attention to certain issues or to their political futures.[49] Overall, Navalny's boycott does not represent a departure from the theoretical expectations of the book, but instead highlights how uncompetitive elections can provide significant venues for opposition protest.

The case studies in this chapter allowed for a look at the long-term effects of opposition boycotts. This is important as the logic of boycotts assumes that a short-term loss in the game arena of the election can still produce long-term benefits. In theory, opposition actors hope this might occur through growing public frustration at the regime who won an election with such a reduced field of competitors. Additionally, such a lopsided victory could damage the legitimacy enjoyed by the victorious incumbent candidate or party. Ideally, either of these scenarios might lead to future openings for opposition actors to gain power in subsequent elections. Yet in the short term, this did not appear to be the case in either Armenia or Belarus. In Armenia, the victory for incumbent president Sargsyan was large, but not completely lopsided. The runner-up candidate Raffi Hovannisyan actually won a greater share of the vote than that won by the runner up in the previous presidential election, Levon Ter-Petrosian. Still, public outrage at allegations of ballot box stuffing and rigging an election led to public discontent, protests, and the lack of acceptance of the election's result by Hovannisyan. More recent events in Armenia have presented the second-ever alteration of power, and may be the start of a political awakening for pro-democracy forces. The boycott of 2013 in all likelihood probably had no direct effect on these events of 2018, but it could possibly have contributed indirectly to a loss of legitimacy to Sargsyan more broadly, adding one additional factor to the many that tipped the scales against him and led to his resignation. The events in Armenia may also have revealed a situation that was only possible given the low degree of incumbent dominance.

In contrast, the political opposition continues to struggle in Belarus. As noted, it currently holds two seats in Belarus's parliament, which is admittedly an improvement from their previous complete lack of representation. But the opposition remains severely limited in its ability to operate and get its message out to voters. The dual reality of higher incumbent dominance as well as very low competition seems to continue to hamper opposition opportunities. As of this writing, neither case has witnessed any measurable improvements in the conditions of democracy.[50] This echoes much of the previous findings on opposition boycotts; while boycotting parties and candidates aspire to produce greater openness through an election lacking serious choices, such openness fails to emerge as a result.

This chapter ultimately emphasizes that boycotts are blunt instruments. As a protest strategy, a boycott can simultaneously draw negative attention to the authoritarian regime while also driving away sympathetic supporters.

When opposition actors boycott, they may instead inadvertently push voters away and destroy their own chances at a future comeback. This dual effect contributes to the mixed calculus of choosing to boycott, as observed in the two positive cases of boycotts. In Armenia, two of the boycotting parties subsequently lost representation in the next elections; the third party remains the second largest bloc in the parliament but they too received fewer seats in the next election. However, Armenia also witnessed its historic alteration of power in April of 2018; this occurred outside of the electoral cycle and thus its effects on democracy remain to be seen. The boycott in Belarus was much comprehensive in its scope, and was also much more explicit in its call for voters to stay home. Yet the results of the 2012 election did not look much different from previous parliamentary elections in Belarus, making it difficult for the contest to signal the particular illegitimacy of the outcome. A boycott in Belarus was also understandable when considered in the aftermath of the 2010 presidential election, which saw violence and imprisonment against most of the presidential candidates. The political opportunities for opposition actors in electoral authoritarian regimes reveal significant tradeoffs. Elections clearly remain the primary venue for carving out political space, but in many cases the election itself can only do so much in the wake of regime interference and manipulation.

NOTES

1. Models that omitted incumbent dominance, perceived competitiveness, and previous competitiveness, respectively, did not produce substantially different results.

2. As discussed previously, this book uses an inverted measure for the margin of victory. Therefore, in Table 6.2, the indicator is signed negative, but this does not capture elections where the margin of victory was small; instead, it refers to elections where the difference was especially great.

3. Beginning in 2013, GDP per capita in Ukraine would drop below the figure in Armenia and would remain there into the present. (Source: World Bank World Development Indicators).

4. Source: Caucasus Barometer 2012 Armenia.

5. "Republic of Armenia Parliamentary Elections 6 May 2012," *OSCE/ODIHR Election Observation Mission Final Report*. Warsaw: 26 June 2012.

6. "Ter-Petrosian Bows Out of Presidential Race," *Radio Free Europe/Radio Liberty*, December 25, 2012.

7. Astghik Bedevian, "Dashnaks Call for Opposition Deal on Presidential Candidate," *Radio Free Europe/Radio Liberty*, October 26, 2012.

8. "Tsarukian Steers Clear of Armenian Presidential Race," *Radio Free Europe/Radio Liberty*, December 12, 2012.

9. Ibid.

10. "10% of Prosperous Armenia Voters to Go to Polls—Expert," *Pan Armenian Net*, January 9, 2013.

11. "Interim Report No. 1 10–16 January 2013," *OSCE Election Observation Mission Republic of Armenia*, January 23, 2013.

12. "Interim Report No. 2, 17 January–5 February 2013," *OSCE Election Observation Mission Republic of Armenia.*

13. Irina Hovhannisyan, "Opposition Presidential Candidate Shot in Armenia," *Radio Free Europe/Radio Liberty*, February 1, 2013.

14. "Statement of Preliminary Findings and Conclusions," *OSCE Election Observation Mission Republic of Armenia,* February 19, 2013.

15. Hovannes Shoghikian and Hovannes Movsisian, "Opposition Candidates Predict Election Defeat for Sargsyan," *Radio Free Europe/Radio Liberty,* February 15, 2013.

16. Ruzanna Stepanian, "Sargsyan Enraged by Key Vote Challenger," *Radio Free Europe/Radio Liberty*, February 11, 2013.

17. Nare Stepanian, "Sargsyan Vows to Cut Poverty," *Radio Free Europe/Radio Liberty*, January 30, 2013.

18. Zaven Kalayjian and Sassoon Kosian, "FPC Briefing: Results of Preliminary Analysis of February 18th, 2013 Presidential Election," *The Foreign Policy Center*, February 2013.

19. Ruzanna Stepanian, "Sargsyan Enraged by Key Vote Challenger," *Radio Free Europe/Radio Liberty*, February 11, 2013.

20. Turnout figures from the International Foundation for Electoral System's Electionguide.org.

21. "Republic of Armenia Presidential Election 18 February 2013 Final Report," *OSCE/ODHIR Election Observation Mission*, May 8, 2013.

22. Astghik Bedevian, "Constitutional Court Rejects Opposition Election Appeals," *Radio Free Europe/Radio Liberty*, March 14, 2013.

23. Ruzanna Stepanian, "Armenian Opposition Leader Ends Hunger Strike," *Radio Free Europe/Radio Liberty*, March 31, 2013.

24. "Thousands Celebrate As Armenia's Longtime Ruler Sargsyan Steps Down." *Radio Free Europe/Radio Liberty.* April 23, 2018.

25. "Armenian Protest Leader Formally Appointed Prime Minister." *Radio Free Europe/Radio Liberty.* May 8, 2018.

26. The disappeared opposition figures include Yury Zakharanka, Viktar Hanchar, Anatol Krasowski, and Zmitser Zavadzki. The death of Henadz Karpenka in 1999 has also been considered questionable.

27. "Republic of Belarus Presidential Election 19 March 2006," *OSCE/ODIHR Election Observation Mission Report*, Warsaw 7 June 2006.

28. This election will be discussed in greater detail in the remaining negative case study.

29. David Marples, "Parliamentary Elections Announced in Belarus," *Eurasian Daily Monitor* 9 (125), July 2, 2012.

30. "The Most Important Results of the Public Opinion Poll in June 2012," *Independent Institute of Socio-Economic and Political Studies*, http://www.iiseps.org/?p=2699&lang=en.

31. Data from the World Bank World Development Indicators.

32. According to the World Bank World Development Indicators.

33. This was not the first opposition boycott to take place in Belarus. In the previous two legislative contests, some opposition actors chose not to take part. However, the magnitude of the 2012 boycott was larger, with more groups adopting the strategy.

34. David Marples, "Parliamentary Elections Announced in Belarus," *Eurasian Daily Monitor* 9 (125), July 2, 2012.

35. "Belarus Opposition Activists Jailed Until after Elections," *Radio Free Europe/Radio Liberty*, September 19, 2012.

36. David Marples, "Parliamentary Elections in Belarus Arouse Cynicism, Anger Among Population," *Eurasian Daily Monitor* 9 (173), September 24, 2012.

37. "Interim Report Parliamentary Elections Republic of Belarus," *OSCE/ODIHR Election Observation Mission*, September 14, 2012.

38. "Statement of Preliminary Findings and Conclusions, Parliamentary Elections Republic of Belarus," *OSCE/ODIHR Election Observation Mission*, September 23, 2012.

39. David Marples, "Parliamentary Elections in Belarus Arouse Cynicism, Anger Among Population," *Eurasian Daily Monitor* 9 (173), September 24, 2012.

40. Grigory Ioffe, "Belarusians Elect Their House of Representatives," *Eurasian Daily Monitor* 13 (146) September 13, 2016.

41. Data from freedomhouse.org.

42. Data from World Bank World Development Indicators.

43. Зянон Пазьняк. "Фальшывыя выбары, фальшывыя паводзіны" Радыё Свабода. 11 кастрычнік 2010.

44. "Opposition Leader in Belarus Says Won't Run for President." *Radio Free Europe/Radio Liberty*. September 17, 2010.

45. Indeed, Medvedev ultimately chose not to criticize Belarus for the election and its aftermath, considering it a domestic issue (Padhol and Marples 2011).

46. "Republic of Belarus Presidential Election 19 December 2010." *OSCE/ODIHR Election Observation Mission Final Report*. Warsaw: February 22 2011.

47. According to Russian electoral laws, candidates can be denied registration due to a criminal record.

48. "Russian Supreme Court Denies Navalny's Appeal to Run for President." *Radio Free Europe/Radio Liberty*. January 26, 2018.

49. "Russian Federation Presidential Election 18 March 2018." *ODIHR Election Observation Mission Final Report*. Warsaw: 6 June 2018.

50. Armenia's ratings from Freedom House and Polity IV remained unchanged as of August, 2018. Any updates based on the recent events will be observed in the 2019 releases of their respective indices.

Chapter Seven

Conclusion and Implications

SUMMARY OF FINDINGS

This book has demonstrated that incumbent and opposition actors within electoral authoritarian settings vary their electoral behavior based on the conditions of the election. On the incumbent side of the equation, strategies of manipulation do not appear to be interchangeable. When the attainability of the election is in question, incumbent and pro-government actors prefer instrumental forms of electoral manipulation. Because instrumental manipulation directly interferes with the conduct of opposition actors and voters, it is better positioned to serve the short-term goal of electoral victory than the more indirect interference of informational manipulation. Chapter 3 demonstrates that two factors are linked to the selection of instrumental manipulation: a higher degree of competiveness and legislative elections. Both of these factors were indeed expected to alter the attainability of the election, and this expectation is confirmed. The quantitative estimations also confirm that instrumental manipulation is associated with incumbents winning elections; this is further evidence that this type of manipulation directly interferes with the conduct of an election. Moreover, the case studies suggest that the excessive usage of instrumental manipulation can be damaging to the incumbents or pro-government actors in the long term when they lose the election. This reveals that in addition to risking short-term blowback through protests and demands for new elections, this strategy carries long-term costs as well.

Informational manipulation includes categories that are highly visible, such as biased state media and campaigning while in an official capacity by incumbents. Unlike instrumental manipulation, it better serves long-term goals of consolidating power through the political institutions. Chapter 3 also revealed that informational manipulation is not likely to have an effect on the outcome of an election. Thus, when it comes to informational manipulation, this strategy is linked to contests in which the attainability is not in question. Depending on the degree of informational manipulation, contests with high incumbent dominance, low competitiveness, and executive positions are all settings in which this strategy is more likely. One takeaway from this is that incumbents are discerning. Dominant incumbents seemingly have the coordination and ability to manipulate elections to the fullest extent possible. Yet this is not what occurred. Instead, incumbent dominance is only related to highly visible, informational manipulation, but not the direct interference of instrumental manipulation. This reveals that these two options are indeed different strategies and that they appear to serve different purposes for authoritarian regimes. The case studies also suggest that informational manipulation is associated with greater institutional control in the long term. In the years following the elections in Azerbaijan and Russia, the Aliyev and Medvedev/Putin regimes, respectively, continued to reshape the political institutions so as to further consolidate their power. Thus, while informational manipulation does little to help incumbents win elections in the short term, it serves long-term goals through the control of political institutions.

Opposition strategies also demonstrate dissimilar relationships regarding the conditions of the election. Opposition pre-election coalitions can serve the short-term goals of anti-regime actors by offering better mathematical odds in the election as well as by combining resources and expertise. Opposition actors are more likely to unite and form pre-election coalitions in legislative elections as well as in elections with less incumbent dominance. However, the empirical analysis shows that coalitions are not more likely in elections with greater competition. Clearly, opposition actors survey the landscape of the election in deciding whether to overcome the logistical and organizational hurdles of uniting. The two case studies in Georgia and Armenia demonstrate how these strategies can yield benefits for the opposition. In Georgia, the coalition was successful in unseating the ruling pro-government party, while in Armenia, the opposition coalition was able to secure some modest concessions from the regime prior to the election itself. However, in the long term these two case reveal diverging effects. Since the coalition was successful in Georgia, they have succeeded in reshaping the political institutions and have, as of this writing, not suffered from any internal challenges that could have undermined their rule. However, Armenia reminds us that a failed coalition can face long-term atrophy as voters lose confidence in the actors to challenge or unseat the incumbent regime.

Opposition boycotts occur less frequently than pre-election coalitions within the former Soviet Union, but their presence and relevance remain important. When elections are typically unfair, opposition actors regularly face the dilemma of whether to participate at all. Boycotts are considered in far more cases than those where it is actually staged, reminding us that opposition actors reevaluate the conditions they face from one election to the next. While all but one boycott took place in a state with medium or high incumbent dominance, the most important factor for this strategy is the degree of competitiveness of the election. As competition decreases, opposition actors are more likely to boycott the election. This strategy seeks to discredit the electoral contest through the refusal of opposition actors to participate, so that, in the long term, the regime's legitimacy may be damaged enough to produce an opening for the opposition. However, the case studies offer little support for this last point. In both Armenia and Belarus, even with their differences in incumbent dominance, the incumbent regime has shown little sign of being vulnerable to electoral threats. In fact, the recent political changes in Armenia have come about not from the electoral process, but through popular demonstrations and protests. Such a scenario was potentially far more likely in Armenia already, as the political institutions have not been completely consolidated in favor of the incumbent, and because opposition forces have continued to win a notable share of votes.

Collectively, these findings reveal that the conditions of the election affect the perspective of both sides. When the level of the electoral contest is in play, instrumental manipulation and opposition pre-election coalitions may be more likely to form. This follows more intuitive logic, as it establishes winning the election as the most important goal. However, when the attainability of the electoral contest is not in question, then each side focuses on the level of the political institutions. Here, more counter-intuitive strategies become more likely. Opposition actors may abandon the election entirely, while incumbents may manipulate a contest they already know that they will win. As these strategies further long-term goals, albeit with different rates of success, they still may make rational sense from the perspective of the political actors.

IMPLICATIONS ON DEMOCRACY

This book considers the topic of electoral strategies in electoral authoritarian regimes. It comes at a time where an increasing amount of attention is paid to the state of democracy globally. While Zakaria (2004) warned over a decade ago that democracy was increasingly threatened by illiberal tendencies, this caution has spread to political systems in the West as well. Freedom House studies have especially measured drops in the political rights and civil liberties of citizens in more established democracies for the past few years

(Puddington and Roylance 2016; 2017). Such a trajectory has been observed both at the elite and at the mass level of politics. Multiple and distinctive political actors antithetical to democracy have been identified across Europe, including anti-democrats, populists, and nativists; the messages are quite different but each grouping represents political actors demonstrating a challenge to the principles of liberal democracy (Pappas 2016). Public trust in democratic institutions, voter turnout, and the general regard for democracy itself have all dropped over the last few decades. Voters have demonstrated a decline in tolerance with growing support for anti-immigrant and xenophobic political appeals (Foa and Mounk 2016). These trends more generally may signal the rise of "democratic deconsolidation," a trajectory previously deemed impossible by most political scientists (Foa and Mounk 2017). This book reveals that electoral manipulation is frequent, but that it can have consequences. Moreover, it primarily presents examples of authoritarian resilience, but also some opposition successes. So what are the implications of this book regarding the future of democracy and autocracy in the post-Soviet region?

One possible interpretation is that the mere survival of this new regime type, *electoral* authoritarianism, may signal a greater acceptance of democratic norms and institutions. As in democracies, elections serve as the site of political maneuvering and action in these states as well. Both incumbent and opposition actors recognize these contests as necessary for political success. If a regime hinders the opposition through cooptation, these actors still typically participate in elections only with their new political affiliation. This may signify the broader global acceptance of democracy and democratic norms and the routinization of elections (Schedler 2013). Indeed, some political scientists maintain that democratic values are stronger than ever within consolidated democracies and that the value changes that have occurred in some formerly authoritarian regimes can, and likely will, also take place in contemporary non-democracies, given greater economic modernization. Inglehart (2016: 21) argues that modernization "transforms social life and political institutions, promoting mass participation in politics and fostering values that—in the long run—make democratic political institutions increasingly likely."

The recent discussion on the implications surrounding the rise of "Autocracy Promotion" are relevant in this discussion. Way (2016) argues that this type of promotion, which has been promulgated by Russia, China, and Saudi Arabia, among others, still solidifies elections as the ultimate arena of political competition. He maintains that Russian efforts at autocracy promotion focus on ways to manipulate elections rather than eliminating them altogether, which may privilege these institutions more permanently. He also asserts that such efforts can often be counter-productive by reinvigorating anti-regime actors, thereby producing the unintended product of greater pluralism in the process. Indeed, Hale (2016) notes how Russian acts of autocracy promotion have a decidedly mixed track record, and are not a primary or even secondary explanation for the survival of non-democratic regimes. Relatedly, EU democracy assistance has been found to effectively mitigate any negative effects from anti-democracy promotion within the former Soviet Union (Lankina, Libman, and Obydenkova 2016). Bermeo (2016) is also optimistic about the prospects for democracy. She argues that so long as democratic institutions remain, they can survive authoritarian interludes. Finally, Inglehart (2016) asserts that democracy is most likely to be threatened when faced with declining economic conditions, but that this trajectory can be reversed. Ultimately, this perspective holds that elections have become such a norm that they remain even in authoritarian settings, and that this represents an ideological victory for democracy.

However, an alternative perspective to those arguments highlights the fundamentally different role that elections play in authoritarian regimes. Regular manipulation and the need to even entertain electoral boycotts at all may instead signal the demise of liberal democratic principles altogether. Ambrosio (2014) asserts that electoral authoritarian regimes have far more in common with closed authoritarian regimes than they do with liberal democracies. He argues that elections work to consolidate authoritarian power for these regimes, rather than genuinely allowing the public to hold leaders accountable and make their preferences known. Dawson and Hanley (2016) agree, claiming that the proliferation of these regimes and electoral manipulation represent an unambiguous failure for liberalism. They note that elections that sustain authoritarian rule cannot and do not serve the ideological goals of democracy. They remind us not to be fooled by the existence of elections, noting that in many cases "liberal institutional forms mask the illiberal parameters constraining political and culture change" (Dawson and Hanley 2016: 30).

This perspective aligns with many of the assertions about the distinctive role that elections play in electoral authoritarian regimes. Elections can serve as tools of control and cooptation of the opposition, which can further authoritarian control (Reuter et al. 2016). They provide valuable information to the regime on voter satisfaction and the perceived legitimacy of the authoritarian elites (Schedler 2013; Simpser 2013; Little et al. 2015; Miller 2015). Hale (2016) highlights the enduring nature of patronalism in combination with the strong presidential systems across the region for democratic deficits. In this view, elections or other institutions of democracy cannot bring about the liberalization of the political system; instead, they can prevent it from occurring through the facilitation of patronal networks and personal connections.

In these veins, elections have transformed from vehicles for transparency and accountability to vehicles of retrenchment and authoritarian consolidation.

The argument and findings of this book tend to favor the latter perspective, but admit that the former holds value as well. Informational manipulation is theorized to serve the long-term goal of enhanced legitimacy and further regime consolidation. The empirical findings show that this strategy is more likely in executive elections, in elections with high incumbent dominance, and in elections with lower competition. Moreover, the case studies also reveal that after the deployment of this strategy, political institutions can be further adjusted so as to perpetuate regime control. There is no denying that in these circumstances, elections do not function in the same way that they do in democracies. Similarly, opposition boycotts represent a strategy with a bleak view of the electoral process. When political actors decide that the most effective strategy, in circumstances of low competitiveness, is to abandon elections altogether, hoping to tarnish the regime and its legitimacy, this too signals the paradox of electoral authoritarianism. If the primary political institution associated with democracy can be regarded as a lost cause, then elections clearly do not represent a universal path toward democracy.

And yet, I contend that the theory and evidence are telling in other ways as well. The impetus of this book is that while these regimes are not democracies, and in most cases are not necessarily moving toward democracy, they nonetheless feature genuine political strategy and decision making. Elections may have been adopted due to the prominence of democratic institutions in the wake of the collapse of the Soviet Union, highlighting the view that they have become a norm of global politics. But this book hopes to move beyond the transition paradigm that often aimed to view any setbacks simply as that—temporary hiccups along the path to democracy. Many of these regimes have been quite persistent, leading both incumbent and opposition actors to adapt to the varying conditions of the elections. This demonstrates that we should focus more on the dynamics of these regimes as they currently stand, rather than their progress, or lack thereof, toward democracy. This regime type, electoral authoritarianism, necessitates the scrutiny of elections not as the institutions of democratic openness,[1] but of political arenas with different stakes and motivations for each side. As such, they now provide us with a public venue for observing the political calculus and machinations that characterize electoral authoritarian regimes, and allow us to evaluate the long-term consequences of different strategies.

One conclusion that should be clear is that the electoral authoritarian regime type is likely here to stay for at least the time being. This regime type may eventually prove to be a pathway toward full authoritarianism, or it could eventually provide the necessary foundation for more genuine democratic competition. Regardless, these regimes feature elections that operate under a different logic and thus feature distinct options for both incumbent and opposition political actors. I intend this study to contribute to the broader study of authoritarian resilience, consolidation, and breakdown. Authoritarian practices have been the common unifier for this region, and while some governments have demonstrated recent improvements (Ukraine, Georgia, and Moldova), it is too early to consider them long-term successes. None of the ten states included in this study currently hold a rating of "Free" from Freedom House, nor have they earned the designation of electoral democracy. As recent studies have noted, this region still shares many more similarities than differences concerning political developments (Hale 2016; Anders 2016). While the political trajectories are more in question in the three above-mentioned states, the unifying feature among these seemingly disparate cases is the genuine possibility for authoritarian resilience and consolidation, as well as the potential for authoritarian breakdown. Elections now serve one of the primary arenas for these very situations, so the scrutiny of strategies, the consideration of goals, costs, and benefits, and the examination of short-term and long-term effects all further our understanding of these phenomena.

IMPLICATIONS FOR
PRACTIONERS OF PRO-DEMOCRATIC EFFORTS

One of the primary conclusions of the book concerns the selection of different strategies of electoral manipulation depending on the conditions of the election. The reduction of manipulation and fraud is one of the foremost goals for election monitors and democracy promotion organizations more generally. So what implications are there for practioners of election observation and democracy promoters from the findings of this book? One conclusion echoes more recent findings that a large amount of manipulation now occurs prior to the election day itself (Donno and Roussias 2012). This shift has been attributed to regime learning and attempts to thwart negative assessments that have often been based mainly on election day fraud. Both informational and instrumental manipulation hinder the ability of all political actors and the electorate to participate in the election freely, fairly, and without consequence, even if the manipulation is indirect. The frequency of pre-election manipulation should encourage election monitors to be more proactive in dealing with manipulation that takes place weeks or months before any votes are cast.

Yet this book also agrees with the sentiment of others (Birch 2011a; Simpser 2013) that election monitoring can only do so much. Governments and pro-government actors learn from the behavior of election monitors and adjust accordingly, so if greater observation missions focused on manipulation during the pre-election campaign, it could produce further unintended consequences. This gets to one of the paradoxes of international election monitoring; organizations like the OSCE are invited to conduct such missions with the permission of the government, which in theory has the potential to influence reports.[2] With this is also the fact that assessments from international election observers are non-binding, as home governments have little motivation or incentive to agree to more stringent terms. Moreover, election observation missions are by definition short-term endeavors focused on a concrete end point. They are inherently limited in their ability to speak to or capture long-term effects from electoral manipulation. Thus the monitors set the vast majority of their attention on the actual process of voting and whether the outcome was genuine and reflects the will of the people. This may be more effective at curbing fraud on election day than it is at reducing pre-election manipulation.

I do not consider election monitoring to be completely hamstrung in their activities. Quite the opposite, I still see ways for their actions to potentially influence electoral manipulation and reduce its frequency. Naming and shaming has been a fairly successful tactic against human rights abuses by putting negative, unwanted international attention on regime actions (Murdie 2012).[3] Even if such a tactic produces minimal or cosmetic changes, this could be a welcome improvement to the conduct of elections in electoral authoritarian regimes. Of course, such an approach is most useful when the West has sufficient leverage with the receiving state, a dynamic that is definitely reduced by incumbent dominance rooted in the reliance on natural resource exports (Levitsky and Way 2012). Greater scrutiny and naming and shaming tactics may work to reduce the occurrence of electoral manipulation, even if these efforts may be limited by the incumbent dominance present. Additionally, I applaud the increased focus on institutional changes and recommendations that monitors provide. The OSCE frequently suggests adjustments to the Election Code, registration processes, and the handling of electoral disputes both during and after the election. This last point in particular is very important: helping to establish a process through which anti-regime candidates and parties can make complaints and report manipulation without political influence is paramount. These actions provide a longer view of elections and their political impacts.

The importance of international actors in assisting opposition actors in electoral authoritarian regimes has also been increasingly discussed. Democracy assistance to civil society and opposition parties has been linked to many of the opposition electoral victories across the region (Bunce and Wolchik 2012). Given that opposition forces are more likely to unify under conditions of low incumbent dominance, this could be a priority for such actors. By encouraging actors to unite and mount electoral challenges, this could actually serve to postpone increases in incumbent dominance. Once incumbent dominance is high, opposition actors are more likely to harden their ideological differences and to focus more exclusively on their base (Greene 2007); this is unconducive for opposition unity and for opposition electoral gains.

Moreover, the presence of electoral monitors has been linked to the decision for opposition actors to both boycott and not boycott certain contests (Beaulieu and Hyde 2009; Kelley 2012). Democracy promoters should definitely continue to support participation in elections, as boycotts rarely seem to have the intended long-term effects, and could instead be detrimental. Even as tools of authoritarian consolidation, elections still provide the opposition with the opportunity to take part, present a counter perspective, and vie for the chance at power. Gaining even some power could present occasions for electoral reform, which could potentially reverse the authoritarian tendencies of the institution.

FUTURE RESEARCH

One potentially fruitful avenue for future research concerns the types of strategies included in the study. In this book, I purposely selected strategies that could easily be classified at serving long- or short-term goals, where the optimal benefit was clearly understood. One interesting approach could be to select more ambiguous strategies and examine whether they also follow any identifiable patterns. Incumbent strategies that may help win an election but are also very public could be one prototype to consider. Similarly, incumbent strategies that are not manipulation, such as the decision to participate in pre-election debates or to grant concessions to the opposition, could also be considered. Opposition strategies could be expanded to include the types of campaign messages used, including whether they are overtly critical of the government, how they select certain candidates, and whether they vary their campaign style. The framework established in this book could be applied to many other strategies, which could reveal supportive or negative findings.

This book built upon the foundational work of Magaloni (2006), Greene (2007), Birch (2011a), Bunce and Wolchik (2012), Schedler (2013), Simpser (2013) and others in its theoretical expectations on incumbent and opposition electoral strategies. I have purposely focused on strategies that all occur in the pre-election campaign period in the theoretical and empirical considerations so as to avoid any potential collinearity from selection strategies that precede or follow one another. However, subsequent research could explore the ways in which any of these strategies may influence election day or post-election behavior. For example, does instrumental manipulation actually influence the decision by opposition figures to unite and protest the official elections results, a relationship that has been asserted but not tested? Additionally, are opposition boycotts associated with greater instances of election day fraud? The selection of electoral strategies is very probably a multistep process, with each side responding to the other at subsequent stages of the process and this would be an area worthy of future research.

A third avenue for further study could be the dynamics of incumbent and opposition strategies at the subnational level. Many recent studies have explored authoritarian behavior at the regional level, noting how manipulation and fraud can vary depending upon the presence of loyal pro-government forces (Moser and White 2016; Goodnow, Moser and Smith 2014; Reuter 2015). Opposition cooptation can also be observed regionally, demonstrating the diffusion and contagion effects of such actions across time in electoral authoritarian regimes (Reuter et al. 2016). This begs the question of whether and to what degree the strategies explored in this book also vary at the subnational level. Some, but not all, post-Soviet states are federal in institutional design, creating more opportunities for political competition at the regional level in some states. Does this affect strategies of regional incumbents as they presumably seek to maintain power and influence? Do incumbent strategies depend on whether the actor is explicitly supportive of the national government and do they learn from the national figures? What influences opposition behavior at the subnational level? Are the benefits and costs the same, or do strategies such as pre-election coalitions and boycotts face a different calculus at the regional level? Moreover, these questions could benefit from either a cross-national approach or a single case-study approach. Either methodological design would offer new insights into the decision making and strategic actions of incumbents and opposition actors operating sub-nationally in electoral authoritarian regimes.

NOTES

1. This is not to say that elections never lead to democratization; instead, it suggests that our baseline assumption when considering elections should not be the inevitable march in that direction.

2. Although, as mentioned in chapter 2, this does not usually occur. Executive summaries may be more deferential and positive, while the report itself is usually more explicit.

3. Of course, naming and shaming can have the opposite effect, or can simply cause the behavior to shift from one strategy to another (Hafner-Burton 2008).

References

Abazov, Rafis. (2007). "The parliamentary election in Kyrgyzstan, February/ March 2005," *Electoral Studies* 26: 507–533.

Ambrosio, Thomas. (2014). "Beyond the transition paradigm: A research agenda for authoritarian consolidation." *Demokratizatsiya*, 22(3): 471–494.

Anders, Aslund. (2016). "The three regions of the old Soviet bloc." *Journal of Democracy* 28(1): 89–101.

Argersinger, Peter H. (1985). "New perspectives on election fraud in the gilded age." *Political Science Quarterly* 100(4): 669–687.

Ash, Constantine. (2015). "The election trap: The cycle of post-electoral repression and opposition fragmentation in Lukashenko's Belarus" *Democratization*, 22(6): 1030–1053.

Aslaksen, Silje. 2010. "Oil and democracy: More than a cross-country correlation?" *Journal of Peace Research* 47(4): 421–431.

Bader, Max. (2012). "Trends and patterns in electoral malpractice in post-Soviet Eurasia," *Journal of Eurasian Studies* 3: 49–57.

———. (2014). "Democracy promotion and authoritarian diffusion: The foreign origins of post-Soviet election laws" *Europe-Asia Studies,* 66(8): 1350–1370.

Baekken, Havard. (2015). "Selections before elections: Double standards in implementing election registration procedures in Russia?" *Communist and Post-Communist Studies* 48: 61–70.

Beaulieu, Emily. (2014). *Electoral Protest and Democracy in the Developing World.* New York: Cambridge University Press.

Beaulieu, Emily, and Susan Hyde. (2009). "In the shadow of democracy promotion: Strategic manipulation, international observers and election boycotts." *Comparative Political Studies* 42(3): 392–415.

Beissinger, Mark. (2007). "Structure and example in modular political phenomena: The Diffusion of Bulldozer/Rose/Orange/Tulip Revolutions," *Perspectives on Politics* 4(2): 259–276.

Birch, Sarah. (1997). "Nomenklatura democratization: Electoral clientelism in post-Soviet Ukraine. *Democratization* 4: 40–62.

———. (2007). "Electoral systems and electoral misconduct." *Comparative Politics Studies* 40(12): 1533–1556.

———. (2011a). *Electoral Malpractice*. Oxford, UK: Oxford University Press.

———. (2011b). "Post-Soviet electoral practices in comparative perspective." *Europe-Asia Studies*. 63(4): 703–725.

Blaydes, Lisa, and Drew A. Linzer. (2012). "Elite competition, religiosity, and anti-Americanism in the Islamic world." *American Political Science Review* 106(2): 225–243.

Boix, Carles. (2009). "The emergence of parties and party systems." In *The Oxford Handbook of Comparative Politics*. Carles Boix and Susan Carol Stokes (Eds.). Oxford; New York: Oxford University Press.

Boix, Carles, and Milan W. Svolik. (2013). "The foundations of limited authoritarian government: Institutions, commitment, and power-sharing in dictatorships." *The Journal of Politics.* 75(2): 300–316.

Bratton, Michael. (1998). "Second elections in Africa." *Journal of Democracy*, 9(3): 51–56.

Bratton, Michael, and Nicolas Van de Walle. (1997). *Democratic experiments in Africa: Regime transitions in comparative perspective*. New York; Cambridge, UK: Cambridge University Press.

Brownlee, Jason. (2007). *Authoritarianism in an age of democratization*. Cambridge, UK: Cambridge University Press.

———. (2009a). "Portents of pluralism: How hybrid regimes affect democratic transitions." *American Journal of Political Science* 53(3): 515–532.

———. (2009b). "Harbinger of democracy: Competitive elections before the end of authoritarianism." In *Democratization by elections: A new mode of transition*. Staffan Lindberg (Ed.). Baltimore: Johns Hopkins University Press.

Boyko, Nazar, and Erik S. Herron. (2015). "The effects of technical parties and partisan election management bodies on voting outcomes." *Electoral Studies* 40: 23–33.

Bueno de Mesquita, Bruce. 2003. *The logic of political survival*. Cambridge, MA: MIT Press.

Bunce, Valerie, and Sharon L. Wolchik. (2011). *Defeating authoritarian leaders in postcommunist countries.* Cambridge, UK: Cambridge University Press.

Cameron, David, and Mitchell Orenstein. (2012). "Post-Soviet authoritarianism: The influence of Russia in its 'near-abroad,'" *Post-Soviet Affairs*, 28(1): 1–44.

Carothers, Thomas and Saskia Brechenmacher. (2014). *Closing space: Democracy and human rights support under fire.* Carnegie Endowment for International Peace. http://carnegieendowment.org/files/closing_space.pdf.

Case, William. 2006. "Manipulative skills: How do rulers control the electoral arena" in *Electoral authoritarianism: The dynamics of unfree competition.* Andreas Schedler (Ed.). Boulder, CO: Lynne Rienner Publishers, Inc.

Chausov, Yury. (2011). "Party theatrics for political process." *Belarusian yearbook 2010*. Minsk: Belarusian Institute for Strategic Studies

Clark, William. (2005). "The Russian election cycle, 2003–2004." *Electoral Studies* 24: 511–519.

———. (2009). "The presidential transition in Russia, March 2008." *Electoral Studies* 28: 342–345.

———. (2013). "The 2012 presidential election in Russia: Putin returns." *Electoral Studies* 32: 374–377.

Cornell, Svante. (2001). "Democratization falters in Azerbaijan," *Journal of Democracy* 12(2): 118–131.

Cox, Gary W. (1997). *Making votes count: Strategic coordination in the world's electoral systems.* New York: Cambridge University Press.

———. (2009). "Authoritarian elections and leadership succession, 1975–2004." *APSA 2009 Toronto Meeting Paper.*

Crabtree, Charles, Christopher Fariss, and Paul Schuler. (2016). "The presidential election in Belarus, October 2015" *Electoral Studies* 42: 304–307.

Darden, Keith. (2001). "Blackmail as a tool of state domination: Ukraine under Kuchma." *East European Constitutional Review* 2: 67–71.

———. (2008). "The integrity of corrupt states: Graft as an informal state institution." *Politics and Society* 36: 35–59.

Dawisha, Karen, and Stephen Deets. (2005). "Political learning in post-communist elections," *East European Politics and Societies* 20(4): 691–728.

Dawson, James, and Sean Hanley. (2016). "The fading mirage of the liberal consensus." *Journal of Democracy* 27(1): 30–34.

Donno, Daniela. (2013). "Elections and democratization in authoritarian regimes."*American Journal of Political Science* 57(3): 703–716.

Donno, Daniela, and Nasos Roussias. (2012). "Does cheating pay? The effect of electoral misconduct on party systems." *Comparative Political Studies* 45(5): 575–605.

Eifert, Benn, Edward Miguel, and Daniel N. Posner. (2010). "Political competition and ethnic identification in Africa." *American Journal of Political Science* 54(2): 494–510.

Ergun, Ayca. (2009). "The presidential election in Azerbaijan, October 2008." *Electoral Studies* 28(4): 647–651.

Fairbanks, Charles. (2004). "Georgia's Rose revolution." *Journal of Democracy* 15(2): 110–124.

Foa, Roberto Stefan, and Yascha Mounk. (2016). "The democratic disconnect." *Journal of Democracy* 27(3): 5–17.

———. (2017). "The signs of deconsolidation." *Journal of Democracy* 28(1): 5–15.

Flores, Thomas, and Irfan Nooruddin (2016). *Elections in hard times: Building stronger democracies in the 21st century.* Cambridge: Cambridge University Press.

Frear, Matthew. (2013). "The parliamentary elections in Belarus, September 2012." *Electoral Studies* 33: 350–353.

Frye, Timothy, Scott Gehlback, Kyle L. Marquardt, and Ora John Reuter. (2017). "Is Putin's popularity real?" *Post-Soviet Affairs* 33(1): 1–15.

Fumagalli, Matteo. (2012). "The 2011 presidential elections in Kyrgyzstan." *Electoral Studies* 31: 864–867.

———. (2016). "The 2015 parliamentary election in Kyrgyzstan." *Electoral Studies* 42: 300–303.

Gandhi, Jennifer, and Ellen Lust-Okar. (2009). "Elections under authoritarianism." *Annual Review of Political Science.* 12 (1).

Gandhi, J., and A. Przeworski. (2007). "Authoritarian institutions and the survival of autocrats." *Comparative Political Studies* 40(11): 1279–1301.

Gandhi, Jennifer, and Ora John Reuter (2013). "The incentives for pre-electoral coalitions in non-democratic elections." *Democratization* 20(1): 137–159.

Gasiorowski, Mark J. 1995. "Economic crisis and political regime change: An event history analysis." *The American Political Science Review* 89(4): 882.

Gehlbach, Scott, and Alberto Simpser. (2015). "Electoral manipulation as bureaucratic control." *American Journal of Political Science* 59(1): 212–224.

Gel'man, Vladimir. (2015). "Political opposition in Russia: A troubled transformation." *Europe-Asia Studies* 67(2): 177–191.

———. (2016). "The vicious circle of post-Soviet neopatrimonialism in Russia," *Post-Soviet Affairs* 32(5): 455–473.

Gilbert, Leah, and Payam Mohseni. (2011). "Beyond authoritarianism: The conceptualization of hybrid regimes." *Studies in Comparative International Development* 46(3): 270–297.

Golosov, Grigory. (2011). "The regional roots of electoral authoritarianism in Russia." *Europe-Asia Studies* 63(4): 623–639.

———. (2013). "Machine politics: The concept and its implications for post-Soviet studies." *Demokratizatsiya* 21(4): 459–480.

Goodnow, Regina, Robert Moser, and Tony Smith. (2014). "Ethnicity and electoral manipulation in Russia," *Electoral Studies* 36(4): 15–27.

Greene, Kenneth F. (2007)*. Why dominant parties lose: Mexico's democratization in comparative perspective.* Cambridge, UK; New York: Cambridge University Press.

Greene, Samuel. (2014). *Moscow in movement: Power and opposition in Putin's Russia.* Palo Alto, CA: Stanford University Press.

Haber, Stephen H., Noel Maurer, and Armando Razo. 2003. *The Politics of property rights: Political instability, credible commitments, and economic growth in Mexico, 1876-1929.* New York; Cambridge, UK: Cambridge University Press.

Haber, Stephen, and Victor Menaldo. 2011. "Do natural resources fuel authoritarianism? A reappraisal of the resource curse." *American Political Science Review* 105(1): 1–26.

Hafner- Burton, Emilie. (2008). "Sticks and stones: Naming and shaming the human rights enforcement problem." *International Organization* 62: 689–716.

Hale, Henry. (2007). "Correlates of clientelism: Political economy, politicized ethnicity, and postcommunist transition." In Herbert Kitschelt and Steven Wilkinson (Eds.). *Patrons, clients and policies: Patterns of democratic accountability and political competition.* (pp. 227–250) Cambridge, UK: Cambridge University Press.

———. (2015). *Patronal politics: Eurasian regime dynamics in comparative perspective.* Cambridge, UK: Cambridge University Press.

———. (2016). "25 years after the USSR: What's gone wrong?" *Journal of Democracy* 27(3): 24–35.

Harutyunyan, Sargis. (2013). "Hovannisyan sees no clean vote." *Radio Free Europe/Radio Liberty*, https://www.azatutyun.am/a/24901350.html.

Harvey, Cole. (2016). "Changes in the menu of manipulation: Electoral fraud, ballot stuffing, and voter pressure in the 2011 Russian election." *Electoral Studies* 41: 105–117.

Hauser, Megan. (2018). "Does electoral manipulation vary? Examining the conditions for instrumental and informational manipulation in post-Soviet election," *The Soviet and Post-Soviet Review* 45: 5–50.

Hermet, Guy, Richard Rose, and Alain Rouquie. (1978). *Elections without choice* 15. London: Macmillan.

Hicken, Allen. (2007). "How do rules and institutions encourage vote buying?" in *Elections for sale: The causes and consequences of vote buying*. Frederic Schaffer (Ed.), (pp. 47–60). Boulder, CO; London: Lynne Rienner.

Huskey, Eugene, and David Hill. (2011). "The 2010 referendum and parliamentary elections in Kyrgyzstan." *Electoral Studies* 30: 876–879.

Huskey, Eugene, and Gulnara Iskakova. (2010). "The barriers to intra-opposition cooperation in the post-communist world Evidence from Kyrgyzstan." *Post-Soviet Affairs* 26(3): 228–262.

Hyde, Susan D. (2011). *The pseudo-democrat's dilemma: Why election observation became an international norm*. Ithaca: Cornell University Press.

Hyde, Susan D., and Nikolay Marinov. (2012). "Which elections can be lost?" *Political Analysis* 20(2): 191–210.

Inglehart, Ronald. (2016). "How much should we worry?" *Journal of Democracy* 27(3): 18–23.

Isaacs, Rico. (2008). "The parliamentary election in Kazakhstan, August 2007." *Electoral Studies* 27(2): 381–385.

Jarabinsky, Ivan. (2015). "Appearances are deceptive: Credibility of the Russian Election Commission" *East European Politics* 31(1): 88–103.

Jawad, Pamela. (2012). "Elections and treatment of the opposition in post-Soviet Georgia." In *Presidents, oligarch and bureaucrats: Forms of rule in the post-Soviet Space*. Susan Stewart, Margarete Klein, Andrea Schmitz, and Hans-Henning Schroder (Eds.). Burlington, VT: Ashgate.

Kanapyanov, Timur. (2018). "Role and place of the parliament of Kazakhstan in the system of checks and balances." *Communist and Post-Communist Studies* 51(1): 81–87.

Kellam, Marisa. (2015). "Why pre-electoral coalitions in presidential systems?" *British Journal of Political Science* (pp. 1–21). doi:10.1017/S0007123415000198.

Kelley, Judith Green. (2011). "Do international monitors increase or decrease opposition boycotts?" *Comparative Political Studies* 44(11): 1527–1556.

———. (2012). *Monitoring democracy: When international election observation works, and why it often fails*. Princeton, NJ: Princeton University Press.

Kendall-Taylor, Andrea. (2012). "Purchasing power: Oil, elections and regime durability in Azerbaijan and Kazakhstan." *Europe-Asia Studies* 64(4): 737–760.

Korosteleva, Elena. (2009). "Was there a quiet revolution? Belarus after the 2006 presidential election," *Journal of Communist Studies and Transition Politics* 25(2-3): 324–346.

Kynev, Alexander (2015). "Combating the opposition: United Russia's electoral and party reforms 2012-13." In *Systemic and non-systemic opposition in the Russian Federation: Civil society Awakens?* Cameron Ross (Ed.), (pp. 139–152). Farnham & Burlington, VT: Ashgate.

Lankina, Tomila, Alexander Libman, and Anastassia Obydenkova. (2016). "Authoritarian and democratic diffusion in post-communist regions." *Comparative Political Studies* 49(12): 1599–1629.

LaPorte, Jody. (2015). "Hidden in plain sight: Political opposition and hegemonic authoritarianism in Azerbaijan." *Post-Soviet Affairs* 31(4): 339–66.

Lassila, Jussi. (2016). "Aleksei Naval'nyi and populist ordering of Putin's stability," *Europe-Asia Studies* 68(1): 118–137.

Levitsky, Steven, and Lucan Way. (2006). "Linkage versus leverage: Rethinking the international dimension of regime change." *Comparative Politics* 38(4): 379–400.

———. (2010). *Competitive authoritarianism hybrid regimes after the Cold War.* Cambridge, UK: Cambridge University Press.

———. (2012). "Beyond patronage: Violent struggle, ruling party cohesion, and authoritarian durability." *Perspectives on Politics* 10(4): 869–889.

Lindberg, Staffan I. (2006a). "Tragic protest: Why do opposition parties boycott elections?" In *Electoral authoritarianism: The dynamics of unfree competition.* (pp. 149–166) Boulder, CO: Lynne Riener.

———. (2006b). "Opposition parties and democratisation in sub-Saharan Africa." *Journal of Contemporary African Studies* 24(1): 123–138.

———. (2009). "Democratization by elections: A new mode of transition?" In *Democratization by elections: A new mode of transition.* Staffan Lindberg (Ed.). Baltimore: Johns Hopkins University Press.

Linz, Juan J. (1973). "Opposition in and under authoritarian regime: The case of Spain." in *Regimes and Oppositions.* Robert Dahl (Ed.). New Haven, CT: Yale University Press.

———. (2000). *Totalitarian and authoritarian regimes.* Boulder, CO: Lynne Rienner Publishers.

Little, Andrew. (2015). "Fraud and monitoring and non-competitive elections." *Political Science Research and Methods* 3(1): 21–41.

Little, Andrew, Joshua Tucker, and Tom LaGatta. (2015). "Elections, protest, and the alteration of power." *The Journal of Politics* 77(4): 1142–1156.

Lust-Okar, Ellen. (2006). "Elections under authoritarianism: Preliminary lessons from Jordan." *Democratization* 13(3): 456–471.

———. (2009). "Legislative elections in hegemonic authoritarian regimes: Competitive clientelism and resistance to democratization." In *Democratization by Elections.* Staffan Lindberg (Ed.), (pp. 101–127). Baltimore: Johns Hopkins University Press.

Magaloni, Beatriz. (2006). *Voting for autocracy: hegemonic party survival and its demise in Mexico.* Cambridge: Cambridge University Press.

Mansfield, Edward, and Jack Snyder. (2002). "Democratic transitions, institutional strength, and war." *International Organization* 56(2): 297–337.

March, Luke. (2009). "Managing opposition in a hybrid regime: Just Russia and parastatal opposition." *Slavic Review* 68(3): 504–527.

Marples, David. (2006). "Color revolutions: The Belarus case." *Communist and Post-Communist Studies* 39: 351–364.

———. (2012). "Parliamentary elections in Belarus arouse cynicism, anger among population." *Eurasian Daily Monitor* 9: 173. https://jamestown.org/program/parliamentary-elections-in-belarus-arouse-cynicism-anger-among-population./.

Marshall, Monty, Keith Jaggers, and Ted Gurr. (2017). *Polity IV project political regime characteristics and transitions, 1800–2016 dataset users' manual.* 1st ed. Center for Systemic Peace.

McFaul, Michael. (2005). "Transitions from postcommunism," *Journal of Democracy* 16(3): 5–19.

Miller, Michael K. (2015). "Elections, information, and policy responsiveness in autocratic regimes." *Comparative Political Studies* 48(6): 691–727.

Mommsen, M. (2010). "Ispolnitel'naia vlast' v sisteme rossiiskogo gosudarstva i tandem Putin/Medvedev" *Rossia: Itogi poslednego desiatiletiia (1998–2008). i perspektivy razvitiia: Sbornik statei.* (pp. 33–66) Moskva: ROSSPEN.

Morse, Yonatan L. (2012). "The era of electoral authoritarianism." *World Politics* 64(1): 161–198.

Moser, Robert, and Allison White. (2017). "Does electoral fraud spread? The expansion of electoral manipulation in Russia." *Post-Soviet Affairs* 33(2): 85–99.

Mueller, Sean. (2014). "The parliamentary and executive elections in the Republic of Georgia, 2012." *Electoral Studies* 34: 342–346.

Murdie, Amanda. (2012). "Transnational NGO activism outside of democracies: The behavior and effect of human rights INGOs on political repression and democracy." in *Liberal interventionism and democracy promotion.* Dursun Peksen (Ed.). Lanhan, MD: Lexington.

Musabayov, Rasim, and Shulman, Rakhmil. (2010). "Azerbaijan in 2006–2010." *Sociological monitoring, comparative analysis of findings of sociological survey held in the republic by totals of 2006–2010 years.*

Myagkov, Mikhail, Peter Ordeshook, and Dimitri Shakin. (2009). *The forensics of election fraud: Russia and Ukraine.* Cambridge, UK: Cambridge University Press.

Nedolyan, Ara. (2013). "Political parties before, during and after the elections of 2012–2013." *Caucasus Analytical Digest:* 53–54.

Nikolyuk, Sergey. (2011). "Presidential election: Sociology of electoral stability." *Belarusian Yearbook 2010.* Minsk: Belarusian Institute for Strategic Studies.

Nyblade, Benjamin, and Steven R. Reed. (2008). Who cheats? Who loots? Political competition and corruption in Japan, 1947–1993. *American Journal of Political Science* 52(4): 926–941.

Ohman, Magnus. (2013). *Political finance oversight Handbook.* (International Foundations for Electoral Systems) OSCE.

———. (2006). "Republic of Belarus presidential election 19 March 2006." *OSCE/ODIHR Election Observation Mission Report.* Warsaw.

———. (2008). "Republic of Azerbaijan presidential election 15 October 2008." *OSCE/ODIHR Election Observation Mission Final Report.* Warsaw.

———. (2009). "Republic of Moldova early parliamentary elections 29 July 2009." *OSCE/ODIHR Election Observation Mission Final Report*. Warsaw.

———. (2012). "Russian Federation elections to the state duma 4 December 2011." *OSCE/ODIHR Election Observation Mission Final Report*. Warsaw.

———. (2015). "Republic of Kazakhstan early presidential elections 26 April 2015." *OSCE/ODIHR Election Observation Mission Final Report*. Warsaw.

———. (2016a). "Kyrgyz Republic parliamentary elections 4 October 2015." *OSCE/ODIHR Election Observation Mission Final Report*. Warsaw.

———. (2016b). "Russian Federation state duma elections 18 September 2016." *OSCE/ODIHR Election Observation Mission Final Report*. Warsaw.

———. (2018a). "Kyrgyz Republic presidential election 15 October 2017." *OSCE/ODIHR Election Observation Mission Final Report*. Warsaw.

———. (2018b). "Russian Federation presidential election 18 March 2018." *ODHIR Election Observation Mission Final Report*. Warsaw.

Padhol, Uladzimir, and David Marples. (2011). "The 2010 presidential election in Belarus." *Problems of Post-Communism* 58(1): 3–16.

Pappas, Takis. (2016). "Distinguishing liberal democracy's challengers." *Journal of Democracy* 27(4): 22–36.

Petrov, Nikolay, Maria Lipman, and Henry Hale. (2014). "Three dilemmas of hybrid regime governance: Russia from Putin to Putin." *Post-Soviet Affairs* 30(1): 1–26.

Pleines, Heiko. (2008). "Manipulating politics: Domestic investors in Ukrainian privatization auctions 2000-2004." *Europe-Asia Studies* 60(7): 1177–1197.

———. (2012). "From competitive authoritarianism to defective democracy: Political regimes in Ukraine before and after the Orange Revolution." In *Presidents, oligarch and bureaucrats: Forms of rule in the post-Soviet space*. Susan Stewart, Margarete Klein, Andrea Schmitz, and Hans-Henning Schroder (Eds.). Burlington, VT: Ashgate.

Puddington, Arch, and Tyler Roylance. (2016). "Anxious dictators, wavering democrats." *Journal of Democracy* 27(2): 86–100.

———. (2017). "The dual threat of populists and autocrats." *Journal of Democracy* 28(2): 105–119.

Radnitz, Scott. (2012). "Oil in the family: Managing presidential succession in Azerbaijan." *Democratization* 19(1): 60–77.

Remington, Thomas F. (2001). *The Russian parliament: Institutional evolution in a transitional regime, 1989-1999*. New Haven, CT: Yale University Press.

Reuter, Ora John. (2013). "Regional patrons and hegemonic party electoral performance in Russia." *Post-Soviet Affairs* 29(2): 101–135.

Reuter, Ora John, Noah Buckley, Alexandra Shubenkova, and Guzel Garifullina. (2016). "Local elections in authoritarian regimes: An elite-based theory with evidence from Russian mayoral elections." *Comparative Political Studies* 49(5): 662–697.

Reuter, Ora John, and Jennifer Gandhi. (2013). "The incentives for pre-electoral coalitions in non-democratic elections." *Democratization* 20(1): 137–159.

Reuter, Ora John, and Thomas Remington. (2009). "Dominant party regimes and the commitment problem: The case of united Russia." *Comparative Political Studies* 42(4): 501–526.

———. (2012a). "Armenian election alignments take shape." *Radio Free Europe/Radio Liberty.* https://www.rferl.org/a/armenia_election_blocs_take_shape/24508594.html.

———. (2012b). "Armenian politics enters new phase." *Radio Free Europe/Radio Liberty.* https://www.rferl.org/a/armenia-politics-new-phase/24595810.html.

———. (2012c). "Belarus opposition urges election boycott, says 'go fishing' instead." *Radio Free Europe/Radio Liberty* https://www.rferl.org/a/belarus-opposition-urges-election-boycott/24711220.html.

———. (2012d). "Six Belarusian groups call for vote boycott." *Radio Free Europe/Radio Liberty.* https://www.rferl.org/a/six-belarus-opposition-groups-urge-elections-boycott/24716030.html.

———. (2012e). "Belarus election commission slams opposition's vote boycott." *Radio Free Europe/Radio Liberty.* https://www.rferl.org/a/belarus-commission-slams-opposition-vote-boycott/24710962.html.

———. (2013). "Armenian opposition takes stock after election defeats," *Radio Free Europe/Radio Liberty.* https://www.rferl.org/a/armenia-opposition-takes-stock/24998864.html.

Roessler, Phillip G., and Marc M. Howard. (2009). "Post-cold war political regimes: When do elections matter?" In *Democratization by elections.* Staffan Lindberg (Ed.), (pp. 101–127). Baltimore: Johns Hopkins University Press.

Ross, Michael L. (2001). "Does oil hinder democracy?" *World Politics* 53(3): 325–361.

Rovdo, Vladimir. (2011). "Presidential campaign." *Belarusian yearbook 2010.* Minsk: Belarusian Institute for Strategic Studies.

Sakwa, Richard. (2005). "The 2003–2004 Russian elections and prospects for democracy." *Europe-Asia Studies* 57(3): 369–398.

Sargsyan, Isabella. (2013). "Armenian elections. No room for optimism?" *Caucasus Analytical Digest*: 53–54.

Schedler, Andreas. (2002). "The menu of manipulation." *Journal of Democracy* 13(2): 36–50.

———. (2006). *Electoral authoritarianism: The dynamics of unfree competition.* Boulder, CO: L. Rienner Publishers.

———. (2009a). "Sources of competition under electoral authoritarianism." In *Democratization by Elections.* Staffan Lindberg (Ed.), (pp. 101–127). Baltimore: Johns Hopkins University Press.

———. (2009b). "The contingent power of authoritarian elections" in *Democratization by Elections.* Staffan Lindberg (Ed.), pp 291–313. Baltimore: Johns Hopkins University Press.

———. (2013). *The politics of uncertainty: Sustaining and subverting electoral authoritarianism.* Oxford: Oxford University Press.

Scott, James. (2012). "Funding freedom? The United States and democracy aid, 1988–2001." In *Liberal interventionism and democracy promotion.* Dursun Peksen (Ed.). Lanhan, MD: Lexington.

Seeberg, Merete Bech. (2014). "State capacity and the paradox of authoritarian elections." *Democratization* 21(7): 1265–1285.

Senyuva, Ozgehan. (2010). "Parliamentary elections in Moldova, April and July 2009." *Electoral Studies* 29: 190–195.

Shevtsova, Lilia. (2005). *Putin's Russia*. Washington, D.C. Carnegie Endowment for International Peace.

Silitski, Vitali. (2005). "Preempting democracy: The case of Belarus." *Journal of Democracy* 16(4): 83–97.

Simpser, Alberto. (2013). *Why governments and parties manipulate elections: Theory, practice, and implications*. New York: Cambridge University Press.

Sjoberg, Fredrik M. (2016). "Bring the party back in: Institutional design for 'smart election fraud.'" *Electoral Studies* 44: 307–318.

Smagulov, Kadyrzhan, Kultai Adilova, and Nesipbala Kambarova. (2016). "The 2015–2016 electoral cycle in Kazakhstan summed up." *Central Asia and the Caucasus* 17(4): 20–27.

Smith, Ian. (2014). "Election boycotts and hybrid regime survival." *Comparative Political Studies* 47(5): 743–765.

Sperling, Valerie. (2014). *Sex, politics and Putin: Political legitimacy in Russia*. New York: Oxford University Press.

Stepanian, Nare. (2013). "Sargsyan vows to cut poverty." *Radio Free Europe/Radio Liberty*. https://www.azatutyun.am/a/24888557.html.

Stern, David. (2010). "Belarus: Lukashenko's certain victory." *Global Post from Public Radio International*. https://www.pri.org/stories/2010-12-15/belarus-lukashenkos-certain-victory.

Stewart, Susan. (2012). *Presidents, oligarchs and bureaucrats: Forms of rule in the post-soviet space*. Burlington, VT: Farnham, UK: Ashgate.

Teorell, Jan, and Axel Hadenius. (2009). "Elections as levers of democratization: A global inquiry." In *Democratization by elections: A new mode of transition*. Staffan Lindberg (Ed.). Baltimore: Johns Hopkins University Press.

Thompson, Viktoriya. (2008). "Political opposition in Ukraine and its effectiveness." *Master's Thesis*. Ottawa: Carleton University. ProQuest MR40614.

Timm, Christian. (2012). "From corruption to rotation: Politics in Georgia before and after the Rose Revolution." In *Presidents, oligarch and bureaucrats: Forms of rule in the post-Soviet space*. Susan Stewart, Margarete Klein, Andrea Schmitz, and Hans-Henning Schroder (Eds.). Burlington, VT: Ashgate.

Tolstrup, Jakob. (2015). "Black knights and elections in authoritarian regimes: Why and how Russia supports authoritarian incumbents in post-Soviet states" *European Journal of Political Research* 54: 673–690.

Turovsky, Rostislav (2015). "The systemic opposition in authoritarian regimes: A case study of Russian regions." In *Systemic and non-Systemic opposition in the Russian Federation: Civil society awakens?* Cameron Ross (Ed.), (pp. 121–138). Farmham, VT: Ashgate.

Tsebelis, George. (1990). *Nested games: Rational choice in comparative politics*. Berkeley: University of California Press.

Tucker, Joshua. (2007). "Enough! Electoral fraud, collective action problems, and post-communist colored revolutions." *Perspectives on Politics* 5(3): 535–51.

Wahman, Michael. (2011). "Offices and policies—Why do oppositional parties form pre-electoral coalitions in competitive authoritarian regimes?" *Electoral Studies* 30: 642–657.

Way, Lucan. (2005a). "Kuchma's failed authoritarianism." *Journal of Democracy* 16(2): 131–45.

———. (2005b). "Authoritarian state building and the sources of regime competitiveness in the fourth wave: The cases of Belarus, Moldova, Russia and Ukraine." *World Politics* 57(2): 231–261.

———. (2015). "The limits of autocracy promotion: The case of Russia in the 'near abroad.'" *European Journal of Political Research* 54: 691–706.

———. (2016). "Weaknesses of autocracy promotion." *Journal of Democracy* 27(1): 64–75.

White, Stephen. 2009. "The duma election in Russia, December 2007." *Electoral Studies* 28(1): 171–173.

White, Stephen, and Elena Korosteleva-Polglase. (2006). "The parliamentary election and referendum in Belarus, October 2004." *Electoral Studies* 26: 147–191.

Wilson, Andrew. (2005). *Ukraine's Orange Revolution*. New Haven: Yale University Press.

———. (2011). *Belarus: The last dictatorship in Europe*. New Haven: Yale University Press.

Wilson, Kenneth. (2006). "Party system development under Putin," *Post-Soviet Affairs* 22(4): 314–348.

Yefimova, Nadezhda. (2011). "Public opinion: Yearly dynamics and certain results." *Belarusian Yearbook 2010*. Minsk: Belarusian Institute for Strategic Studies.

Zakaria, Fareed. (2004). *The future of freedom: Illiberal democracy at home and abroad*. New York: W. W. Norton and Co.

Ziegler, Charles E. (2016). "Great powers, civil society and authoritarian diffusion in Central Asia." *Central Asian Survey* 35(4): 549–569.

Index

Armenia, 56, 198, 199; 2012 parliamentary election, 148–151; 2013 presidential election, 177–181; Armenian National Congress, 148–151, 175–178; Civil Contract, 182; Ghukasyan, Andrias, 179; Harutyunyan, Aram, 179; Hayrikian, Paruyr, 179; Hovannisian, Raffi, 158, 177, 179–181; Kocharian, Robert, 145–146, 148, 175; Law-Based State Party, 145, 148, 151; Pashinyan, Nikol, 182; police interference, 66, 68; Prosperous Armenia, 146, 148–151, 175–178, 181; Republican Party, 145, 148, 151, 175–177, 182; Sargsyan, Serzh, 145–146, 148, 151, 161, 175–176, 178–180, 182; Ter-Petrossian, Levon, 145–150, 177–178, 180–181; Tsarukian, Gagik, 149, 151, 175, 178, 180–181

autocracy promotion, 9, 200–201

Azerbaijan, 67; 2008 presidential election, 116–118; Aliyev, Heydar, 111, 116, 119; Aliyev, Ilham, 111, 116–119; Gambar, Isa, 117; Mammadov, Ilgar, 120; New Azerbaijan Party, 117–119; opposition, 119–120; Yagunblu, Tofig, 120

Beaulieu, Emily, 12, 20–22, 169, 173

Beaulieu, Emily and Susan Hyde, 12, 20

Belarus, 67, 68, 169; 2010 presidential election, 189–191; 2012 parliamentary election, 184–187; Anisim, Elena, 187; Kazulin, Alyaksandr, 183–184; Konopatskaya, Anna, 187; Lukashenka, Aleksander, 182–187, 188–190; Milinkevich, Alyaksandr, 183, 189–190; Nyaklayeu, Uladzimir, 190–191; opposition, 13, 169, 185–186, 193; Pazniak, Zyanon, 189–190; political parties, 183, 185; Sannikau, Andrei, 190–191; Yarmoshyna, Lidziya, 184

Birch, Sarah, 3, 5, 8, 14–17, 58, 67, 69, 95, 203, 205

Bunce, Valerie and Sharon Wolchik, 2, 9–11, 19, 68, 125, 135–136, 169, 183, 204

Color Revolutions, 1–2, 3, 8, 9, 10–12, 18, 19, 57, 68, 81, 136, 183

correlates of electoral strategies, 13; competitiveness, 42–44, 51–54; incumbent dominance, 44–45, 54–56; incumbent strategies, 14–17; opposition strategies, 17–22; type of election, 46–47

About the Author

Megan Hauser is currently a lecturer at the University of North Georgia in Dahlonega. She publishes and researches on the form and function of elections in non-democratic states, and how these elections contribute to growing authoritarianism, with a particular emphasis on the region of the former Soviet Union. She completed her Ph.D. in Political Science at the University of Arizona and received her B.A. in Political Science and Russian from the University of Wisconsin-Madison.

www.ingramcontent.com/pod-product-compliance
Lightning Source LLC
Chambersburg PA
CBHW022311280326
41932CB00010B/1062